# DO Make Your Job Interviews Real ShowStoppers

★ Do your research. Demonstrate your interest in the company by showing your knowledge of it — and of the skills it wants.

★ Find out what role they want you to play. Ask, as soon as possible, about the scope of the job and ideal person's qualifications for it. Then use specifics to describe your matching skills.

★ Focus on your skills and other factors that will make you immediately productive. Employers no longer wait for you to practice for six months before delivering benefits to them.

★ Present the appropriate image for the part you seek. Walk it, talk it, and *look* it — and you have a better chance to *be* it.

★ Master a 1- or 2-minute commercial in response to "tell me about yourself" requests.

★ Rehearse answers to likely (and unlikely) questions.

★ Prepare a list of job-related (not self-interest) questions — and ask them.

★ Concentrate on what you can do for the company, not on what the company can do for you.

★ Present any potentially damaging information in the most favorable light.

★ Act confident and friendly — establish eye contact, smile, and address the interviewer by title and name (Ms. Smith or Dr. Harrison, for example — don't use first names).

# Job Interviews For Dummies,® 2nd Edition

Cheat Sheet

## DON'T Close Your Show in the First Act

▼ Don't be late. And don't sit down before you're asked to — or put anything in your mouth (gum, cigarettes, toothpicks, or breath mints).

▼ Don't audition without having researched the company and rehearsed your script.

▼ Don't try to dazzle an interviewer who screens (like a human resource specialist); behave conservatively. Save your sparkle for the manager to whom you would report.

▼ Don't chatter to fill a silence — you may nervously blurt out harmful information. Ask a question: "Would you rather hear about my skills in A or B?"

▼ Don't stray from the point with nonmarketing talk; for instance, if a company's agenda is a six-month contract offer, don't blather on about your loyalty.

▼ Don't bring up negatives or bad-mouth previous employers.

▼ Don't fail to develop a storytelling knack — true stories that support your claims of relevant skills.

▼ Don't ask about salary, benefits, and perks too soon. Wait until you're offered a job or you're "talking deal."

▼ Don't leave without asking when a decision will be made and if you can call back to check progress on the decision.

Copyright © 2000 Wiley Publishing, Inc. All rights reserved.

Item 5225-2.

For more information about Wiley Publishing, call 1-800-762-2974.

## For Dummies: Bestselling Book Series for Beginners

# Praise, Praise, Praise about Joyce Lain Kennedy's For Dummies Books

"My sister Peggy recommended I read *Job Interviews For Dummies*. The night before my interview, I reread several chapters and also took it with me in the car and refreshed myself before the interview. The interview went great. One of the things that Ms. Kennedy mentions in her book that attracted my attention was "You have the determination, the willingness to work hard, and the quick-learning skills to make up for any lack of experience." I walked into that interview with my head held high — and got the job. I believe in Joyce Lain Kennedy's wisdom."

— Julie Beecroft, Portland, Ore.

"Joyce Lain Kennedy: I love your books. Because I used a cover letter that you suggested, I got my job. You mean a lot to my career."

— Pilar Mendiola Fernandez, Washington, D.C.

"Dear Joyce: I just finished your book *Cover Letters For Dummies*. It was terrific. I laughed and I cried when I saw some of my writing habits as the things not to do."

— Gretchen Nordby, Leesburg, Va.

"Joyce's book *Job Interviews For Dummies* is out, and I think it's terrific! Joyce's job-interview directions should get you on an employer's Top Choice list every time."

— Jack Chapman, Wilmette, Ill.

"I borrowed a copy of *Job Interviews For Dummies* from the public library. After reading the book, I am now willing to invest in a personal copy for myself. It is an excellent book, and I think you did such a fabulous job with presentations that now I actually look forward to job interviews."

— Sherry Akbar, Brampton, Ontario

"I never thought writing resumes could be fun and easy! *Resumes For Dummies* shows many magic formulas to create unbeatable resumes that get interviews! Highly recommended by the Professional Association of Resume Writers, it is a must reference for all pro writers."

— Paul Chin, Papua, New Guinea

"Wow! *Resumes For Dummies* is a great resource. Since it has been 15 years since I wrote my last resume, I was at a definite loss as to where to begin — this book was the perfect resource for creating my resume. I really like the Web-oriented resume information. Now I need to get *Cover Letters For Dummies* and *Job Interviews For Dummies*."

— Tracy Pipkin, Houston, Texas

"Thank you so much for *Resumes For Dummies*. Chapters 12 and 13 have become the two most valuable chapters of information in my life. I am currently relocating from Portland, Oregon, to Tampa, Florida. I cannot imagine trying to do this little feat without the help of the Internet. Your help in preparing a digital resume and your listing of job sites is invaluable. The resume that I've been posting looks great, the content is mine, but the display is a result of you! Again, thank you very much."

— Lisa Johnson, Tampa, Fla.

"I have read *Resumes For Dummies* with joy, laughter, and a deep sense of gratitude. What a godsend you are to those of us who are resuming a career. Thanks for your gifted advice."

— Carol Treadwell, San Diego, Calif.

"I'm an engineering/computer science college senior and have had several internships in college. For my last interview, I prepared by reading Joyce's *Job Interviews For Dummies*. It is spectacular! I thought I knew how to interview, but now I know how much I didn't know — from making a "commercial" about myself, to gathering information on companies, to telling about my strong points, and negotiating my salary. Thank you, thank you. This book is *the* interviewing book!"

— Carole Beaudoin, Tottenham, Ontario

"Take it from an insurance guy: *Resumes For Dummies* is the job insurance of the new millennium"

— Al Ferrari, St. Louis, Mo.

"I'm writing to show my appreciation for your book *Job Interviews For Dummies*. I had been working for a company for five years and was being retrenched due to the bad economy condition in Asian countries.

Being through several job interviews but in vain, I was totally depressed and eager to know what was the problem. After I finished reading your book, I realized that I had made several mistakes during job interviews.

I decided to follow your guidance for my last job interview. And what happened? I got the job offer, and the pay was (equivalent to) my last drawn salary."

Thank you for your book for giving me confidence and guidance."

— Lim Lie Ching, Singapore

"I just wanted to thank you for writing the wonderful book *Resumes For Dummies*. I am changing careers in the near future (as soon as I find a job), and this book is helping me out immensely in rewriting my resume. I have used numerous resources in identifying my resume needs and find this book to be the best — the most useful tool. Thanks again."

— Mohammed Fares, Rockville, Md.

"*Resumes For Dummies* is an all-purpose, content-filled resume book that has enough humor to focus your interest on what is a very serious matter: you as a marketable product. One chapter (Chapter 3) stood out for me. It clarifies the use of hooks — when to use an objective and when to use a skills summary, citing advantages and disadvantages of each. I also liked the detailed chart on updating you resume for scanning technology and for sending it online. A very timely read!"

— Patricia S. Pigg, Florissant, Mo.

"I love *Resumes For Dummies*! It's my job search bible."

— Bonnie J. Mclurg, Mayfield, Ohio

"I really did love *Job Interviews For Dummies*. It was the first book that actually taught me how to answer specific questions. It was *very* valuable in my job search process. I have a lot of experience, but was always lacking in interview skills. (I would get really nervous before and during the interview, and would bomb it because of this.) I can see why this book won the year's best career book award."

— Susan Postma, Burnaby, British Columbia

"After a disappointing job search, I picked up *Job Interviews For Dummies*. In two days, I read the first eight chapters, went to the interview, and my answers flowed very smoothly — I showed confidence when meeting with three key people individually for three hours. The next day I had an offer for the pay I wanted plus stock options. I am overjoyed — your book was a tremendous help. Thanks for writing the book the way you did."

— Ali Khan, Fairfax, Va.

"I wish to thank Joyce Lain Kennedy for writing the books *Job Interviews For Dummies* and *Cover Letters For Dummies*. I relied solely on the two books in my attempt at a career move.

I have been driving a truck for eight years and just recently finished night school with a Magna Cum Laude, B.S. degree in accounting. Every job interview and cover letter were tailored by Joyce.

I'm now a portfolio accountant with an investments company in Andover, Mass. I have begun my dream career thanks to you and your effective material."

*[second letter]*

"Joyce's book saved me again. I had been interviewing for the past couple of months to take my career to the next level. After an interview that went awry, I dug out *Job Interviews For Dummies* and crammed all the pertinent chapters the night before the next big interview for a job I really wanted. The interview the next day with the director of human resources went *perfectly*. For each forthcoming interview, I read this book again the night before interviews with the supervisor, manager, and director of the department. I began working at my present great job a month ago, thanks to Joyce and her book.

I was so excited about the results that I let two coworkers at my previous employer borrow it before their interviews. They both received offers after those interviews. I'm touting the praises of Joyce's book all over Boston, and it's having a great effect."

> — Mark W. Emmith, Newburyport, Mass.

"There are lots of books on how to create a sharp resume. I would recommend *Resumes For Dummies* by Joyce Lain Kennedy. . . "

> — Werner Koepf (Web posting — How I found my job:
> www.physics.ohio-state.edu/~koepf)

"Two books I found helpful in writing my resume were: *Resumes For Dummies* by Joyce Lain Kennedy and . . . [A resume book for scientists and engineers]"

> — Chris Pippenger (Web posting — Civilian Transition
> Resources [military to civilian jobs]:
> www.geocities.com/~cga86/civ.html)

# Job Interviews

## FOR

# DUMMIES®

## 2ND EDITION

# Job Interviews

## FOR

## DUMMIES®

### 2ND EDITION

**by Joyce Lain Kennedy**

**WILEY**

Wiley Publishing, Inc.

**Job Interviews For Dummies,® 2nd Edition**

Published by
**Wiley Publishing, Inc.**
111 River Street
Hoboken, NJ 07030
www.wiley.com

*Library of Congress Cataloging-in-Publication Data:*

Library of Congress Control Number: 99-69707

ISBN: 0-7645-5225-2

Manufactured in the United States of America

10

3B/TR/RS/QU/IN

# About the Author

**Joyce Lain Kennedy** is the author of the *Los Angeles Times* Syndicate's column **CAREERS**, now in its 32nd year and appearing in more than 100 newspapers.

Her twice weekly column is carried in the *St. Louis Post-Dispatch, The L.A. Times,* the *Dallas Morning News,* the *Seattle Times,* the *Louisville Courier Journal, Tulsa World,* and more.

Recognized as America's favorite careers journalist, Kennedy has received more than three million reader letters. In her column, she has answered in excess of 4,200 queries from readers.

Kennedy's wise counsel about job and career development addresses universal problems experienced by most working people — problems ranging from dealing with demotion to celebrating or coping with defining career moments. First to report on many new technologies and trends, Kennedy advises job seekers to relearn many strategies and tactics to prosper in a distinctly new job market.

She is the author or coauthor of eight books, including *Joyce Lain Kennedy's Career Book* (VGM Career Horizons) and *Electronic Job Search Revolution, Electronic Resume Revolution,* and *Hook Up, Get Hired! The Internet Job Search Revolution* (the last three published by John Wiley). The last three books are groundbreaking works for the new technology that's bringing people and jobs together. With Dr. Herm Davis, she wrote *College Financial Aid For Dummies.*

*Job Interviews For Dummies* is one of a trio of job market books by Kennedy published under the wildly popular *For Dummies* imprint: *Resumes For Dummies, Cover Letters For Dummies,* and *Job Interviews For Dummies.*

Writing from Carlsbad, California, a San Diego suburb, the dean of careers columnists is a graduate of Washington University in St. Louis. Her e-mail address is jlk@sunfeatures.com.

# Author's Acknowledgments

A million sunny smiles to

**James M. Lemke,** HR Staffing and Systems consultant, Redondo Beach, California (jmlemke@aol.com). Once again, Jim has proved himself to be number one at "He who knows the answers."

**Kelly Ewing,** Hungry Minds project editor of this edition, Indianapolis, Indiana. Working online with Kelly is a genuine pleasure.

**Karen Hansen,** Hungry Minds acquisitions editor of this edition, Chicago, Illinois. Karen steps up to the plate and hits one out of the park when challenges arise.

**Lisa Roule,** Hungry Minds acquisitions coordinator, Chicago, Illinois. Lisa, your production support is tops.

**Walter Tamulis,** Sun Features Inc., Carlsbad, California, my technical associate. Wally knows weighty ways around the Web.

**Jeffrey R. Cox,** Indianapolis, Indiana, a lawyer-in-the-making who is quip-meister for this book. Jeff writes the most wonderful comedy material. (See Chapter 25.)

For help in Chapters 12 and 13, my sincere appreciation goes to **Rebecca Mickey, Lori La Rose Roy, Kim Kasse, Scott Darling, Bill Metcalf, Mary Ward, Charles Rutstein,** and **Jeffery Arnson.**

## Publisher's Acknowledgments

We're proud of this book; please send us your comments through our online registration form located at www.dummies.com/register.

Some of the people who helped bring this book to market include the following:

### Acquisitions, Editorial, and Media Development

**Project Editor:** Kelly Ewing

    *(Previous Edition: Kathleen M. Cox)*

**Acquisitions Editor:** Karen Hansen

**Acquisitions Coordinator:** Lisa Roule

**General Reviewer:** James M. Lemke HR Staffing and Systems consultant

**Editorial Director:** Kristin A. Cocks

**Editorial Administrator:** Michelle Hacker

### Composition

**Project Coordinator:** Maridee V. Ennis

**Layout and Graphics:** Amy Adrian, Joe Bucki, Barry Offringa, Tracy K. Oliver, Jill Piscitelli, Brent Savage, Jacque Schneider, Brian Torwelle, Erin Zeltner

**Proofreaders:** Laura Albert, Corey Bowen, John Greenough, Mildred Rosenzweig, Marianne Santy, Toni Settle, Charles Spencer

**Indexer:** Christine Karpeles

---

### Publishing and Editorial for Consumer Dummies

**Diane Graves Steele,** Vice President and Publisher, Consumer Dummies
**Joyce Pepple,** Acquisitions Director, Consumer Dummies
**Kristin A. Cocks,** Product Development Director, Consumer Dummies
**Michael Spring,** Vice President and Publisher, Travel
**Brice Gosnell,** Associate Publisher, Travel
**Suzanne Jannetta,** Editorial Director, Travel

### Publishing for Technology Dummies

**Richard Swadley,** Vice President and Executive Group Publisher
**Andy Cummings,** Vice President and Publisher

### Composition Services

**Gerry Fahey,** Vice President of Production Services
**Debbie Stailey,** Director of Composition Services

# Contents at a Glance

Introduction ...................................................................1

## Part I: ShowStopper Interviews Win You the Part ..........5
Chapter 1: Interviews Are Drama .................................................7
Chapter 2: A Chorus Line of Interviewing Styles ............................33

## Part II: SuperStars Research and Rehearse ..................51
Chapter 3: Research Frames Your Performance .............................53
Chapter 4: Rehearse, Rehearse, Rehearse ...................................67
Chapter 5: Costuming for the Role ...............................................77
Chapter 6: Getting Psyched for the Screen Test .............................83
Chapter 7: Lining Up Your Credits ...............................................95

## Part III: Powerful Performance Prompters ..................101
Chapter 8: Scenarios to Expect .................................................103
Chapter 9: Questions You Ask — and When .................................113
Chapter 10: Getting Paid What You're Worth ................................119

## Part IV: Technology Makes an Entrance .....................131
Chapter 11: Telephone Interviewing: A Growth Industry .................133
Chapter 12: Say Hello to Video Online Interviews ..........................141
Chapter 13: Special Tips for Camera Closeups ..............................149

## Part V: Rave Answers to Interview Questions .............157
Chapter 14: Now, Tell Me about Yourself .....................................159
Chapter 15: Questions about the Job and the Company ..................171
Chapter 16: Questions about Skills .............................................175
Chapter 17: Questions about Experience ......................................181
Chapter 18: Questions about Your Education and Training ...............189
Chapter 19: Questions about Your Age .........................................199
Chapter 20: Questions about Special Issues ..................................209
Chapter 21: Upstaging Inappropriate Questions .............................223
Chapter 22: Closing the Show ...................................................229
Chapter 23: When You're Offered the Part ....................................241

## Part VI: The Part of Tens ...................................................... 249

Chapter 24: Ten Interviewer Personality Types ............................... 251

Chapter 25: Tens of Interview Lines That Never Made History ............ 257

Chapter 26: Ten Odd Interviews ................................................ 261

## Encore ........................................................................ 269

## Index .......................................................................... 271

# Cartoons at a Glance

## By Rich Tennant

"I'm not saying my performance will be linked to my salary, but do you want the $30,000, $40,000, or $50,000 a year answer?"

**page 101**

"I have an interview with a law firm. I hope to make an impression."

**page 51**

"They had recruiters working the beach all through Spring break. It's the first time I ever had a job interview cut short by an incoming tide."

**page 249**

"Let me give you some advice for a job interview. Before you open your mouth, know what you're going to say, make good eye contact, and remember to remove your tongue stud beforehand."

**page 5**

"Very good answer! Now, let me ask you another question..."

**page 131**

"All my interviews are second interviews. One second and I'm out."

**page 157**

**Fax:** 978-546-7747
**E-mail:** richtennant@the5thwave.com
**World Wide Web:** www.the5thwave.com

# Table of Contents

Introduction ...................................................................1
    What Is a ShowStopper in Job Interviewing? ..................2
    Dummies Here. Dummies There. Dummies, Dummies Everywhere ..........2
    What's in This Book .................................................2
    Icons Used in This Book ...........................................3
    Staging Your Own Production ....................................4

Part I: ShowStopper Interviews Win You the Part ............5

Chapter 1: Interviews Are Drama ..............................7
    Take a Tip from The Flamingo Kid ..............................7
    Interviewing Is Show Biz .........................................8
    "Be Yourself" Can Be Poor Advice ..............................9
        Being natural can leave you out of the act ...............10
        Being the Best You is the role you should take .........11
    New Faces, New Factors .........................................11
        New kinds of interviewers ....................................11
        New emphasis on immediate skill facility .................12
        New kinds of questions .......................................12
        Farewell gold watch ...........................................13
        Technology impacts thinking time .........................14
        Flexible competency is an asset ............................14
        Telephone interviews becoming popular .................14
        Behavior-based interviewing still popular ...............14
        Learn new lines for small business jobs .................15
    Here's How to Take Home an Oscar from Any Interview .......16
        Light up your face with a smile .............................16
        Watch your every move .......................................16
        Remain positive .................................................16
        Start your interview off on the right foot at the right hour ..........17
        Don't limit yourself to one- or two-word answers .........17
        Yes, you will take pre-employment tests ..................17
        Your degree can't do all the heavy lifting ................18
        Bring a pen and notebook with you .......................18
        Listen and observe .............................................18
    Eight Concepts to Make You a Star ...........................18
        Preparation is big at the box office ........................19
        Verify early what's wanted; then show how you deliver .............19
        Master a one- to two-minute commercial about yourself ..........19
        Distinguish screening from selection interviews .........20
        Win the hiring manager's regard, and you're in! .........20

Never wrestle the interviewer for control ......................................21
Show sensitivity for the hiring manager's
    dislike of interviewing ....................................................21
Don't talk money until you've been offered a job ..........................22
Interview Ethics and Exploitation ...............................................22
Portfolio scam ...................................................................22
State government rip ...........................................................22
Consulting caper ...............................................................23
Educational trick ...............................................................23
Early warning ....................................................................23
Protecting yourself from Unreasonable Demands .........................24
Generations at Job Interviews ...................................................25
Who's who ......................................................................26
Younger bosses and older workers ...........................................28
Prime-of-lifer scores in age-diverse interview ............................29
Understanding the Event .........................................................29
When Interviewers Chase You ...................................................30
Building Lifetime Confidence ...................................................31

**Chapter 2: A Chorus Line of Interviewing Styles** ...............**33**
Mastering Interviews by Purpose ...............................................33
Screening interview ...........................................................33
Selection interview ...........................................................35
Combination interview ........................................................36
Promotion interview ...........................................................36
Recruiter courtesy interview ................................................37
Recruiter general screening interview ....................................37
Recruiter search interview ..................................................38
Second interview ...............................................................38
Mastering Interviews by Interviewer ...........................................39
One-to-one interview .........................................................39
Group interview ...............................................................39
Serial interview ...............................................................40
Mastering Interviews by Technique ...........................................41
Behavior-based interview ....................................................41
Directive interview ...........................................................43
Nondirective interview .......................................................44
Stress interview ...............................................................45
Mastering Interviews at All Locations ........................................46
Mealtime interview ...........................................................46
Party interview .................................................................47
Golf course interviews ........................................................47
Airport interviews .............................................................47
On-campus interview ..........................................................48
Job fair interview .............................................................48
What's Playing at the Roxy? ....................................................49

## *Part II: SuperStars Research and Rehearse* .................*51*

### **Chapter 3: Research Frames Your Performance** .................**53**

Get on Board with Information ..............................................53
Here's the Good News .........................................................54
What's to Know? ...................................................................55
Research Questions to Ask ..................................................55
    Size and growth patterns ............................................56
    Direction ......................................................................56
    Products or services ....................................................56
    Competitive profile .....................................................57
    Culture and reputation ...............................................57
    Company history ..........................................................58
    Net worth ....................................................................58
    Start with a few simple basics ...................................58
Researching Employers Online .............................................59
A Job Interview Online Address Book ..................................60
    Company Web sites ......................................................60
    Finding out about companies .....................................61
    Employee message boards — new! ............................61
    Career sites ..................................................................62
    Niche sites ...................................................................62
    Guides to professional organizations .........................63
    Search engines .............................................................63
    Publications .................................................................63
Popular Printed Resources ...................................................64
Preparation Takes You Out of the Chorus ...........................65

### **Chapter 4: Rehearse, Rehearse, Rehearse** .....................**67**

More Techniques to Develop Stage Presence ........................68
    Building your repertoire ..............................................69
    Rehearsing aloud ........................................................69
    Practicing with a camcorder .......................................70
    Funneling off extra physical tension ..........................70
    Eliminating mental tension ........................................71
Building a ShowStopper Attitude .........................................71
    Tips useful to all .........................................................71
    Tips that rookies need to know ...................................72
    Tips that aces can apply ..............................................72
    Tips especially for women ...........................................72
    Tips mainly for men ....................................................73
Anticipating Interviewing Trapdoors ...................................73
    Interference .................................................................73
    Silent treatment ..........................................................74
Take One . . . Take Two . . . Take Three . . . ........................75

### Chapter 5: Costuming for the Role ......................... .77
Keeping Up Appearances ...................................78
Striking a Pose ...........................................79
Taking the Conservative Approach .........................81
Choosing Business Casual .................................82
Getting Your Act Together ................................82

### Chapter 6: Getting Psyched for the Screen Test .............. .83
Understanding the Great Testing Controversy ..............84
Meeting and Beating the Test Types .......................85
General Tips to Help You with Tests ......................85
Questions you can ask before the test ..................85
Watch for combination tests ............................86
Beware of absolutes ....................................86
Leapfrog questions .....................................86
Computerize yourself ...................................86
Visualize high scores ..................................87
Answer as the perfect employee .........................87
Choose answers suggesting positive traits ..............87
Avoid answers suggesting negative traits ...............88
Suggest adaptability to stressful situations ...........89
Show confidence in yourself ............................89
Be alert to replayed questions .........................90
Personality Tests ........................................90
Integrity Tests ..........................................90
Sample Questions for Tests ...............................91
Concerned That You Didn't Do Well? .......................93

### Chapter 7: Lining Up Your Credits ........................ .95
Collect the Best Possible References .....................96
Maintaining Confidentiality ..............................97
Meet with References .....................................97
When a Reference Can Kill You ............................98
Understanding Legal Knots ................................99
Find Out Who's Saying What ..............................100

## Part III: Powerful Performance Prompters ..................101

### Chapter 8: Scenarios to Expect ......................... .103
The Day Before ..........................................103
The ShowFlopper way ...................................103
The ShowStopper way ...................................104
Critic's review .......................................104
Opening the Interview ...................................104
The ShowFlopper way ...................................105
The ShowStopper way ...................................105
Critic's review .......................................106

During the Interview ........................................................106
    The ShowFlopper way ..............................................106
    The ShowStopper way ..............................................107
    Critic's review ...........................................................107
Sizing Up Audience Reaction .......................................108
    The ShowFlopper way ..............................................108
    The ShowStopper way ..............................................108
    Critic's review ...........................................................109
Ending the Interview ....................................................109
    The ShowFlopper way ..............................................109
    The ShowStopper way ..............................................110
    Critic's review ...........................................................110
After the Interview ........................................................111
    The ShowFlopper way ..............................................111
    The ShowStopper way ..............................................111
    Critic's review ...........................................................112
Pre-Interview Checklist ................................................112

**Chapter 9: Questions You Ask — and When** ..................**113**
Selling Questions You Ask before the Offer ................113
Questions to Ask after the Offer .................................115
Questions to Draw Out Hidden Objections ................116
Questions to Ask Very Carefully .................................117

**Chapter 10: Getting Paid What You're Worth** ................**119**
Background on the Bucks ............................................120
Those Big Little Extras .................................................121
Discovering the Going Rate for Your Kind of Work .....122
    Where to find salary information online ................122
    Where to find salary information in print ..............122
Timing Is Everything ....................................................123
What to Say to Stall Money Talk .................................124
What to Say to Downplay Your Salary History ............126
Tips to Get Your Worth's Money ................................126
    Find a home in the range .......................................127
    Plot your salary history carefully .........................128
    Stonewalled? Try to upgrade the job ...................128
    Use dramatic silences ...........................................129
    No flexibility? Make creative suggestions ............129
The Magic of Market Value ..........................................130

**Part IV: Technology Makes an Entrance** ......................**131**

**Chapter 11: Telephone Interviewing: A Growth Industry** .........**133**
Tougher Than Face-to-Face Talking ...........................133
    Calling your shots ..................................................134
    Keep your telephone well stocked ........................135
    Make telephone appointments ..............................136

How do you sound? .................................................136
The screening script ...........................................136
The salary question .............................................138
Psychological Readiness Carries the Day .........................138

### Chapter 12: Say Hello to Video Online Interviews .............141

Interviewing Live . . . From Anywhere to Anywhere ...............142
Here's Looking at You, Kid ......................................143
What You Should Know about Video Online Interviews ..............144
Computer Online Interviewing: Pushing the Right Buttons ........145
Outsourced service .........................................146
Company direct .............................................146
Who's in charge? ...........................................147
Big Time Cyber-time Ahead ......................................147

### Chapter 13: Special Tips for Camera Closeups .................149

Watch Your Look ................................................150
Watch Your Setting .............................................152
Watch Your Performance .........................................152
Looking on the Bright Side .....................................155

## Part V: Rave Answers to Interview Questions .............157

### Chapter 14: Now, Tell Me about Yourself .....................159

More Telling about Yourself ....................................160
Narrow the Question ............................................161
Write a Commercial — about You .................................161
Sample Commercials .............................................162
The Questions ..................................................164
In Getting to Know You, Storytelling Counts ....................169

### Chapter 15: Questions about the Job and the Company .........171

Know the Job and the Industry .................................171
The Questions .................................................172

### Chapter 16: Questions about Skills .........................175

Recognizing Questions about Your Skills .......................175
Answering Questions about Your Skills .........................176
The Questions .................................................177

### Chapter 17: Questions about Experience .....................181

Make Your Experience Relevant .................................181
The Questions .................................................182

### Chapter 18: Questions about Your Education and Training .....189

Aces: High on Adaptability ....................................189
If You Are Degree-less ........................................190
Hot-Wiring the Ivory Tower ....................................191

Aces: Updated Education Is Marketable ................................................. 192
The Questions ........................................................................................... 192
Rookies: High on Education, Low on Experience .............................. 193
The Questions ........................................................................................... 194

**Chapter 19: Questions about Your Age** ........................**199**
Boos and Hisses ...................................................................................... 199
Emphasizing the Positive ...................................................................... 200
Avoiding the Trapdoors ......................................................................... 202
The Questions for Rookies ................................................................... 203
The Questions for Aces .......................................................................... 205

**Chapter 20: Questions about Special Issues** ..................**209**
When You've Been in the Same Job Forever ...................................... 210
When You've Served Prison Time ......................................................... 211
When You're Shoved out the Door ....................................................... 212
When Sexual Orientation Is Up for Discussion ................................. 213
When You've Worked Everywhere ........................................................ 214
When Gaps Shred Your History ............................................................ 215
When You're Demoted a Notch ............................................................. 216
When People in Recovery Interview .................................................... 217
When Women Are Put on the Spot ....................................................... 218
When Disabilities Are Up for Disclosure ........................................... 219

**Chapter 21: Upstaging Inappropriate Questions** .............**223**
Defining Illegal Questions ..................................................................... 223
Why Interviewers Ask Inappropriate Questions ............................... 224
Redirect Inappropriate Questions ....................................................... 225

**Chapter 22: Closing the Show** .............................**229**
Make a Strategic Exit ............................................................................. 229
Your parting sales pitch ................................................................... 230
Leaving the door open ...................................................................... 231
How Aggressive Should You Be? .......................................................... 232
Your After-Interview Checklist ............................................................ 233
Follow Up or Fall Behind ...................................................................... 234
Let's hear it for e-mail follow-up! ................................................... 234
Letters ................................................................................................. 235
Telephone calls .................................................................................. 238
Reminding your references ............................................................... 239
Onward and Upward ............................................................................... 240

**Chapter 23: When You're Offered the Part** ..................**241**
Don't Say Yes Right Away ...................................................................... 241
Stick to Your Career Script? ................................................................. 242
To Accept or Not to Accept ................................................................... 243
Is the job itself a good one? ............................................................ 243
Is the company a good choice? ........................................................ 245
Is the pay enough? ............................................................................ 245

Employment Contracts: Theirs and Yours ..............................................246
    Company pre-employment contracts ...............................246
    Your pre-employment contract ...............................247
Last Chance to Back Out ...............................247

## *Part VI: The Part of Tens* ..............................*249*

### Chapter 24: Ten Interviewer Personality Types .................251
Achieveus Youngius (Young Achiever) ...............................251
Businessius Serious (Serious Business Person) ...............................252
Bossus Potentialus (Potential Boss) ...............................252
Contemplativius Coldius (Cold Contemplator) ...............................252
Fuzzius Warmus (Warm Fuzzies Person) ...............................253
Interviewus Incompetus (Incompetent Interviewer) ...............................253
Intimidatus Serious (Serious Intimidator) ...............................254
Recruiterus Professionalus (Professional Recruiter) ...............................254
Talkus Alotus (Person Talks a Lot) ...............................255
Technicus Strictus (Strictly Technical Person) ...............................255
Too Muchus of a Good Thing? ...............................255

### Chapter 25: Tens of Interview Lines That Never Made History ....257
From the Time Machine: News You Can't Use ...............................257

### Chapter 26: Ten Odd Interviews ..............................261
More Beans Than You Need to Spill ...............................261
Signs of Misfortune ...............................262
Be Funny or Else ...............................262
Beware the Easy Answer ...............................263
Forgive Me, I Have Sinned ...............................263
Name Your Job ...............................264
Too Good in the Part ...............................264
Never Take No for an Answer ...............................265
Why It's Called SLAPstick ...............................265
A Storybook Ending to the Interview from Hell ...............................266

## *Encore* ..............................*269*
An Audition Is Like a Job Interview ...............................269

## *Index* ..............................*271*

# Introduction

●●●●●●●●●●●●●●●●●●●●●●●●●●●●●●●●●●●●●●●●●●●●●●●●●●●●●●●●

*W*ould you go into an interview with a face looking like a busted grapefruit, swollen with stitches and splotched with bruises?

One of today's most celebrated actors did, according to a celebrities star bio on Go Network's Mr. Showbiz. Surviving a barroom brawl the night before the interview, **Mel Gibson** must have come across as the perfect image of the futuristic hero Mad Max when exhibiting his enormous talent because in that interview/audition he nabbed the part that catapulted his career skyward.

Except for showing his competence with action scenes, Gibson's auditioning experience wasn't all that different from the job interview you face today. Like Gibson, you must do everything possible to convince a decision-maker within minutes of seeing you that looking further to fill the job is a waste of time.

This book explains why job interviewing is performance art and how you can use it to gather job offers.

Another celebrities star bio on Mr. Showbiz features TV and film hunk **George Clooney**. The dazzling actor also understands that performance presentation is everything in both theatrical auditioning and job interviewing.

When Clooney landed his first professional gig in a television stereo commercial, he showed up at the audition with a six-pack of beers under his arm (don't try this at home in your own job interview). Clooney had researched the type of actor the advertiser wanted for the role, one whose attitude revealed casual poise.

The celebrity later explained his rationale, saying that the best actor doesn't get the job but the one who makes the best impression: "You get the job when you walk in the door. Because in a weird way, we're not selling acting. What we're selling is confidence."

Appearance. Performance skills. Confidence. All are winning — and learnable — traits in auditions and in job interviews. You can acquire them in this book. The second edition incorporates a multitude of updates, but perhaps none more important than my expanded coverage of the use of technology in job interviewing (see Part IV). This book covers all the bases in getting employers to say — *You're the One! You're a ShowStopper!*

# What Is a ShowStopper in Job Interviewing?

In the drama of job interviewing, a *ShowStopper* performance is the one that makes the audience (in this case, the employer) mentally shout "Bravo! Bravo!" Your stunning impact quickly leads to a preliminary decision in your favor. If follow-up interviews, testing, and reference checking support that initial decision, you get a job offer. The employer may see other candidates to round out the interview process, but in reality, no one else stands a chance at landing the job once you succeed in figuratively stopping the show.

*Job Interviews For Dummies,* 2nd Edition is packed with the building blocks of ShowStopper interviews. These range from strategies and techniques to sample dialogue and research tips. Want metaphorical standing ovations? Follow the guidelines offered in these pages.

# Dummies Here. Dummies There. Dummies, Dummies Everywhere

This book is for virtually all job seekers — new entrants, midlevel people, very experienced individuals, and technical and nontechnical job seekers. I've heard from readers in all categories who tell me they found the first edition a valuable aid in their job searches.

By now the Dummies idea has caught fire and just about everyone knows that "dummy" means delightful, not duncey. And just about everyone knows that the information in a *For Dummies* book has to be top of the line to get away with its lighthearted approach. In a faster-and-faster world, most people are glad to get needed information in a crash course that doesn't come with a prescription for sleepytime pills. *Job Interviews For Dummies,* 2nd Edition is that kind of book. To anyone who says not, let's arm wrestle.

# What's in This Book

**Part I, ShowStopper Interviews Win You the Part,** takes you backstage to review the basics of interviewing. Even though jobs in the United States are plentiful, employers still take a cautious stance on new hires. You also discover why interviewing is drama and how eight concepts can make you a star.

**Part II, SuperStars Research and Rehearse,** describes off-Broadway tryouts before you raise serious curtains. You are encouraged to practice your best acts, costume for the role, recognize the mind games of job testing, and woo reviewers who give you references.

**Part III, Powerful Performance Prompters,** offers probable scenarios to expect. You find questions you can use to sell yourself. You discover how to negotiate pay or other things you want, like time off.

**Part IV, Technology Makes an Entrance,** brings you face-to-face with the new job interview formats ricocheting about in countless telephone calls and video transmissions. Success tips differ when machines are involved. As technology continues marching toward global domination, you don't have to fake it with humming when this part teaches you the words to sing real loud.

**Part V, Rave Answers to Interview Questions,** helps you learn your lines for all sorts of questions. Questions about you, your interest in the company, your experience, your education and training, your skills, your age, questions you're afraid that they'll ask — and questions they shouldn't ask.

**Part VI, The Part of Tens,** offers some surefire tips for dealing with specific types of interviewers and takes an irreverent look at statements that superstars of history might have made on a job interview, if they'd had one. And, closing the show, ten job interviewing experiences that weren't exactly ShowStoppers.

# Icons Used in This Book

One helpful feature of the *For Dummies* series is the liberal use of cute pictures called icons that draw your attention to information too useful to ignore. These are the icons used in this book and what they signify:

These star-quality tips will make your job interview a real ShowStopper.

This icon highlights tips to target online opportunities and issues.

This dinosaur icon chomps away at job-killing goofs; ignore these warnings and you may be eaten alive.

Reminds you that preparation tames panic; do your homework before hopping into an interviewing chair.

The bare essentials you must know about ShowStopper job interviews.

Indicates a savvy suggestion on how to steal a scene made by insiders who are behind the scenes.

Underscores a lack of absolute agreement on an issue.

Pay attention to this icon so that you don't come across as a clueless beginner, even if you are one.

This icon highlights tips for the individual who's been around the business block but whose experience may need recasting.

# Staging Your Own Production

On the stress scale of life, job interviewing ranks with making speeches before a vegetable-throwing crowd. Stress is such a big issue that some inter viewees take tranquilizers or beta blockers to reduce stage fright. A better way exists: Master the job-interviewing process. Get the winning ways down pat, and you'll have a special kind of insurance the rest of your working days.

# Part I

# ShowStopper Interviews Win You the Part

The 5th Wave   By Rich Tennant

"Let me give you some advice for a job interview. Before you open your mouth, know what you're going to say, make good eye contact, and remember to remove your tongue stud beforehand."

## In this part . . .

*J*ob interviewing is not real life, but a theatrical event with recognizable roles assigned to each player. The first chapter is an executive summary of the entire book — in case your interview is tomorrow, you can use it for first-aid today.

Interviewing used to mean a couple of people sat down in a room and swapped information. Now you may face a panel of 12 eyes that glare at you all at once, or you may be invited to a nice lunch to see if you're so uncouth that you go home wearing it. The second chapter describes various types of interviews — by purpose, by intent, by time of day, and by location. The growing popularity of behavior-based (structured) interviewing with an emphasis on storytelling is noted.

# Chapter 1

# Interviews Are Drama

• • • • • • • • • • • • • • • • • • • • • • • • • • • • • • • • • • • • •

### In This Chapter

▶ An executive summary of this book

▶ Why job interviewing is show biz

▶ Eight concepts to make you a star

▶ Avoiding exploitation

▶ Doing great at any interview

• • • • • • • • • • • • • • • • • • • • • • • • • • • • • • • • • • • • •

*B*eat the drums! Sound the trumpets! Huzza huzza huzza! Today's job market is bursting at the seams in the longest running United States employment show since World War II. If help-wanted signs are everywhere, why bother to polish your job interviewing skills? Here's why:

 ✔ You can get a much better job by interviewing as the best of the bunch.

 ✔ You can interview your way above obstacles if you're over 40 or in an industry or nation where you still have to try harder.

 ✔ You can be ready to compete and win when the good times slow and jobs become harder to get than they are today.

What, then, is the essence of effective interviewing?

# Take a Tip from The Flamingo Kid

Rent a classic movie, *The Flamingo Kid*, and you'll see that even seemingly complex issues can be boiled down to basics. When the young man played by **Matt Dillon** questions his role in life and takes a job as a cabana boy at the Flamingo beach club to widen his horizons, his father, **Hector Elizondo,** tells his son you only have to know two things in life — what you do well and what makes you happy. He adds that if God smiles on you, they're the same thing.

Things aren't so different for employment challenges. You only have to do two things in a job interview — convince an employer that you can do a job better than your competitors and that you'll be happy to do the work, fitting in and creating profits, not problems. I add that if God smiles on you, you'll pull it off.

These are the basics of the message you must deliver with a bang at each job interview — the make-or-break point in your job search. If you don't make an outstanding impression, someone else will be offered the job. With such high stakes, little wonder that sheer terror ties your tongue and your body into knots, stopping you from succeeding under the microscope of job interviewing.

Throughout this book, I report proven techniques on delivering your message of being able to do the work well and being a good fit for the job. I tell you how to get the duct tape off your mouth, unshackle your sweaty palms, and step out with a quality of confidence you never thought could be yours. And I disclose the real dynamics of that great and venerable institution, the job interview.

# Interviewing Is Show Biz

The job interview is the do-or-die step in the difficult process of getting hired, which is why leading job search consulting firms spend the majority of client-coaching time on interviewing drills.

Once you're inside an office and engaged in an interview, your entire future may rest on how well you present yourself to a stranger across a desk in 15, 30, or 60 minutes.

These self-presentations have been described as everything from school final exams to mating rituals, but here's the real secret:

> ***Job interviews are show biz.***

These real-life dramas never appear on film, on Broadway, or in local dinner theaters. Yet perhaps 130 million of them take place each year across the nation.

Interviewing, like acting, requires solid preparation with the goal of delivering a flawless performance that just rolls off your tongue and gets the employer applauding as you outshine all the other auditioners.

## Executive summary for one-minute job hunters

I've written this chapter as an executive summary of the entire book. If you're pressed for time, these opening pages give you a useful overview of job interviewing trends. When you have a few more minutes, the other chapters give you invaluable and specific inside information on acing the interview, from what you should wear to how you can respond to inappropriate questions.

## Playing the role of consultant

A number of respected career advisers say that a job interview should be seen not as an audition, but as a fact-gathering meeting between a consultant and a prospective client. The pro-active consultant asks questions and draws out answers. That mind-set can work well at the professional and managerial levels, and especially in a hot job market when employees are in the driver's seat. If you elect to play the consultant's role, remember that you are still in a job interview to sell your qualifications. Until the person on the other side of the desk says "yes," you don't have a "client" — or a job offer.

# "Be Yourself" Can Be Poor Advice

A scene in the movie *Children of a Lesser God* reveals a speech teacher (**William Hurt**) and a deaf janitor (**Marlee Matlin**), at the special school she once attended, duking it out in a jolting battle of wits.

In a climactic verbal battle, the janitor signs to the speech teacher, "Let me be me," to which the speech teacher replies, "Well, who the hell are you?" There is no answer.

The troubled janitor isn't the only one who has trouble with that question. The bromide — "Be yourself" — is very difficult to articulate with consistency. Be yourself? *Which self?* Who is the real you? Our roles change at various times.

Jerry is a father, an engineer, a marathon runner, a public speaker, a law student at night, and a writer of professional papers. Will the real Jerry please stand up?

Jennifer is a loving daughter, the best salesperson in her company, a pilot, a tennis player, and a football fan. Will the real Jennifer please stand up?

Jerry or Jennifer could duck the which-self question by asserting unchangeable inborn traits: *I am the same as my feelings. If I suppress or alter my urges I am being untrue to myself.*

But that, of course, is superficial thinking. After all, each of us has all kinds of urges, some of which are lofty while others are base and unattractive.

Don't make the mistake of pretending you are stuck with one identity — that's not who you are.

Who you are at this particular time is a person playing the role of job seeker. The stranger across an interviewing desk is playing the role of interviewer.

Playing the role most appropriate to you at a given time, and playing it effectively enough to get you the job you deserve, is not dishonest. To do less courts unemployment — or underemployment.

When you give a ShowStopper job interview performance, you are not being phony. You are simply standing back from the situation and looking at it with a detached eye, seeing which type of information and behavior is likely to result in a job offer and which is likely to leave you out in the cold. You can't do so if you are too busy staying true to your most easily assumed self-identity.

## *Being natural can leave you out of the act*

What about being *natural?* Isn't natural better than artificial? Not always. Is combed hair natural? Shaved legs? Trimmed beard? Polished shoes? How about covering a cough in public? Or not scratching where you itch?

Being natural in a job interview is fine as long as you don't use your desire to be natural as an excuse to blurt out negative factors.

Never treat a job interview as a confessional in which you are charged with disclosing imperfections and indiscretions that don't relate to your future job performance.

Nor should you treat a job interview as social dialogue in which you share cultural, sociological, political, sexual, or other viewpoints. Don't download your personal beliefs on interviewers in the name of "being yourself" or "being natural" — or, for that matter, "being honest."

Society cannot survive totally natural behavior. Neither can your unrefined behavior survive at job interviews. To really know someone in a brief encounter of 15, 30, or 60 minutes is simply impossible — even when you repeat that encounter multiple times. How can you compress a lifetime into 15 to 60 minutes? You can't, unless you present your life story with the same speed that television news covers the state of the world.

Instead of real life, each participant in an interview sees what the other participant(s) wants seen. If you doubt that, think back: How long did you need to really get to know your roommate or spouse?

Unless you are dealing with a trained, professional interviewer, the job interview is far from being an impartial, impersonal, rational exchange of information. The interview may be riddled with bias, subjectivity, and prejudice — on both sides of the desk. If you insist on being natural, an employer may pass you over because of your unkempt beard or because you don't feel like smiling that day or because you foolishly volunteer the information that you're active in a specific political party.

## Being the Best You is the role you should take

So what role should you play during a job interview?

> *The role to play is your Best You.*

The acting you do comes from assimilating enough interviewing skills to make interviewers want to hire you.

People who advise you to "just be yourself" in a job interview are giving you well-intentioned but worthless advice. Joining an amateur theater group to practice displaying your best attributes is a much better idea for job hunters.

All the things you've done to date — your identification of your skills, your job lead management, your resume (see my book *Resumes For Dummies,* 3rd Edition), your cover letter (see my book *Cover Letters For Dummies,* 2nd Edition) — are pointless if you fail to perform a ShowStopper job interview that delivers a job offer.

# New Faces, New Factors

Are you having trouble staking out your future because you can't "close" the sale during job interviews? This proverb states the right idea:

> *If at first you don't succeed . . . get new batteries.*

Wind yourself up with a knowledge of the new trends and changing developments that impact your job interviews. Here are highlights of contemporary happenings.

## New kinds of interviewers

If the last time you trod the boards of job interviewing you went one to one with a single interviewer, usually a white man or woman, get ready for a different set of questioners.

- Are you prepared to explain to a veteran team of six managers — individually or collectively — why you're the best candidate for the job?

- Are you comfortable with a hiring manager (especially in technical and retail fields) who is two decades younger than you?

- Are you all set to respond to someone of another color or heritage?

Anticipate interviewing panels, interviewers younger than you, and a diversity of interviewers.

# New emphasis on immediate skill facility

Because you can't count on being on the job more than a few years — or, in contract assignments, a few months — the hiring spotlight lasers in on skills, skills, skills: What can you do for this company *immediately?*

You can come across as an instant wonder if you do industrial-strength research on the company's goals (increase revenues, reduce costs, acquire new market share, land larger accounts, create a technical breakthrough), think about how you can help the company reach those goals, and are ready to speak the insider jargon of the industry.

If the job you're applying for is not at the professional — or managerial — level, at least know the nature of the company's business, assume that it wants to make or save money, and have a few good words used in the industry ready to speak.

# New kinds of questions

The familiar job interview questions, *Where do you want to be in five years?* and *Why do you want to work for our company?* are not outdated. But they certainly are spear carriers in the ensemble of contemporary leading questions, described more fully in Chapters 14 through 21. Some of the players on the questioning scene are logical and work related:

- What do you plan to accomplish within the first year that gives me a good reason to hire you?
- Can you tell me about a time when you worked under intense deadline pressure and what actions you took to succeed?
- How do you deal with a boss who lies to you?

Other questions are designed to reveal the quality of your mind (see Chapter 6):

- Why are manhole covers round? (1)
- How many barbers are there in Chicago? (2)
- If you could be an animal, what kind of animal would you be?

Still other questions are brainbusters favored by technical and financial people to see if you can keep up in the analytical-thinking department:

- You wake up one morning, and the power is out. You know you have 12 black socks and 8 blue ones. How many socks do you need to pull out before you've a match? (3)

- You're on the road to Truthtown. At a fork in the road, one road leads to Truthtown (where everyone tells the truth), the other to Liartown (where everyone lies). At the fork is a man from one of those towns. Which town? You can ask one question to discover the way. What's the question? (4)

- You have two containers, one holds five gallons, the other holds three. You can have as much water as you want. You are told to measure exactly four gallons of water into the five-gallon container. How do you do it? (5)

(You can find the answers to these questions in the sidebar "Answers to answerable questions.")

In addition to verbal mind-benders, hands-on assessment exercises occasionally turn up. One example: Checking teamwork skills by asking a group of candidates, observed behind a one-way mirror, to solve a problem together.

Interviewers for youth-driven Internet firms, in particular, may throw out wild challenges, such as handing you a box of Lego blocks and being told you have five minutes to build whatever you want and then explain it. They're looking for cowboys with never-say-quit energy, wit, and intelligence who question everything.

In this huge world, answering all the old questions is impossible, much less answering all the new questions. But you can get a step ahead on the brain-busters if you stop in at your local bookstore's trivia shelves — I'm not making this up.

## *Farewell gold watch*

Answers to certain questions are pretty much the same year after year, but watch out for one humdinger requiring a new response: *Why do you want to work here?* The old "looking for a home" statements claiming enduring loyalty and lack of wanderlust don't play as well as they once did. (Loyalty as an asset may still sell for older workers; see Chapter 14.)

Companies typically no longer expect that you will stay with them forever — nor do they want you to. They may not even want to see your face a year from now. Doing the math, managements don't want to have to deal with high health insurance and pension costs.

Rather than play the loyalty card, talk about your desire to do the work — to funnel substantial amounts of *productivity into the job quickly*. Talk about wanting to use your superior technology skills. Talk about your interest in work that excites you, work that matters. Talk about work that — with its combination of work-life balance and stimulating tasks — is too tempting to pass by. But fidelity? Pass on that as a theme song; it won't make the charts.

## Technology impacts thinking time

In face-to-face interviews, allowing a few moments of silence to pass, pausing to look at the ceiling or glance out an open window — taking time to think — can make you look wise and measured in your response. Today's interviewer, however, may call on a telephone or use a videoconferencing system where dead air time can make you appear dull-witted rather than contemplative. (See Part IV.)

## Flexible competency is an asset

Self-reliance is a keen selling point today. With computers impacting office work as dramatically as robots muscled in on manufacturing work, interviewers do not want to hear that you expect an administrative assistant to handle your e-mail and other simple clerical chores. Do not let the ITH (I'm technically helpless) words escape your lips.

Keyboarding (or talking to your computer) is now as appropriate for managers and professionals as for secretaries. And if you don't know how to sail around the Internet, take a class or hire a tutor. It's true: The geek shall inherit the earth. The days of the technophobe are numbered.

## Telephone interviews becoming popular

Quicker and cheaper than on-site visits, telephone interviewing is common in companies everywhere. Also on the marquee of change: videoconferencing for job interviewing. You need to learn new techniques to come out of these a winner. Turn to Chapters 11, 12, and 13 for proven technology techniques.

## Behavior-based interviewing still popular

Behavior-based probing intended to end hiring-by-gut remains a prevalent practice. This approach to interviewing predicts future behavior based on past behavior. Interviewers place new emphasis on "storytelling." That is, the more you can use success stories from your past, the greater interviewers see your chances of having more such success in the future. Read more about behavior-based interviewing in Chapter 2.

## *Learn new lines for small business jobs*

As I point out in Chapter 19, aces who've grown up in a large-company environment should carefully consider answers given when applying to small companies. Revise your answers to reflect different aspects of your work personality than those shown when interviewing for a big company. Interviewers of big companies and small companies have different agendas.

Among the reasons that owners of small ventures reject former big-company people are these stereotypical perceptions: People who come out of Big Corporate America are unaware of the needs of small business, too extravagant in their expectations of resources and compensation, too spoiled to produce double the work product their former jobs required, unwilling to wear more than one job hat at a time, and deadwood or they wouldn't have been cut loose from the big company.

## Answers to answerable questions

(1) Manhole covers are round so that they don't fall into the manhole.

(2) Numbers change. The interviewer wants to know how your mind works. The classic answer is based on math reasoning.

People with mathematical minds may say that you need to know the population of Chicago, the percentage of the population who are male, the number of haircuts the average man has per year divided by the number of days the barbershops are open, and the number of haircuts the average barber can give in a day. After a lot of research and math, the number of barbers in Chicago rounds out to more than 4,100.

People with practical minds may say that because barbers are licensed, you could

call the State Board of Barbers in Illinois and ask.

(3) You only have two colors. To get a pair of matching socks, pick three.

(4) Ask the man, "Which way is your hometown?" Go the way he points. If he's from Liartown, he'll point to Truthtown. If he's from Truthtown, he'll point the correct way.

(5) Fill the three-gallon container and pour it into the five-gallon container. Do so again. One gallon will be left in the three-gallon container. Empty the five-gallon container. Pour in the one-gallon container of water. Fill the three-gallon container and pour that into the five-gallon container. Now you have four gallons of water.

Be prepared to challenge these perceptions during the interview. Study up on small businesses with fewer than 500 employees — that's where most jobs are today.

# Here's How to Take Home an Oscar from Any Interview

Rookie? Prime-of-lifer? Clerk? CEO (chief executive officer)? No matter. You can do exceptionally well by following certain performance routines that succeed in any interview scene. Some of these suggestions will be familiar, but that's okay — most of us can use the reminders. Slipping up on one or two may have caused you to miss job awards — drat!

## Light up your face with a smile

A pleasant, relaxed, sincere smile carries you on a carpet of goodwill: You'll seem like an agreeable person, and everyone likes to work with agreeable, sunny people. Be enthusiastic, but don't gush. Speak of ability, not need — people are hired for what they bring to the table, not because they need the job to make ends meet.

## Watch your every move

Everything about you is observed, not only your dress and interview answers, but your body language, facial expressions, posture, carriage, and gestures. If you're a rookie, think dignity. If you're an ace, think energy.

## Remain positive

Steer clear of negative words (such as *hate, don't want,* or *refuse*) and of loaded issues such as why you left your last job and the knock-down, drag-out fights you had with that bonehead you worked for — never knock the old boss. Your prospective new boss may empathize with your old boss and decide to never be your boss at all.

## Start your interview off on the right foot at the right hour

Some advisers say that the first five minutes is the critical period of your job interview; others say that your window of opportunity for acceptance is only during the first 60 seconds. Here are some tips to help you make a good impression right off the bat:

- Find out in advance what to wear and where the interview site is located. Make a trial run if necessary. (See Chapter 5.)

- Be on time, be nice to the receptionist, read a business magazine while you're waiting, and — surprise, surprise — don't smoke, chew gum, or otherwise look like a barbarian at the gate.

- Develop a couple of icebreaker sound bites, such as comments about a nice office, attractive color scheme, or interesting pictures.

- Do not sit until you're asked or until the interviewer sits. Do not offer to shake hands until the interviewer does (especially if you're meeting with Donald Trump who thinks handshaking is unsanitary — and kissing is just as germy).

During the interview, use the interviewer's name (never use a first name unless you are old friends) as often as possible without seeming like a suppli-cant. And remember to make lots of eye contact by looking at the bridge of an interviewer's nose (divert your gaze occasionally, or you'll be perceived as more weird than honest).

## Don't limit yourself to one- or two-word answers

Communication skills are among the most desired qualities employers say they want. Answer questions clearly and completely. Be sure to observe all social skills of conversation — no interrupting, no profanity, no unsubstantiated-by-example bragging. Just as you shouldn't limit yourself to one- or two-word answers, neither should you try to cover your nervousness by talking too much.

## Yes, you will take pre-employment tests

If you want the job, you're going to have to take job tests when asked. See Chapter 6 for survival clues.

## Your degree can't do all the heavy lifting

Education is a fulcrum for movement throughout your career, but relying on it to pull you through a competitive job search is unrealistic. *Storyboard* — spell out with examples — what you learned and what you can do with your degree.

## Bring a pen and notebook with you

Making a note here and there is advisable, but don't make a project of taking notes. You may really need to take some notes (when you can't answer a question from memory and need to get back to the interviewer, for example). Plus, writing down what someone says is flattering.

## Listen and observe

Don't just sell, sell, sell. Listen. If you're constantly busy thinking of what you're going to say next, you need to work on your listening skills. If you don't understand an interviewer's question, ask for clarification.

In observing the interviewer, watch for three key signs: high interest (leaning forward), boredom (yawning or glazed look), or a wish to end the interview (stacking papers or standing up).

- ✔ High interest suggests you're stopping the show and should continue.

- ✔ The remedy for boredom is to stop and ask, "Would you rather hear more about (whatever you've been talking about) or my skills in the ABC area?"

- ✔ When the interviewer is ready to end the meeting, take the hint and go into your interview closing mode (described in Chapter 22). Gain a sense of timing and keep the door open for a follow-up contact by asking three questions: *What is the next step in the hiring process? When do you expect to make a decision? May I feel free to call if I have further questions?*

# Eight Concepts to Make You a Star

Your aim is to impress, to get hired! Read these eight super tips to make the hiring gods choose you at job interviews.

## Preparation is big at the box office

Preparation makes all the difference in today's job market, where you face intense scrutiny, probing questions, and employers who are afraid of making hiring mistakes. You must show that you're tuned in to the company's needs, that you have the skills to get up to speed quickly, and that you are a good fit in the company culture. Fortunately, never in history has so much material on companies and industries been so easily accessible, both in print and online. Virtual research has arrived — just in time!

Chapter 3 gives tips on researching your audience.

## Verify early what's wanted; then show how you deliver

Almost as soon as you're seated, ask the interviewer to describe the scope of the position and the qualifications of the ideal person for that position.

You've already done this research if you're a ShowStopper. Use this question to confirm your research. If you're wrong, you must know immediately that you need to shift direction.

If you are dealing with multiple interviewers, direct your question to the senior panel member and wait for an answer. Then gaze around the group and ask, "Does anyone have something to add to the description?"

Confirming your research or gaining this information on the spot is the key to the entire interview. This technique permits you to focus on the factors upon which the hiring decision will be made, without taking verbal detours that will not advance your candidacy.

## Master a one- to two-minute commercial about yourself

Almost certainly you will be asked to respond to some version of the "Tell me about yourself" question (see Chapter 14). Memorize a short description of your background (education, experience, and skills) that matches your strengths to the job.

After briefly relating the facts of your background, add a sentence or two of lily-guilding prose about your curiosity, commitment, and drive to build mountains atop your already good skills base. Don't get too fancy-schmancy in your choice of language, but do use a few well-chosen words to enliven a dry recitation of facts with a splash of your personality.

# Distinguish screening from selection interviews

As hiring action is concentrated increasingly in smaller companies, the separation between screening and selection interviews fades, and the same person may do both types. But traditionally, here's how the types differ.

### Screening interviews

In large organizations, interviewing is usually a two-stage process. A human resource specialist screens out all applicants except the best qualified. The screening interview is frequently handled by telephone rather than in-person. Survivors are passed to a manager (or panel of managers) who selects the winning candidate.

Screeners are experienced interviewers who look for reasons to screen you out. Screeners can reject, but they cannot hire. They will not pass you on to hiring managers if your experience and education are not within the specifications of the job.

When you're being interviewed by a screener, be pleasant and neutral. Volunteer no strong opinions. Raise no topics, except to reinforce your qualifications. As I mention later in this chapter, avoid revealing your salary history or requirements until you're in the interview setting and have been offered a job. (See Chapter 10.) Answer no questions that aren't asked — don't look for trouble.

### Selection interviews

By the time you're passed on to a hiring manager who makes the selection, you're assumed to be qualified or you wouldn't have made it that far along the channels of employment. You're in a pool of "approved" candidates chosen for the selection interview.

At a selection interview, move from neutral into high gear if the person doing the interview will be your boss or colleague. No more bland behavior — turn up the wattage on your personality power. This is the best time to find out if you'll hit it off with the boss or colleagues or fit into the company culture.

# Win the hiring manager's regard, and you're in!

Given a choice of technically qualified applicants, employers almost always choose the one they like best. Despite the best efforts of "scientific" interviewing techniques to eliminate hiring by mutual chemistry, most experts say that more people lose job offers for personality factors than for lack of capability.

The psychological principles involved in winning friends and influencing interviewers have been around since the pharaohs ran the pyramid projects. For your purposes, remember this one:

> *We like people who are like us.*

How do you encourage the interviewer to think "you and me against the problem" rather than "you against me"?

Beyond pleasantries, mutual interests, connecting with eye contact, and other well-known bonding techniques, watch for special opportunities.

- ✔ Suppose your interviewer looks harried with ringing telephones and people rushing about interrupting your talk. Flash a sympathetic smile and commiserate: "It looks like you're having one of those days." The subtext of your comment is "I understand your frustrations. I've been in a similar place. You and I are alike."

- ✔ Or suppose you're showing a work sample. Ask if you can come around to the interviewer's side of the desk to discuss your sample. You are looking at it "together."

Forget about age, color, gender, or ethnic background. Do whatever you reasonably can to make the hiring manager believe the two of you are cut from similar cloth.

To borrow from the late Broadway wit Damon Runyon:

> *The job offer goes not always to those we like, nor the hiring to our twins, but that's the way to bet.*

## Never wrestle the interviewer for control

Some advisers seem to suggest that you take charge of the interview, directing the discussion in your favor. Doing so is not a good idea if you look as though you're usurping the interviewer's prerogative. If a big void exists in what you're being asked to relate, you can ask questions of the "Would you like to hear about *X?*" variety.

## Show sensitivity for the hiring manager's dislike of interviewing

From supervisors to top executives, hiring managers tend to see interviews as encroachments on their already impossibly busy schedules. But they know they have to conduct them.

Suggest follow-up interviews be done on weekends or during the evenings to take the pressure off the interviewer's prime business hours.

## Don't talk money until you've been offered a job

See Chapter 10 for more on this topic, but when the salary question comes up at the beginning of an interview, say that money isn't your most important consideration — nor should it be at this point. Only when you know the scope of the position and that the company wants to hire you are you in a position to bargain in your best interest.

# Interview Ethics and Exploitation

You can lose your intellectual property through abuse of the job interview. In the trendy "performance interview" for professional and managerial jobs, candidates are required to prove themselves with projects that demonstrate on-job skills, problem-solving capabilities, and communications abilities.

The employer asks for a proposal of how you would handle a company project or requests that you design a process the company can use. You are told to be ready to "defend your ideas" at the interview.

Unfortunately, sometimes the free-sample demand is incredibly time-consuming (say 80 hours) and costly ($100 plus materials and research). What if you still don't get the job? Unbelievably, your work samples may be given to the victorious candidate who steals your creative ideas. In the following sections, I give you a few examples from stung readers of my newspaper column.

## Portfolio scam

"When applying to an advertising agency for a copywriting job, the owner asked me to leave my portfolio for review. He kept the portfolio and called on all the clients whose work was shown in the portfolio! Since then, I always respond to requests to leave or send my portfolio with this statement: 'I need to be there to clarify the work shown. I will be glad to bring it, and we can discuss my work at your convenience.'"

## State government rip

"When I applied for a significant and highly symbolic job with my state government, I was informed I had been selected but had to go through the formality of an interview with a key aide to the governor. As requested, I took materials and a plan for approaching the job's goals to the confirmation interview. A long, official silence followed before a form letter arrived stating that a less qualified professional, to whom I was a mentor, had won the position. The victor showed me the state's plan of action: mine."

## Consulting caper

"My husband, an expert in human resources, spent two long days interviewing in a small town with the owner of a family company and his son. He gave them an unbelievable amount of advice and information to help their meager HR program, process management, and integrated product development. All we got out of that was reimbursement for a 200-mile car trip, a bad motel, and meals. That was our first realization of how small businesses in particular get almost free consulting work."

## Educational trick

"I've had more than my share of time-consuming presentations; once when I interviewed for the position of dean of a community college district and another when I was a candidate for a city's new training division chief. I had to spend several hours in the employers' computer labs designing programs and leaving them on disks. I knew that with my education and experience, I had done well both times. In the first case, I received a form letter the following day announcing the college district had selected a candidate [which suggests the victorious candidate was preselected, that the job was "wired," and the college district was going through the motions]. In the second instance, a long-term firefighter with zero training experience got the job with the city and used my materials for new employees!"

## Early warning

"At the end of a two-hour interview at a major company, I was asked to return three days later and give a 20-minute formal presentation to upper management on why they should hire me. I've been in Toastmasters and don't mind giving presentations, but I did mind not being told it was a requirement until the end of the interview. With a full-time job, I simply did not have adequate time to prepare for something like this and wouldn't have wasted my time interviewing had I known. I told them I would not be giving a presentation, but if interested, they could contact me in the future. They did a few days later, and I got the job."

As Paul Harvey would say, now for the rest of the story . . .

"Four weeks after I came onboard, the company announced that anyone under the age of 40 (I'm 36) would no longer be eligible for the company pension plan. I pointed out to my manager that all the literature I was given described the pension benefit, a major factor in my decision to join the company. I was told nothing could be done. In this day and age, there is a tremendous lack of ethics in the business environment. My antenna should have gone up about this company when they tried to throw me a last-minute curve ball about the presentation."

# Protecting Yourself from Unreasonable Demands

How do you avoid abuse without taking yourself out of the running for a job you want when you're not sure about the real interview agenda? As an insightful Seattle consultant observed: "It's a delicate balancing act in making proposals or responding to written job application 'supplemental questions' — teetering between appearing too ignorant or unintelligent to get the work and giving away all the know-how so that they no longer need your services."

I've found no bulletproof answer, but here are two ideas:

- You can copyright your plan and place a valid copyright notice (c), along with the publication date and your name, on its cover as an indication of your underlying claim to ownership. For free information, contact Registrar of Copyrights, Copyright Office, Library of Congress, Washington, D.C., 20559. But for more understandable advice, see *The Copyright Handbook: How to Protect & Use Written Works,* by Stephen Fishman (Nolo Press; nolo.com).
- You can bluff, hoping to create a theft deterrent by slapping a copyright notice and "Confidential — Property of (Your Name)" on your plan's cover.

When you are desperate or really, really, really want the job but do not have the time, inclination, or money to respond in full measure, offer something like this:

*I'm glad that you see I have the brains and talent to bring value to your company. I'm happy, too, that you have the confidence in my work to ask me to handle such a potentially important solution to your marketing challenge.*

*With my background, I'm sure I could do a bang-up job on this assignment. But you do realize, I hope, that such an important project would require 80 to 100 hours of intensely focused work. I'd enjoy doing it, but, quite frankly, I have several other job interviews scheduled that I really can't shift around. Do you think a sample of substantially smaller scope would serve as well for your purposes?*

What you do with a statement like this is

- ✔ remind the interviewer that you're a top candidate,

- ✔ promise superior results,

- ✔ bring a reality check to a sensitive interviewer about what's being asked of you,

- ✔ let the interviewer know others are interested in you,

- ✔ propose to do much less work until a job offer crosses your palm.

You can, of course, flatly refuse to part with advance goodies, jokingly saying that you'd love to do the free work sample, but that your accountant says it's bad mojo to give away so much unpaid work. When it's a seller's market, you'll probably be considered anyway. But in a buyer's market for your services, the likelihood is that you'll be passed over when you decline to turn in a hefty free sample.

# Generations at Job Interviews

The devil is in the demographics: People of different ages are butting heads at job interviews these days. The prime-of-lifers and seasoned aces think the rookies need attitude adjustments, and the rookies think the prime-of-lifers and aces should show more confidence in their competence:

*They have no work ethic. They're waiting for someone to wait on them, the spoiled brats!*

*To them, thinking globally means the world owes them.*

*She's treating me like I'm the 15-year-old who mows her lawn.*

The people in each generation have definite and different ideas about how work should be done, including how job interviews should proceed. Their ideas are founded in more than mere physical years — they are founded in *generational memory*. People of the same vintage share remembrances of the same coming-of-age experiences, the same early work pathways, and, of special interest to you, the same job interview protocols.

## A class act

Speaking of sensibilities, Queen Victoria of England showed enormous courtesy and respect to one of history's greatest writers, Charles Dickens. Summoned for an audience with the Queen at Buckingham Palace, Dickens realized that court protocol forbade his sitting in the ruler's presence and stood for nearly two hours. So did Queen Victoria.

## *Who's who*

Although there's debate over which years mark the borders of each category, here is a commonly used classification.

- **Preboomers:** Born before 1945
- **Baby boomers:** Born between 1946 and 1964
- **Generation X:** Born between 1965 and 1978
- **Generation Y:** Born since 1979

No matter to which age group you belong, when you are interacting with an interviewer of another generation, ignore the sensibilities of that generation at your own peril. Think of each generation as having its own culture and guarding it against outsiders.

When you want a job offer, take pains to lace your interview performance with generational sensibilities, showing courtesy, tact, and respect.

What are the sensibilities of each group? No classification is perfect and you may want to revise the profiles below based on your own research. But in the following sections, I give you my overview of how the cultures of each generation can influence the outcome of job interviews.

### *Preboomers*

Preboomers are authority respecters who are rooted, stable, and steady. Money matters to them as an issue of security; getting preboomers to increase pay offers is hard work but speak often of market rate and fairness. They value loyalty, seniority, manners, honor, law and order, and doing the right thing. Preboomers expect you to deliver the goods (no excuses) or get out of the way.

### Baby boomers

Optimistic can-do stars who grew up being adored children, they are teamwork lovers and work-to-succeed afficionados. Money matters as a method of keeping score; proving you bring value loosens their purse strings. Boomers believe they'll always be young (no wrinkles) and cool; even so, showing respect and acknowledging social conventions matter to half-century boomers — they don't like it when you use first names upon first meeting.

### Generation X

Technologically gifted individuals who do not suffer boring work gladly, these commitment-shy young people want to keep their options open, and open — and open. Teamwork is overrated. Personal lives are more important than careers. Xers are cynical about boomers, particularly those who put work ahead of family and moneymaking over community. Much disparaged by boomers as slackers, Xers expect change, don't impress easily, and have made cyberspace their stomping ground.

"GenX decision-makers will be looking for candidates who are results-oriented," says Bruce Tulgan (`rainmakerthinking.com`), an expert consultant specializing in this group.

"GenX decision-makers care much less about formalities from the workplace of the past — authority for the sake of authority, where you prefer to work, and so on. What matters is, 'Can you get the job done for me right now, with speed and quality?' Above all, be real. Tell real stories about real things you've done," Tulgan advises.

### Generation Y

Technological frights, this is the first generation that grew up digital, cutting its teeth on the Internet and living in virtual reality. Also called "n-gen" (Net generation) and "nexters," early buzz on these rookies puts them philosophically closer to the preboomers (World War II grandparents and great-grandparents) than boomers or Xers. They have zero tolerance for *technophobes,* people who are afraid of technology.

The jury's still out on specifics of how to appeal to GenY decision-makers because so few are yet on the scene. But keywords used to describe them include hard-working, self-directed, contrarian, flexible, collaborative, and high in self-esteem. But never fall into the trap of thinking "uppity children." Your interview mind-set should realign ideas of authority — mutual respect is the right tone.

## Younger bosses and older workers

The face on the interview floor is changing, and to boomer candidates, it looks 12 years old.

For the first two millenniums, authority was handed down from one generation to the next in a linear fashion. Which meant that everyone had a mutual understanding of interviewing standards. But as we launch the third millennium, an age-diverse workplace — with its attendant generation gaps — has, as Elvis would sing, caused the interviewing process to be *All Shook Up*.

What differentiates today's generational workplace handover from those of earlier times is its speed and technological base.

As ironic as it seems, growing numbers of Xers are managing those same boomers who, when the first edition of this book was written a few years ago, were complaining about the Xers' work ethics.

How fast are Xers climbing the managerial ranks? Bosses aged 20–34 shot up from 4.8 million in 1994 to 5.2 million in 1998; at the same time, chieftain numbers in older groups declined. Expect more of the same: News magazines report that 80 percent of all new businesses started in the past three years belong to Xers.

Not only will this decade see 7.4 percent fewer prime-of-life people in the labor pool as boomers retire, a boomer turns 50 every 7.5 seconds.

When the interviewing relationship flip-flops and twentysomethings are on the other side of the desk handing out jobs to prime-of-lifers, more red flags than you'll find in China signal "danger ahead." The first clue that all will not work happily ever after is when the boomer's face registers shock at the horror of taking orders from a manager young enough to be the boomer's child.

Before you launch your round of job interviews, take a day or so to become more conscious of generational cultures. For each person you meet, approximate the person's age and generational outlook; ask yourself what would be a pleasing statement — or annoying remark. This is a mind game to oil your hinges, tweak your radar, or monetize your value proposition (depending upon your generation's wording).

The radically different sensibilities of multiple generations make it more important than ever to understand the true nature of job interviewing.

## Prime-of-lifer scores in age-diverse interview

Career changer Paul Nichols has nailed generational interviewing. Read these excerpts from his e-mail letter to me:

> I made a career change at age 56. I was in the restaurant industry for 15 years when I discovered the absolute wonder of the computer. I spent the next four years working temporary jobs, getting ready for desktop publishing and technical writing.
>
> Last week I landed an excellent position as a technical writer for a new young company where I'll be the 5th employee. The boss is 33 (so is my son). The other three employees are in their late 20s (so are my daughters).
>
> I think I was offered the job because of my attitude during the interview. I made it clear that I would rather work with people in "your age bracket" because there is so much energy and new, fresh ideas — my kind of environment. I emphasized that I'm open to learning whole new concepts and methods from younger workers.
>
> At the same time, I bring life skills, customer service skills, quality control skills, excellent grammar, English and communication skills, a great work ethic, and a positive, enthusiastic, energetic attitude to the company. I told them, "I could make you look good to your clients."

Paul Nichols may have grown up listening to the *Lone Ranger* instead of hearing "Weird Al" Yankovic songs, but in his interview with a younger boss, the career changer said all the right things. Way to go, Mr. Nichols! Oops, I mean Paul.

# Understanding the Event

If you have ever wanted to look like someone in a **Madonna**, **Cyndi Lauper**, or **Duran Duran** video, you have enough life experience to know that certain things in this world change rarely, if at all. One constant is the basic dynamic of the job interview:

> *Before you receive a job offer, you're in the persuasion business, not the asking business.*

Some clueless candidates, who actually may be qualified for the lost positions, confuse their identities. They miss the interactive dynamic of selling and buying. Instead of imagining themselves as a seller, they cast themselves as some other character — such as a "prideful achiever" who doesn't need to recount her talents (she believes everyone already knows them) or a "youthful techster" who doesn't need to list his abilities (he figures he's entitled to a job because he knows how to set time on a VCR).

You won't make a mistake leading off with a strong sales effort in a job interview and waiting until later to reveal the topics of personal interest to you.

> *Star to Joyce:* What's wrong with talking at the same time about what you are selling and what you will accept as payment?

> *Joyce to star:* Your message describing the benefits you will bring is diluted. The interviewer needs time for your sales communication to spark excitement. As political consultants tell their politician clients: "Stay on message."

After you receive an offer (or a near-offer), everything changes. You, the seller, temporarily switch sides and put on the buyer's hat. Maybe you do want the job — and maybe you don't. You'll have to consider the compensation package and other enticements before you say "yes" or "no." You have worked for this window of opportunity, and here it is — celebrate your *deal moment.*

> ***Your deal moment is the happy time after you get an offer but before you accept it — that's when your best deal has the best chance of becoming reality.***

Your deal moment is the time to ask those important questions about vacation, your office, or three-day weekends. Your deal moment is the time to negotiate for more benefits, relocation expenses, flextime, a company car, on-site day care, a good bonus package, or stock options.

To sum up, when qualified people walk away from a recruiting meeting without a job offer, the root cause can often be traced to a fundamental misconception of the event — which is a job interview, not merely a social conversation in which each party explores the other's viewpoints.

You are selling a theme of future workplace excellence to an employer who you hope will buy your promises.

# When Interviewers Chase You

If you're lucky enough to be the target of hot pursuit by panting recruiters, you may quarrel with the seller/buyer relationship I described in the preceding section.

Yes — there are times when it's decidedly to your advantage to play a little hard to get — depending on your stature, your competition, the nature of the work, the seniority of the position, and your personality.

When you're hot, you're hot — but even then the essential dynamic of a hiring episode is immutable: The employer has to be sold on you before a job offer will be yours to accept or reject.

That's because when the employer parts with capital to buy your labor, you sell a chunk of your life for monetary rewards. What has changed when you are ruling from a lofty perch is the *timing of your leverage.* What has happened is that your deal moment passed through the interviewing door before you.

Back up, what leverage?

Leverage is the ability to decide the outcome in a situation when you control what someone else wants. In job searching, leverage is your ability not just to get a job, but *to get a job on your own terms.*

Until a job offer materializes, until your deal moment actually clocks in, stay on message in the selling of your qualifications for the position. It's much easier on the ego to reject an offer than to be left standing at the starting line.

# Building Lifetime Confidence

This first chapter serves as an executive summary for the entire book. The remainder of these pages are wide and deep with the details that can help you gain a lifetime of confidence in your ability to sail through interviews and receive job offers.

Turn the page, cue the star. . . .

# Chapter 2

# A Chorus Line of Interviewing Styles

. . . . . . . . . . . . . . . . . . . . . . . . . . . . . . . . . . . . . . . . . . . . . . .

### In This Chapter

▶ Finding out about different styles of interviews

▶ Discovering tips to walk away winning in each style

▶ Influencing outcomes in all styles

. . . . . . . . . . . . . . . . . . . . . . . . . . . . . . . . . . . . . . . . . . . . . . .

In today's fast-moving world, interviewing dramas appear in many styles. This chapter highlights the most popular and provides key tips for stopping the show.

For convenience, I've divided the styles of interviews that follow into clusters describing *purpose, interviewer, technique,* and *location.*

## Mastering Interviews by Purpose

Interviews grouped by purpose include *screening, selection, combination, promotion, recruiter courtesy, recruiter general screening, recruiter search,* and *second interview.*

## Screening interview

In large organizations, interviewing is a two-stage process, although each stage may contain several steps. The two stages are *screening* and *selection.*

In-person interviews to screen applicants are held at the employer's work site, independent employment services, college career services, and job fairs.

Interviewers often rely on technology, such as telephones and computers, to screen applicants (see Part IV). The telephone, in particular, has become a favorite of employers who want to be sure that you're not underskilled and overpriced.

The purpose of screening, or *first-cut interviews,* is to weed out all applicants except the best qualified.

The screener, usually a human resource professional or third-party recruiter, interrogates all comers and passes the survivors to a person who makes the final selection. That person with hiring authority is usually the department manager or the boss to whom the victorious candidate reports.

Screeners are generally more experienced in interviewing than the questioners who select — they've read about interviewing, studied interviewing, and made interviewing an art form. Their job is to gather facts and keep out candidates who are not qualified for the position, or who may be qualified but who have a poor employment history.

When screening is done at a professional level (rather than leaving the task to a receptionist or office assistant), the screeners are experts at finding out what's wrong with you — why you should be screened out.

Screeners determine if you have the minimum qualifications for the position, not if you are the best candidate. Typical subjects for the screening interview include

- ✔ Questions about your job history
- ✔ Questions about your salary history or requirements
- ✔ Questions about your transferable skills — ability to do the job
- ✔ Inquiries about inconsistencies on your resume (work history gaps)
- ✔ Probes designed to reveal lies in your resume
- ✔ Questions to reveal what kind of person you are — reliable, trustworthy, team-oriented

Screeners are usually not concerned with evaluating your personality or thought processes. They have one basic responsibility before putting you on the approved list and waving you to the next interviewing level: to be sure that you qualify. They do so by validating your experience, education, skills, and track record.

Screeners are gatekeepers; they will be criticized for allowing unqualified candidates to slip through the gate. That's why they want the facts, just the facts.

**Tip:** Keep your answers straightforward and save most of your dynamo-drama moves for the selection interview.

When the facts confirm that you are qualified for the position, the opportunity to participate in a selection interview is yours to lose. As long as you don't volunteer reasons to send you away, expect to be passed to the decision-maker — who assumes that you are qualified or you would not have been passed along.

What if you and the screener don't seem to be on the same wavelength? Unless you're plying the human resources trade, it doesn't matter — you won't be working together.

Screeners can't hire you, but screeners can send you to the showers.

## Selection interview

Suppose that you are hired, but fail to live up to expectations. Is the screener in trouble? No. The selector made the call.

In the selection interview, sometimes called the *decision interview,* you meet with the supervisor, department head, or a person with the authority to hire you. Often this interviewer will be your potential boss, so you'll be making some judgments too. (Sometimes this is more than one person, as discussed in the section "Group interview.")

Selection interviewers are rarely pros at interviewing and often just go with their intuition, hoping the task is over as quickly as possible so that they can get back to their "real" work.

**Tip:** Because the selection interview may take several detours, be ready to ask leading questions to get the interview back on track and to set up an opening to describe your qualifications in light of the position.

Even if the questioner seems like the kind of person you'd share a beer with, your interviewer is trying to decide which candidate is the best investment for the company — because a wrong choice could cost the company thousands of dollars in training time, correcting mistakes, and firing to hire again. Selection interviewers are looking for:

- ✔ **Strong presentation of personality** — how you will blend with other employees, as well as your general likability and motivation to work

- ✔ **Qualifications and skills** — how you can do the job better than other candidates

- ✔ **Specific details of your job experience or education** — proof that you've not only done — or been trained for — a similar job, but how you'll apply that background to the new job

- ✔ **How you handle specific job scenarios** — more proof of your superior qualifications

Assuming that the person conducting the meeting will be your boss or a colleague with whom you have to get along, the selection interview is where you move from neutral behavior into high gear. This is where you reveal the best of your personality (you're not holding yourself in, as you were during the screening interview). And this is where you take note of how you and your potential boss blend. If your gut instinct tells you the blend is oil-and-water, think carefully before saying "yes" to this job offer.

Even when everything else is tempting, your future will go better when you and your future boss are using the same software (or as boomers say, are on the same page).

In *Blazing Saddles*, the ultimate Western spoof, **Harvey Korman** plays a gang leader recruiting bad guys to ruin a town. Interviewing **Cleavon Little,** Korman initially worries that they're not "using the same software" when he asks Little to describe his qualifications as a villain. When Little tells him his past work was stampeding cattle, Korman is about to blow him off with a comment that stampeding cattle isn't a big thing in gangland. Little smiles knowingly, then says, "Through the Vatican?" Right then, Korman decides that Little and he are two villains of a kind, shouting "kinky!" and hiring him on the spot.

## Combination interview

Small firms often combine the screening and selecting interviews. The resulting combination tends to be long and grueling, and not only tests your match to the ultimate hire, but also measures your stamina and motivation for the job.

**Tip:** From the first exchange, sell your top qualities.

## Promotion interview

Although, with your inside information and good record, you've got a jump start on being promoted from within, overconfidence can topple the unsuspecting: Never assume that you'll be promoted over other internal candidates — or given preference over outside candidates.

Approach the promotion interview as though you were heading out to a new company. Research diligently, as described in Chapter 3, to be able to talk about industry trends and other big issues.

When you are the only insider wrangling for the job, use your knowledge of the company's policies, plans, and culture to point out that you can hit the floor running — which no outsider can do. Then offer several current company problems you would deal with immediately.

If you're trying to move up from a nonsupervisory or staff job into one requiring the oversight of others, prepare by reading a managerial guide, such as *Managing For Dummies* by Bob Nelson and Peter Economy (IDG Books Worldwide, Inc.).

**Tip:** Emphasizing your 20 years of loyal service with a show-and-tell of your successes, especially when a company is handing off control from boomers to Xers, is unpromising strategy.

A youth-oriented type of management doesn't care about the glories of Ancient Rome or Ancient You — what they care about is whether you can do the *work ahead.*

So while you will include the accomplishments of the past ten years, reframe the discussion to focus on work samples and skills that highlight your ability to do the new job. Give examples of your flexible personality. Identify times when you welcomed new tasks and responsibilities. Help them see you as "tomorrow," not as "yesterday."

## Recruiter courtesy interview

A retained recruiter gets paid whether or not the recruiter matches a candidate to a position. Retained recruiters typically run the other way to avoid seeing job seekers who come unbidden to their offices. (Time is money.) But you may know someone who is a client or friend of a retained recruiter who can get you in the door with a courtesy interview.

Unless your interviewer is recruiting for a position that's perfect for you (which is very unlikely), focus on providing the recruiter with information that may qualify you for a future search. Some rules to follow include

- ✓ Always give the recruiter a current resume.
- ✓ Get straight to the point; don't take more than 20 minutes of the recruiter's time.
- ✓ Explain your experience, achievements, and skills.
- ✓ Thank the recruiter for time invested in you.

**Tip:** Don't play the role of a coy, amateur job seeker. The retained recruiter is doing you a favor. You wouldn't ask for a courtesy interview if you didn't need a job. Your conciseness and ability to communicate efficiently count. Review your resume and get to the point.

## Recruiter general screening interview

Contingency recruiters, unlike retained recruiters, get paid only when they match up a candidate with a position. The more people they see, the larger their candidate pool from which to fill employers' job orders. Getting an interview with a contingency recruiter or employment agency consultant is easier than with a retained recruiter.

This doesn't mean you can waste a contingency recruiter's time. Hand over your resume and give your best performance to show a broad selection of work experiences. You're trying to make the contingency recruiter remember you for a variety of future job openings.

**Tip:** Make sure that you get high scores in the following qualities:

- ✔ Personality/likability
- ✔ Adept communication
- ✔ Enthusiasm and motivated interest in work
- ✔ Leadership and initiative
- ✔ Competence in skills and knowledge
- ✔ Experience (some job history)

## Recruiter search interview

A recruiter may contact you about a specific job opening. Eventually you'll be told who the client is. Chances are you're doing the same or a nearly same job, and that's why the recruiter called you. So you already know the basics of your industry.

If you've been so busy doing your job that you're not up to date on industry trends, there's no time like the present for a cram review. Third-party executive and technical recruiters can't hire you, but you've got to get past them to see their clients. To impress a recruiter in a search interview:

- ✔ Show that you have definite career goals and indicate how this position fits those goals.
- ✔ Ask probing, thoughtful questions about the company and position, showing you've done your homework.

**Tip:** Use the Net to research recruiting firms that specialize in your industry or occupation. One good resource is *Oya's Directory of Recruiters* at `i-recruit.com/oya`.

## Second interview

When you're invited back for a second interview with the same person, the real purpose is a confirmation to be sure that you're as wonderful as you looked at first glance. You know your talents are appreciated, so slow down on the aggressive self-marketing. Take "yes" for an answer, not for a chance on unselling yourself.

**Tip:** The second time around, act as though the job is virtually a done deal. Be poised and confident, give additional examples of your accomplishments, and ask more thoughtful questions about the business. This means you need to devote more research time at the library, on the Net, or with anyone who has inside information on the business.

When you're invited back for a second interview with someone else, that person is usually the first interviewer's boss or others with whom you'd interact. They're taking a wider look at you, chiefly to know how you'd fit in now and in the future. Be likable and ask questions about where the company is headed. Emphasize your ability to be productive and meet goals.

You may be surprised at being asked to come back yet again! Being subjected to more than two interviews for a job is no longer rare. Even five to ten interviews isn't unheard of. In fact, overinterviewing happens often enough that the practice has been given a name: "death by interview." Why is this happening?

Reasons range from plain indecision to scheduling difficulties with all the future coworkers who want a voice in the hiring decision, to fear of making a wrong choice. In addition to a test here and there (see Chapter 6), the only basis that managers have to go on is the resume, reference check, and interview. So when in doubt, they interview and interview and interview.

# Mastering Interviews by Interviewer

You may have to face several pairs of measuring eyes — all at once. Other times, you may share your interview with several other candidates. Or you may have to endure one interview after another, all with the same company. Don't be surprised by these variations — rehearse for them as well.

## One-to-one interview

The one interviewer, one interviewee format is the traditional and familiar style of job interview. You and the employer meet, usually at the employer's office, and discuss the job and your skills and other qualifications that relate to the job. Tips to handle the one-to-one interview are found throughout this book.

## Group interview

Also called a panel, board, team, collective, or committee interview, this style puts you stage center before a comparatively huge crowd — perhaps 5 to 12 questioners. Usually they are people from the department where you would work, or they may come from various departments throughout the organization.

You wouldn't be at this expensive meeting (think of all the salaries for the group's time) if you hadn't already been screened to be sure your qualifications are acceptable. These people are gathered together to see if they like you and if you'll fit into their operation. Greet each person, handing out a fresh copy of your resume. Appear confident. Make a quick seating chart to help you remember names.

Before you answer a first question, smile, thank everyone for inviting you to meet with them, and then begin your answer. Which will probably be "You asked me to tell you about myself. . . ."

Should you try to identify the leader and direct most of your remarks to that person? Not necessarily. The boss may be the quiet observer in the corner. Play it safe — maintain eye contact with all committee members. When your curtain goes up, play to a full house!

Group interviews highlight your interpersonal skills, leadership, and your ability to think on your feet and deal with issues in a stressful setting. The purpose of a group interview is not only to hear what you say, but to see what behaviors and skills you display in a group setting.

When the interview is over, thank the group as a platform presenter would: "Thank you for having me here today. I enjoyed being with you. This interview confirmed my research indicating that this company is a good place to work. I'll look forward to hearing from you, and hopefully, joining you."

**Tip:** Ask questions. Periodically summarize important points to keep the group focused. Use a notebook to record several simultaneous questions, explaining that you don't want to omit responding to anyone's important concern.

## Serial interview

A serial interview also involves a group of people, but not all at once. You are handed off from person to person. You typically are passed from screener to line manager to top manager — and perhaps a half-dozen people in between in the drawn-out process of the serial interview. You strengthen your chances each time you are passed onward.

**Tip:** Use your screening (plain vanilla) interview behavior with all interviewers you meet except those with whom you would work. Then go into your selection (full personality) mode.

Another type of serial interview is a prescheduled series of interviews, usually lasting one to two days, that each applicant must complete before the employer makes a hiring decision.

**Tip:** When the initial interviewer says that you're being passed on to the second interviewer, try to find out a little about the second interviewer. Ask a question like *"Does number two feel the same way about customer service as you do?"* You'll get information you need to find common ground with your next interviewer. Continue the advance-tip technique all the way to the finish line.

When you are interviewed by one person after another, consistency counts. Do not tell a rainbow of stories about the same black-and-white topics. When interview team members later compare notes, they should be discussing the same person.

# Mastering Interviews by Technique

In the heat of an interview, the last thing you'll probably be thinking about is the interviewer's technique, but under the lights, the interviewer is looking for a special kind of talent. In the cool of your evening reading, try to anticipate what the interviewer seeks.

## Behavior-based interview

Behavior-based interviewing relies on storytelling — examples of what you've done that support your claims. Premised on the belief that the past predicts the future, behavior-based interviewing techniques are used to ask the candidate how they have handled specific situations — what kinds of *behaviors* they used to solve problems. The presumption is that if you were a good problem solver in the past, you'll be a good problem solver in the future. Behavior-based interviewing emphasizes "What *did* you do *when,*" not "What *would* you do *if?*"

All candidates are asked virtually the same questions. The tip-off that you've just been handed a behavior-based question, which should be answered with a *demonstrated skill* or *trait,* is when the question begins with such words as "Tell me about a time when . . ." "Give me an example of your skills in . . ." "Describe a time when you . . ." "Why did you . . . ?"

> *Think back to a time when you were on the verge of making a huge sale, and the customer balked at the last minute, promised to get back to you, but didn't. What action did you take?*
>
> *Remember a time when you improved inventory turns; how big an improvement did you make?*
>
> *Tell me about an on-the-job disaster that you turned around, making lemonade from lemons.*

*Describe the types of risks you have allowed your direct reports to take.*

*Can you give me an example of when you were able to implement a vision for your organization?*

*Why did you decide to major in sociology at the San Marcos State University rather than at a small private college?*

Companies using behavior-based interviewing first must identify the behaviors important to the job. If leadership, for instance, is one of the valued behaviors, several questions asking for stories of demonstrated leadership will be asked:

*Tell me about the last time you had to take charge of a project but were lacking in clear direction. How did you carry forward the project?*

Because the behavioral style of interviewing attempts to measure predictable behavior, rather than pure paid work experience, it can help level the playing field for rookies competing against seasoned candidates.

In mining your past for anecdotes, you can draw from virtually any part of your past behavior — education, school projects, paid work experience, volunteer work, activities, hobbies, family life.

**Tip:** As you sift through your memories, be on the lookout for *a theme,* the motif that runs through your choices of education, jobs, and activities. Examples of themes are leadership, problem solving, negotiating, initiative, overcoming adversity, succeeding, dealing with stress, sacrificing to achieve an important work goal, how you have dealt with someone who disagrees with you, commitment, work ethic, task orientation, and communications skills. Put at least half a dozen anecdotes in your pocket that illustrate your theme and pull them out when you need them.

Here are several more suggestions to best answer behavior-based questions:

✔ One good way to tell a story with a beginning, a middle, and an end is the *PAR technique — problem, action, result.* Here's an example. *Problem*: An E-commerce company was operating at a substantial loss. *Action:* I outsourced technical support and added seven new product lines. *Result:* We cut our expenses by 8 percent, increased our revenues by 14 percent, and had our first profitable year with expectations of higher profits next year.

✔ Rookies: Don't simply cite the subject of your classes — "I couldn't solve my accounting problem and so I asked my professor." No! Look back at your student class projects, previous work experience, and extra-curricular activities. Reach into real life for your success stories.

> ✔ Try not to sound as though you memorized every syllable and inflection, or like a machine with all the answers. Admitting that your example was a complex problem and that you experimented until you found its best solution humanizes you.

Realize that the interviewer is more interested in the process than in the details of your success stories. What was the reasoning behind your actions? Why did you behave the way you did? What skills did you use?

Behavior-based interviewing, which arrived more than 30 years ago, is popular today because employers are trying to snatch clues from history to project the future. The underlying rationale is that people tend to play the same roles over and over in life.

Theatrical insiders call this tendency "typecasting." In explaining a recent shift away from action films, celebrated film star **Bruce Willis** quipped, "I've saved the world so many times, they've given me an 800 number."

# Directive interview

The *directive interview* is one in which the interviewer maintains complete control and walks you through the discussion to uncover what the interviewer wants to know. The *patterned interview* is similar except the interviewer works from a written list of questions asked of all candidates and writes down your answers.

A patterned interview is also called *structured interview*. Although the structured interview has been around a long time, the format is finding new followers.

The argument in favor of structured interviews is that it promotes fairness, uncovers superior candidates, and eliminates the cloning effect (in which an interviewer essentially hires candidates in his own image — or one who he thinks will "fit in").

The fairness issue is an elimination of bias because hiring based on one's own sense of comfort is likely to eliminate short young men, middle-aged men, unattractive women, nonsports buffs, overweight anyone, or victims of any bias who isn't "quite like us."

In structured interviews, the interviewer may throw out a *critical incident* asking you to respond. A critical incident is a specific problem or challenge that was successfully handled by employees of the company. Like a quiz show, the host (the interviewer) has the "answer sheet" — the actual behavior that solved the problem or met the challenge.

**Tip:** Some critical incidents can be anticipated by researching industry trends and inferred by reading company press releases (increasingly available on the Net). An example of a critical incident you could meet in the defense industry:

*Problem: Defense contractor often cannot find enough tech workers to meet government contract deadline.*

*Successful behavior: Recruiter works year-round with college career centers and unemployment clubs (for example, FortyPlus) to develop relationships fostering high employment visibility for her company; arranges crash courses to orient computer programmers to specific software; and monitors print, agency, and Internet sources of new technical candidates.*

Whether you are in a directive interview, or a patterned (structured) interview, expect interviewers to ask both closed- and open-ended questions.

A *closed-end question* can be answered yes or no —

*Did you find my office easily?*

An *open-ended question* usually asks how or why —

*How do you like this industry?*

This interviewer has an agenda and is intent on seeing that it's followed. Being too assertive in changing the topic is a mistake. The only way you can introduce one of your skills is to ask a question —

*Would you like to hear about my experience in quality assessment?*

## Nondirective interview

By contrast, a nondirective interview rewards you for leading the discussion. It's often an approach of line managers who don't know much about professional interviewing. Questions tend to be broad and general so that you can elaborate and tell all kinds of terrific stories about yourself. A few questions may reveal key areas of the employer's needs. These questions may sound at first as though they're critical incidents, but in this loose-limbed interview, the interviewer probably doesn't assume that she knows the answers.

*We had a problem employee last quarter who squealed information about our marketing strategies to a competitor — how would you handle this situation?*

*You understand some of the difficulties this department faces — how would you approach these in your first four months?*

*Tell me about your goals in the next decade and how this position fits in with them.*

*Your resume shows you have a degree in Spanish and another in computer science — how do you plan to use both of these in the position?*

**Tip:** Carry agenda cards or a small notebook with a list of your qualifications and a list of questions about the company. When you have to carry the ball, working from notes can be a lifesaver if you have a leaky memory.

## Stress interview

Recognizing the hazing that goes on in a stress interview is important; recognize it for what it is — either a genuine test of your ability to do the job or terminal pranksterism by a dumb jerk.

**Tip:** Don't take the horrors of a stress interview personally. Keep your cool and play the game if you want the job. Don't sweat and don't cry. Your most reliable tactic is to speak with calm, unflagging confidence.

Suppose that you're in sales. Asking you to sell the interviewer something — like the office chair — is fairly common. But having you face blinding sunlight while sitting in a chair with one short leg is, at best, childish.

Stress interviews often consist of

- Hour-long waits before the interview
- Long, uncomfortable silences
- Challenges of your beliefs
- A brusque interviewer or multiple curt interviewers
- Deliberate misinterpretation of your comments and outright insults

---

### Storytelling your way to a job

Prepare for your all interviews — not just behavior-based interviews — by recalling incidents from your past experience that back up your claims of skills and other qualifications. Work on these stories as though you're going to present them in a speech before hundreds of people. Make them fun, interesting — even exciting! Few of us are natural-born storytellers, but do your best to tell a good story.

Experts claim the way to ace behavior-based interviews is to prepare, rehearse, and deliver one- to two-minute stories about your skills, experience, and accomplishments that relate directly to the job. Your commitment to meeting their interests shows as you recognize their goal and pay up in full with stories.

A famous admiral, now dead, used to nail the furniture to the floor and ask the applicant to pull up a chair. If an interviewer crosses your personal line of reasonable business behavior, you may want to make a speedy exit.

# Mastering Interviews at All Locations

Not every interview takes place across a desk — you may interview over a meal, in a campus interviewing room, at a job fair, or even at home where the whole family gets the lookover.

## Mealtime interview

While a mealtime interview may seem more relaxed, stay as alert, if not more so, as you would in any other location. Mealtime interviewers watch your social habits and interpret them for clues to your job performance.

To avoid spilling precious job opportunities, mind your manners.

- ✔ Don't order entrees so hard to eat that you spend the whole interview lost in your plate with long pasta or saucy, messy, or bony food.
- ✔ Don't order alcohol unless you're at dinner — then only have *one* drink. White wine is a good choice.
- ✔ Don't order the most expensive or the most inexpensive thing on the menu.
- ✔ Don't smoke (companies are becoming obsessed with employee health costs).
- ✔ Don't complain about the food, the service, or the restaurant.
- ✔ Don't over-order or leave too much food on your plate.

For a winning mealtime interview, be sure to:

- ✔ Order something that's easy to eat (like a club or veggie sandwich).
- ✔ Chew with your mouth closed, speak with your mouth empty.
- ✔ Order something similar to what the interviewer orders or ask the interviewer to suggest something.
- ✔ Show your appreciation for the treat — once hired, you may find yourself brown-bagging your lunch.
- ✔ Practice a technique known as *mirroring* — what the boss or the interviewer does, you do. Take the interviewer's lead in resting arms on the table, holding forks, the speed of shoveling in the food. Subconsciously, you're establishing similarities, making the interviewer like you.

No matter what, the interviewer always pays, so don't reach for the bill when it comes, even if it's placed closer to you. Let it sit there. Remember, this could be a test of your confidence or of your knowledge of protocol.

Mealtime interviews make asking inappropriate questions much easier for the interviewer to get away with. As you're chatting, you may find yourself telling about your spouse, children, political views, or other social topics. Try to stay with business concerns or the weather.

## Party interview

A party setting designed for mass screening through mingling, away from the workplace, pops up occasionally. A few dozen people are gathered — recruiters and potential candidates — who typically are about to graduate from college or grad school. The environment is like a fraternity or sorority "rush party." Recruiters are sizing you up, and you're picking up signals about their company's culture.

Treat these events as deadly serious interviews. Drink very lightly, if at all. Don't be late or slip indiscrete remarks to your "new buddy." All the recruiters will join in a debriefing the next day, and your confidences will be revealed.

## Golf course interviews

Using a golf course as a site to interview for a managerial position isn't common, but it happens. Employers and recruiters use this game with lots of conventions to judge your professional character. Three examples from business-golfing pros: "Always wear a collared shirt, don't lose on purpose, and never throw your clubs."

If you're not an experienced golfer and certain of your course etiquette, try for a change of venue. Or ask at a golf pro shop for a business-golf book or seminar recommendation.

## Airport interviews

Executive recruiters increasingly use airline hospitality clubs at airports to interview candidates. The recruiters fly in, interview, and fly out — covering a lot of ground in a short period of time.

One of the problems with this site is the public nature of airport clubs. Job hunters risk running into their bosses or colleagues, and recruiters run into rivals. If you agree to interview at an airport, ask if you can meet in a private room. You'll be more relaxed and do a better job of presenting yourself without being worried about being seen by the wrong person.

## On-campus interview

Some employers recruit on campuses by setting up interviews through the college's career center. These screening interviews are conducted by company recruiters.

College seniors, to get the interviews you want, start by learning the system. Sign up for resume and job interviewing workshops; make friends with the counselors. Become a regular at your campus career center early in your college experience. Sure, the past few years have been blockbusters for new graduates, but don't forget: Some jobs are better than others, and why shouldn't you have them? Do the drill your counselors suggest — unless you turn into a supernova, this is the one time in your life that recruiters are likely to come charging after you.

Get the best handle you can on the career track you'd like to follow. You may not know exactly where you want to go, but avoid sounding like **Steve Zahn** in *Reality Bites*, a film about young adults trying to make their way in life. **Winona Ryder** asks Zahn to name his goal. Zahn's answer: "My goal is . . . I'd like a career of something."

**Tip:** If you don't get interview slots you want, check back for last-minute cancellations or additions to the interview schedules.

## Job fair interview

Job fairs are brief but significant encounters in which you hand over documents — either your resume or a summary sheet of your qualifications (carry both types of documents). Your objective is to land an interview, not get a job at the fair.

Try to preregister for the event, get a list of participating employers, and research those you plan to visit. Be better prepared than the competition.

Fair lines are long, so accept the likelihood that you'll be standing in many lines. Make use of your time by writing up notes from one recruiter while standing in line to meet another.

Everyone tries to arrive early, so arrive at half-time when the first flood has subsided. Dress professionally.

Work up a 30-second sales pitch with one strong point to say to recruiters — *I am in the top 10 percent of my environmental engineering class.* If there's no feedback inviting you for an interview, hand over your summary sheet and ask — *Do you have positions appropriate for my background?* If the answer is positive, ask *Could we set up an interview?* If you don't get a positive response, continue with *Could we talk on the phone next week?*

Whether or not you are able to schedule an interview on the spot, when you leave, hand over your resume (see my book *Resumes For Dummies* for ways to put your resume on top of the stack).

Think of your job fair interaction with recruiters as a major star's cameo performance in a film: Move in, make a high-profile impression through dress and preparedness, and move on to the next prospect.

# What's Playing at the Roxy?

You may not know in advance the type of interview you'll encounter under the blinky lights, but at least you won't be caught off guard if you take seriously the message in the next chapter.

# Bravo moves for all interviewing styles

No matter what style of interview you're doing, some factors are all-purpose job winners.

✔ **Make them like you.** No matter how scientific the interviewing style, the quality of likability is a powerful influence in deciding who gets the job. And it's human nature to like people who like us, and who are like us in common interests and outlooks.

*Show your similarities* with the interviewer and company culture. You need not be clones of each other, but do find areas of mutual interest: preferences in movies, methods of doing work, or favorite company products, for instance. When you successfully intimate that you and the decision-making interviewer share similar world views, values, or approaches to work, you create affinity that leads to job offers, as this true story shows:

After trying for months, Julia Benz (not her real name) finally won an interview with a major Los Angeles company, and she was taking no chances on botching the interview. As a part of her preparation, Benz went to the office the evening before her appointment.

She had merely intended to peek inside to see what the building was like but just as she looked in, a janitor cleaning the floor noticed her and asked if she needed help.

Benz told the truth. She said, "I wanted to get a feel for the place where I'm having an important interview tomorrow." Probably against company policy, the janitor invited Benz into the interviewer's office and pointed out several meticulously detailed models of old ships mounted on a high shelf.

The interviewer was clearly an avid collector. Later that night, Benz read up on old ships at the library.

You know what happens next: When Benz met the interviewer, she pointed at one of the models and remarked — *Say, isn't that a Hudson sloop?* The affinity was instant. Benz got the job.

Other ways to make them like you:

✔ **Listen well to interviewers' questions, statements, and feelings.** People like to be listened to more than they like to listen. Show your likability by summarizing, rephrasing, and playing back what interviewers say instead of concentrating just on what you have to say.

✔ **Don't drip honey by overdoing compliments or small talk.** Take cues from interviewer's office mementos just long enough to break the ice. Most interviewers will cloy at such transparent, saccharin plays for empty approval. Rather, get to the point — the job.

✔ **Pause thoughtfully.** Show that you think as you talk. It's okay to pause in thoughtfulness during an in-person interview, where interviewers can tell you're contemplating, thinking things through before answering. Exception: Don't take a thinking pause in a telephone or videoconferencing interview, where any pause is dead airtime.

✔ **Take notes.** Have a small notebook handy and use it when the interviewer is talking, especially after you've asked a question or the interviewer has put special emphasis on a subject. Taking notes not only shows that you're paying attention, but it also flatters the interviewer.

# Part II
# SuperStars Research and Rehearse

The 5th Wave    By Rich Tennant

©RICHTENNANT

"I have an interview with a law firm. I hope to make an impression."

# In this part . . .

To help you be as calm and competent as a Zen master at your job interviews, this part whispers clues you don't want to forget to be interview-ready.

This part begins with the incomparable value of research; what you do first determines who comes out first in the race to win the job interview. A list of online and printed resources to use for researching is included.

Next comes the value of rehearsals. You won't sound canned or stilted if you rehearse until your answers sound natural. Even if you're shy, you talk the talk better when you practice.

This part concludes with chapters that emphasize the value of costuming yourself for the role you want to play . . . that give you a heads up on pre-employment testing . . . and that show you how to stage manage your references for rave reviews.

# Chapter 3

# Research Frames Your Performance

● ● ● ● ● ● ● ● ● ● ● ● ● ● ● ● ● ● ● ● ● ● ● ● ● ● ● ● ● ● ● ● ● ● ● ● ● ● ● ● ● ● ● ● ●

*In This Chapter*

▶ Researching makes you 10 feet tall

▶ Knowing what you should research

▶ Quickly finding the research

● ● ● ● ● ● ● ● ● ● ● ● ● ● ● ● ● ● ● ● ● ● ● ● ● ● ● ● ● ● ● ● ● ● ● ● ● ● ● ● ● ● ● ● ●

*W*hat do three terrific, Oscar-winning actors have in common? **Robert De Niro, Al Pacino,** and **Nicholas Cage** all understand that information is everything.

Robert De Niro traveled to Jerusalem recently where he met with former intelligence officials to research his role in an upcoming movie on the Middle East conflict.

Al Pacino has performed more unforgettable gangster characters than just about any other actor. Even so, the pro prepared for his late '90s role as an aging Mafia hitman in *Donnie Brasco* by chatting up actual New York wiseguys.

Nicholas Cage plays a New York paramedic in *Bringing Out the Dead.* The paramedic, surrounded by the injured and the dying, nears the abyss of spiritual shutdown as his ambulance screams across city streets. To get a feel for what these health workers go through, Cage asked to do a ride-along with paramedics. He was told to put on a bulletproof vest and "just stay calm" because the real paramedics were going to the scene of a drive-by shooting, where Cage witnessed the reality of a young kid with a bullet shot through his leg.

## Get on Board with Information

Information is everything — and everywhere. You may not want to go as far as traveling overseas to check out spooks, gazing eyeball to eyeball with hoods, or holding back tears as you comfort a suffering gunshot victim. Understandable.

But don't pull up short in the opposite direction, either. That's one of the miscues in today's tropical job climate. Too many job seekers have become nonchalant about research, figuring companies are so desperate to hire that it doesn't matter if the job seeker comes in asking to do whatever it is that the company does.

An indifferent attitude toward research won't devalue your candidacy during a screening interview (especially when a recruiter makes the initial contact), but it will hurt you at an in-person selection interview.

So even if you'd rather scrub floors than do quiz-show-quality research on organizations and their people, you'll be heads above the others when you do. You gain these benefits:

- ✔ You'll have the facts to demonstrate a convincing fit between your qualifications and the job's requirements.
- ✔ You can give smart answers when asked, "What do you know about our company?"
- ✔ You can better absorb and evaluate new facts the interviewer adds during the interview.

# Here's the Good News

In the past few years, the Internet has given the old run-all-over-town company research task the old heave-ho! Old way: Dash to the library! Pretend you're an investor to get a stockbroker's annual report! New way: Getting a ton of free information on most public companies — and some private companies — is as easy as "click here."

In just an hour or two, you can uncover annual reports, financial data, news releases, information about products and services, industry trends, competitor information, and sometimes what employees have to say about the company. You often can find out about pending mergers, acquisitions, layoffs, and shifts in management personnel. You may pick up clues to corporate culture and find out Wall Street's outlook for the company.

All the data you obtain at the click of a mouse helps you make good career moves. You may discover that you'd better steer clear of the company under investigation. But if you discover no impending corporate collapse or toxic boss syndromes and decide you do want the job, research is a tiebreaker in a tight race with another candidate. (To find out how to research online, see the section later in this chapter.)

# What's to Know?

In filling a responsible position, many companies develop what is called a *candidate specification.* The specification describes the skills, experience, knowledge, education, and other characteristics believed to be necessary for the job. A part of your advance research should include the preparation of your own *position analysis* — the counterpart of the candidate specification.

Compile a position analysis from commercial job descriptions, recruitment advertising (print and online), occupational career guides, and news columns in business and trade publications. If you're working through a third-person recruiter, ask the recruiter to identify and prioritize the qualifications sought. Ask about major responsibilities, technical problems to be solved, and objectives for the position.

Even if you have to fill in the blanks with educated guesses, write down your understanding of what the interviewing company wants in the candidate.

Once you write a position analysis, review your skills and strengths to match what the hiring company says it wants. (For help on your side of the equation, see my books *Resumes For Dummies,* 3rd Edition, and *Cover Letters For Dummies,* 2nd Edition.) After you do this exercise a couple of times, you'll find that you can do it fairly quickly — probably in less than 30 minutes.

Now build on your foundation position analysis by adding the information you find in library and online research.

By interview time, your position analysis and supporting research give you a reasonable idea of what the hiring company wants from the person who fills the job.

# Research Questions to Ask

Use the following questions as a checklist to gather all the information you need. You won't necessarily need information on all the factors that follow, and you may think of others important for your search.

Here's the rule on how much research to do:

> *The more responsible the job — or the more competitive the race — the greater amount of research you must do to pull ahead.*

## Size and growth patterns

The size of a company and the scope of its operations say a great deal about the company's culture and opportunities for advancement. Try to answer the following questions:

- What does the company do?
- Is it a conglomerate?
- Has the company expanded globally?
- Is it expanding or downsizing?
- What are its divisions and subsidiaries?
- How many employees does it have?
- How many clients does it serve?
- How many locations does it have?
- Does it have foreign satellites?

## Direction

Answers to the following questions about the company's plans may be difficult to find outside of the company's annual report, newspaper business pages, business magazines, or the industry's trade publications. This information is worth pursuing as it lets you know some of the hot issues to address or avoid.

- What are the company's current priorities?
- What is its mission?
- What long-term contracts has it established?
- What are its prospects?
- What are its problems?
- Is it initiating any new products or projects?

## Products or services

You shouldn't go into a job interview without at least knowing what products or services are the bedrock of the company's business.

✔ What services or products does the company provide?

✔ What are its areas of expertise?

✔ How does it innovate in the industry — by maintaining cutting edge products, cutting costs, and so on?

✔ What are its production standards?

## Competitive profile

How the company is positioned within its industry and how hard competitors are pressuring offers valuable information about the company's long-term health and the relative stability of your prospective job there.

✔ Who are the company's competitors?

✔ What are the company's current projects?

✔ What setbacks has it experienced?

✔ What are its greatest accomplishments?

✔ Is the company in a growing industry?

✔ Will technology dim its future?

✔ Does it operate with updated technology?

✔ Can its jobs easily be moved to another country?

## Culture and reputation

The answers to these questions are likely to be subjective, but they say a great deal about how well you'll be able to fit into the corporate culture. Look for clues — does the place run at a frantic pace? laid-back? formal? informal? aggressive? sophisticated? Tuning your performance to a company's environmental factors can make you look as though you'd fit in fine.

✔ Does the company run lean on staffing?

✔ What's the picture on mergers and acquisitions?

✔ What is the company's business philosophy?

✔ What is its reputation?

✔ What kind of management structure does it have?

✔ What types of employees does it hire?

- ✔ Is it family-friendly?
- ✔ Is it woman-friendly?
- ✔ What is the buzz on its managers?
- ✔ How does it treat employees?
- ✔ Has it pushed out older workers?

## Company history

Assess how the company's future may be influenced by its past. Was the company part of a hostile takeover? Has it been doing the same things the same way for years because its founder would have wanted it that way?

- ✔ When and where was it established?
- ✔ Is it privately or publicly owned?
- ✔ Is it a subsidiary or a division?
- ✔ Has it changed much over time?
- ✔ How quickly has it grown?

## Net worth

Information about net worth is another tough area to find hard data on, but it's better to learn a company's shaky financial picture before you're hired than after you're laid off. Last hired, first fired is still the rule for many companies.

- ✔ What are the company's sales?
- ✔ What are its earnings?
- ✔ What are its assets?
- ✔ How stable is its financial base?
- ✔ Is its profit trend up or down?
- ✔ How much of its earnings go to its employees?
- ✔ How far in debt is the company?

## Start with a few simple basics

Publicly owned and big national companies are easier to track than privately owned and local or regional companies. Reporting on corporations as a whole is easier than reporting on their subsidiaries or divisions.

Once you know which pieces of information are of the most value for your search, keep careful notes and focus on the dates of the material you find online and in newspaper business sections, news magazines, and trade journals. Copies of library directories are probably too old to count on without additional fact-checking.

The following sections show you where to find the research you need.

# Researching Employers Online

Doing research online simply means using a computer and the resources of the Internet and other computer data banks to gather information. The *Internet* is a worldwide collection of networked computers sharing a standard for information transfer that makes sending and receiving data from many different types of computer systems possible. The *World Wide Web* is one component of the Internet that adds pictures to the mix and that creates links from one site to another, making Internet resources easy to find and use.

Never has educating yourself about employers, large and small, been as easy as it is now that the Internet's around. The Internet is a global computer network that is stocked with information about hundreds of thousands of public, private, and international companies, as well as government agencies and nonprofit organizations.

The most accessible employer data is found on the World Wide Web at company Web sites. You can find company mission statements, product descriptions, annual reports, job postings, press releases, and employee news.

To check up on your intended employer, try the following Sherlockian techniques:

- **Contact the company directly:** Start compiling a company dossier by looking at a company's own Web site. One easy way to do so is by looking at an online career resource that contains corporate profiles or provides a link page allowing you to connect to corporate Web sites with a mouse click. Examples of career resource Web sites are listed in "A Job Interview Online Address Book" in the next section.

- **Check out the company indirectly:** Continue checking by mousing around with your computer into the myriad research sites that review thousands of companies. You want to know what others say about the company. A search of the archives at publications' Web sites may turn up good stuff. The same is true for Dun & Bradstreet, Hoover's On-line, and Securities Exchange Commission documents. A sampling of research sites appears later in this chapter.

- ✔ **Perform a company search:** Entering a company name — as a keyword — in a Web search program will show you whether there's a site for the company you're researching. (A *keyword* is an identifying noun that a computer can search on. For more about keywords, see my book, *Resumes For Dummies,* 3rd Edition.) These search programs are called *search engines.* The search engine may turn up not only the company's Web page, but articles about the company. Whether you choose small or large organizations, a search engine brings you information like a messenger you send to the library — only at sonic speed. Several search engines are noted later in this chapter.

- ✔ **Contact trade group sites:** Most businesses and industries have a trade group on the Internet. Asking for information on banking from a search program results in a link to a variety of banking organizations, all of which are potential tattletales for your job interview.

- ✔ **Network with others online:** Signing up for online discussion groups (mailing lists, forums, roundtables, and the like) puts you in touch with people in your field. Get known and respected inside the group before asking about a specific company.

# A Job Interview Online Address Book

Start mining the wealth in virtual resources with the sampling of sites that follows. The Web addresses (called URLs — uniform resource locators) are impossible to keep up to date; if the one you want has moved without a forwarding address, just tap into a Web search engine or directory and find out where the site is now or check out a useful alternate site.

## Company Web sites

For job seekers, the company Web site is the annual report of a generation ago. These resources help you find them.

**Company WebPages** (4,000 companies) `www.interbiznet.com/hunt/companies`

**JobOptions** (6,000 companies) `www.joboptions.com`

**WetFeet.com** (industries; companies) `wetfeet.com`

**CorpTech** (high-tech companies) `corptech.com`

**Meta List High-Tech Companies** `job-hunt.org/companies.shmtl`

**Google** (insert company/click on I feel lucky) `google.com`

# Finding out about companies

The following resources are useful both for compiling job sourcing lists and for mining details useful in writing your cover letters.

**Companies Online** companiesonline.com

**PR Newswire** prnewswire.com

**Hoover's Online** hoovers.com

**Thomas Register Online** thomasregister.com

**About.com** (search on employer research) about.com

**Corporate Window** corporatewindow.com

**Business Wire** businesswire.com

**SuperPages.com** (company contact info) superpages.com

**FreeEDGAR** (Securities Exchange Commission) freeedgar.com

# Employee message boards — new!

Web-working the trenches of corporate America is opening an unprecedented era in opportunities for pre-employment research.

Employee message boards are becoming common, but, like talk radio, they tend to attract more complaints than compliments. So use common sense in deciding if you're reading the real skinny on advancement opportunities, coworkers, pay raises, and the names of scrappy managers to avoid. Small companies have yet to grow their own "fine whines," so stay on the prowl for personal one-on-one networking to find a friend of a friend who is an ex- or current employee who's willing to spill the company beans.

**Vault.com** (hundreds of various companies) vault.com

**Yahoo!/Business-Finance/Co.'s/Intraco.Group** clubs.yahoo.com

# Career sites

This sampling of national sites is useful for company research as well as job sourcing.

**Monster.com** `monster.com`

**Headhunter.net** `headhunter.net`

**JobOptions** `joboptions.com`

**HotJobs** `hotjobs.com`

**NationJob Network** `nationjob.com`

**CareerBuilder** `careerbuilder.com`

**Career Mosaic** `careermosaic.com`

**CareerPath** `careerpath.com`

**Careers.wsj.com** `careers.wsj.com`

# Niche sites

Affinity groups, people who share a special interest or background, are good places to find out what's going on in an industry or company. Many niche sites are maintained by nonprofit professional associations. Others are commercial. A few examples:

**Society of Human Resource Management** `shrm.org`

**Medzilla** (biotech, pharmaceutical, medical) `medzilla.com`

**StarChefs** (foodservice) `starchefs.com`

**Chronicle of Higher Education** `chronicle.com`

**Public Relations Society of America** `prsa.org`

**Project Management Institute** `pmi.org`

**Assn. of Internet Professionals** `association.org`

**Law Jobs** lawjobs.com

**Advertising Age** adage.com

**MBA Central** careercentral.com/mba

## Guides to professional organizations

Similar to the niche category, you can use associations to research.

**American Society of Association Executives** asaenet.org

**Associations on the Net** (Int. Public Library) ipl.org/ref/AON

**Yahoo Business&Econ/Organizations/Professional** yahoo.com

## Search engines

What once were sites designed to help you find what you needed online — search engines — are now virtual mega-malls.

**Google** google.com

**Excite** excite.com

**Alta Vista** av.com

**Lycos** lycos.com

**Infoseek** infoseek.com

## Publications

Newspaper and magazine sites are particularly useful for researching archives and learning about environments when you're thinking of relocating.

**AJR News Link** (most newspapers) ajr.newslink.org

**Newspaperlinks.com** (most newspapers) newspaperlinks.com

**Business Week** businessweek.com

**U.S. News and World Report** usnews.com

**Inc.** inc.com

# Popular Printed Resources

Once you exhaust computer-based resources, round out your search with traditional printed publications — directories, newspapers, magazines, and trade journals. A business library may also have company brochures or annual reports. Some of the following directories are also available online or on CD-ROMs, a few of which are moderately priced for consumers, but many cost thousands of dollars and are sold to libraries and other institutions.

*America's Corporate Families* (Dun's Marketing Services)

*Business Periodicals Index*

*Directory of Corporate Affiliations*

*Directory of Leading Private Companies*

*Directory of American Firms Operating in Foreign Countries*

*Dun & Bradstreet Principal International Business*

*Dun & Bradstreet Reference Book of Corporate Management*

*Dun's Top 50,000 Companies*

*Encyclopedia of Associations* (Gale)

*Plunkett's Research Publications*

*Standard and Poor's Register of Corporations, Directors and Executives*

*Thomas's Register of American Manufacturers*

*U.S. Industrial Outlook*

*Value Line Investment Survey*

# *Preparation Takes You Out of the Chorus*

Employers consider company research a reflection of your interest and enthusiasm, intelligence, and commitment. Research shows you are thorough, competent, and revved up to work. And in a market where you find that everybody you compete with looks alike, research is your secret weapon to make yourself different by specifically identifying the added value you bring. And not so incidentally, finding out what you should know about a company may encourage you to make a decision to look elsewhere.

The path to stardom begins with research. Without it, you risk being cast as an extra.

## A tutorial and tips for researching companies

Hundreds of Web sites are flush with helpful information about where your cover letter could help you find a job. But making sense of all of them is a reach. Debbie Flanagan, a human resource professional in Ft. Lauderdale, Florida, gets five gold stars for her terrific free tutorial, *Researching Companies Online*.

Find it at `home.sprintmail.com/~deb flanagan/index.html`. This resource is well worth the mile-long address.

# Chapter 4

# Rehearse, Rehearse, Rehearse

• • • • • • • • • • • • • • • • • • • • • • • • • • • • • • • • • • • • • • • • • • • • • • •

## In This Chapter

▶ Overcoming your nervousness

▶ Building attitude against stage fright

▶ Anticipating interview trapdoors

• • • • • • • • • • • • • • • • • • • • • • • • • • • • • • • • • • • • • • • • • • • • • • •

*Y*ou're nervous. You've got butterflies, a queasy feeling, a mouthful of cotton, and a rabbit pulse. You feel yourself sliding into brain fade, and the curtain's coming down fast. In short, you've got a galloping case of stage fright. Sound familiar?

Welcome to the club. You're not alone in your nervousness. Leading man **William Hurt** told *Parade* magazine that he suffered from such paralyzing stage fright that "My lips literally started to lock during a performance, and I had to turn away from the audience to pry my mouth open with my fingers."

Most people start out with a case of the shakes when interviewing or making a speech, including me. When I began giving speeches, I could feel my throat drying up as panic fried my memory banks. I knew I had to go out and orate to promote my *Careers* column, but doing so was not a pleasure.

One day in Orlando, a teacher with whom I shared a podium watched me shake my way through remarks. The teacher, herself an accomplished speaker, took me aside after the program and delivered one of the best pieces of advice I've ever had. The teacher explained that nervousness is caused by the fear of looking ridiculous to others:

> *When you are nervous, you are focusing on yourself. Try to focus on how you are helping other people by sharing with them the knowledge you've acquired. You've been privileged to gather information not many people have. Think about serving others, not about yourself when you're up there on stage.*

Those words of wisdom were like a lifetime speech-making tranquilizer for me. Never again have I been nervous on stage. Thanks, Teach, for putting nervousness in perspective.

How can *you* use that perspective?

When you think about it, preparing for a job interview is not unlike preparing for a speech. The trick is to first get the kinks out of your basic self-presentation, which you accomplish with plenty of rehearsals. That's the design of this chapter — to help you present a basic all-around, favorable interviewing image.

Once you get your basic act down pat, you will, of course, polish it with new words before each interview — words you find by researching the interviewing company (see Chapter 3).

Once you know your material cold — and how the skills you are selling benefit the potential employer — the outward-looking perspective kicks in. Divert your attention to the needs of your audience. Concentrate on fulfilling the interviewer's needs. Remember

> *Focus on your audience, not on yourself.*

Just as I found that focusing on the audience is a giant step toward eliminating nervousness, so will you. Before going on to other rehearsal tips, here's a recap of the three critical steps you can take to deliver a confident, poised, ShowStopper interview performance:

1. **Polish your basic sales pitch.**

   Know your skills and rehearse until you're comfortable answering questions and have polished your basic presentation techniques.

2. **Personalize each sales pitch.**

   Research each potential employer to personalize your basic presentation.

3. **Spotlight your audience.**

   Focus on how your skills can benefit your audience; do not focus on yourself and how imperfect you may appear.

# More Techniques to Develop Stage Presence

When stars of the theater walk on stage, they claim the stage from wing to wing, backdrop to footlights. They have the gift of presence. With confidence and charisma, they win the audience's undivided interest. In a phrase, stars have stage presence.

*Stage presence* is the result of being comfortable on stage. How can you develop that comfort? The short answer is rehearse until you get it right. If you have so many practice interviews that finally the real one would seem to be "just another time through," that might be best, advises Briar Cliff College professor Phil Hey.

The long answer is contained in the following sections.

## Building your repertoire

Be comfortable with your script. Choose at least five major skills you'd most like interviewers to remember after the interview. Memorize a short statement about each skill. Which five skills are your best?

1. _____

2. _____

3. _____

4. _____

5. _____

## Rehearsing aloud

Practice reading your skill statements aloud. Read them five times at a minimum. Why not just read the statements over and over silently? Experts say "rehearing" helps fix content in your mind. Rehearing your statements at least five times makes them yours.

Rehearsing five times beats the time frame of an orator in ancient Greece. Demosthenes, who knew a thing or two about holding a listener's ear, went into a cave to learn oratory skills. Not having a watch or calendar — and of course, a sundial wouldn't work in a cave — Demosthenes shaved off the hair on half of his head and didn't come out until it grew back three months later. When he emerged, wow, could he spiel!

## Practicing with a camcorder

Discover yourself through an employer's eyes. With a friend feeding you practice questions, work with a video camcorder — rented or borrowed if you don't own one. An audio tape recorder is useful, but isn't in the same league as being able to see as well as hear yourself in interviewing action.

You'll see how — with image improvement and mannerism modification — you can look alert, competent, and confident. You can refine actions that turn hiring on and eliminate those that turn hiring off. Rehearse nonverbal as well as spoken messages.

- ✔ Watch for leg swinging, tapping, or rocking from side to side.
- ✔ Watch fiddling with your hair.
- ✔ Watch nervous hands.
- ✔ Don't lean back, cross your arms, or bow your head frequently.
- ✔ Are you remembering to smile?

Look interested when seated by leaning slightly forward with the small of your back against the chair. Look the interviewer squarely in the nose; you will appear to be making eye contact. You'll look open and honest. More earnest honesty is communicated by upturned, open palms.

Avoid darting eyes — they make you seem shifty. Slow blinking comes across as disinterest — maybe even as slow-thinking. Half-glasses may suggest haughtiness. Keep your hands away from your mouth.

Should you pause and think before answering? Why not? You'll seem thoughtful and unflappable.

Should you refer to your notes? Why not? You'll be seen as one who covers all the bases. Just don't make the mistake of holding onto your notes like they're a life preserver.

Does your voice seem a tad tight and creaky? Warm up by singing in your car on the way to the interview. La la la la. . . .

## Funneling off extra physical tension

Minimize physical tension by resting well, stretching and exercising beforehand, and avoiding foods challenging to your digestion. Try an instant stress reliever — take a deep breath, breathing from your toes all the way through your body, then slowly exhale. Repeat twice more — three deep breaths in all.

Another trick: Go into a nearby restroom and lean into a wall like a suspect being frisked in a cop show. Push hard, as though you would like to push the wall down. Grunt as you push. It sounds funny, but try it — it works. Speech coaches say that when you push a wall and grunt, you contract certain muscles, which in turn reduces anxiety. Don't let anyone see you do this exercise, though — heaven knows what an observer might think.

## Eliminating mental tension

If events in your personal life increase your worries, take care of those issues before the interview. Free your mind to concentrate on the subject of your job interview. If your personal concerns can't be handled immediately — and most can't — write them down and promise yourself that you'll deal with them after your job interview.

# Building a ShowStopper Attitude

As you log rehearsal hours to sell yourself at today's high-powered interviews, keep in mind these basic stage directions.

## Tips useful to all

The following tips are ones that anyone going for a job interview should follow:

- Visualize your interview as an adventurous challenge, where you can toot your horn with a chance at a reward — not as an angst-ridden test of your ability to recite script.

- Practice focusing your discussion on the employer's needs; show that you understand those needs, that you possess the specific skills to handle the job, and that you are in sync with the company culture.

- Don't discuss previous rejections — you'll come off as a constant audition reject.

- If you're a minority, don't play the race card with the interviewer as though you're being targeted for outscreening (see related anti-discrimination tips listed under the sections "Tips especially for women" and "Tips mainly for men").

- Make eye contact, but don't try for a laser lock on the interviewer. Imagine two cats in a staring contest — in the animal kingdom, nobody moves until somebody swats. Break the tension — periodically look away.

## Tips that rookies need to know

Rookies need to concentrate on the skills they bring to a job. Follow these tips to help establish stage presence:

✔ Practice elaborating on the skills and knowledge you bring to the job.

✔ Storytell — prepare detailed examples of all your skills, with as many examples from off-campus as on-campus (see Chapter 2).

✔ Rehearse discussions of your adaptability, high learning capacity, high energy, and hard work.

✔ Don't flag your newbiness by apologizing for a lack of experience — the employer already knows that you lack experience.

✔ Don't dull your competitive edge by practicing statements that rely only on your college education — that alone won't sell you.

## Tips that aces can apply

As good actors and actresses grow older, they no longer have to prove their talent, but they do have to prove that they still have what it takes to play a demanding role. Follow these tips to make you a star with staying power:

✔ Experiment with statements clarifying that contributing to the employer's goals is your first priority.

✔ Storytell — prepare examples of your high energy, fresh enthusiasm, and willingness to compete (see Chapter 2).

✔ Control your own biases against supervisors or interviewers long before interviewing — for example, if they're mere babes, don't offer towels for drying behind the ears.

✔ Carry yourself with a young attitude; sit up in the chair and look *alive* — laugh if the interviewer makes a show biz joke even if you never heard of the celebrities involved.

## Tips especially for women

When auditioning for a role, actresses use a whole different set of skills than actors. Whether you're a starlet in the making or an established *grande dame* of the theater, follow these tips to make sure you get the role you covet:

✔ Don't make a habit of discussing gender issues (such as the "glass ceiling") or call your former boss sexist (pig that he was).

✔ Develop and practice justifiably proud statements of your accomplishments.

✔ Practice descriptions of your leadership qualities and initiative.

✔ If you're a mom, anticipate having to neutralize an employer's hidden worries about maternal absenteeism.

✔ Feminine behavior is in vogue again — practice speaking in a low, thrilling voice that makes anything you say sound intelligent.

## Tips mainly for men

Well-known actors like **Robert Redford, Tom Cruise,** and **Clint Eastwood** had to prove at one time that they could play both the tough guy and the sensitive, romantic lead to win lasting stardom. Use the following tips to create that perfect balance in the interviewing situation:

✔ Don't gripe about reverse discrimination if you're white (no matter how many hits you've taken).

✔ If pressed, you can admit you've made a mistake in your career (when was it — 3:48 p.m. on June 14, 1993?) — but rehearse satisfying explanations of how you learned from your one mistake — or two or three.

✔ Drill yourself to reveal positive aspects of your personal life, such as team sports, group hobbies, and kids — employers like well-rounded candidates.

✔ Don't practice long monologues — be fair: Split air time with your interviewer (yes, the same tip goes for women).

# Anticipating Interviewing Trapdoors

No matter how well you're doing as you sail through an interview, certain things can throw you off balance if you're not forewarned.

## Interference

As you rehearse, keep in mind that not everything that happens during the interview is related to you. Your meeting may be interrupted by a ringing telephone, the interviewer's coworkers, or even the interviewer's needs. Add some interference to your mock interviews. Because the show must go on, find methods to politely overlook these interruptions with patient concentration being your purpose. Practice keeping a tab on what you're discussing between disruptions in case the interviewer doesn't.

## Silent treatment

Remember this mantra:

> *Never should the unnecessary be volunteered by the unwary for the unforgiving.*

Anticipate this trapdoor by closing it with good questions or by waiting it out.

Interviewers use silence strategically. Moments, even minutes of silence, are intended to get candidates to answer questions more fully — and even to get them to spill harmful information. Instead of concentrating on your discomfort during these silences, recognize the technique, and either wait out the silence until the interviewer speaks, or fill it with star-studded questions (see Chapter 9). Do not bite on the silent treatment ploy and spill your innermost secrets.

# Not a pretty picture

Watch videos of your mock interviews with these lists of don'ts in mind:

**Don't say**

- *Uhm*
- *Uh*
- *Yeah or Yup* (instead of *yes*)
- *Y'know*
- *Like*
- *Okay*
- *I guess*
- *Pretty good*

**Don't**

- Jingle pocket change
- Tap feet, fingers
- Twirl, pull, or rearrange hair
- Fold arms
- Sit with arms or legs far apart
- Offer a limp handshake
- Fidget
- Maintain constant eye contact
- Display shy eyes
- Have gum or anything else in or near your mouth
- Mumble
- Interrupt
- Speak too fast
- Slump
- Twiddle props — pens, paper, or desk items

Turning the tables, you can use your own silence to encourage the interviewer to elaborate or to show that you're carefully considering issues under discussion.

# Take One . . . Take Two . . . Take Three . . .

Practice your scenes until they feel right, until they feel spontaneous. Rehearsing gives you the power to become a confident communicator with the gift of presence. No more nervousness, no more zoning out.

No matter how much you protest that you just don't have the personality to sell your talents in an interview, master the simple principles set out in this chapter, and you will go a long way toward achieving the ShowStopper-class meetings you need to land the jobs you want.

## What impresses campus recruiters?

University of Texas at Dallas counseling specialist Allen H. Krause shares this recent study of how a group of recruiters rates applicant behaviors at job interviews. How would interviewers rate you on these factors?

Key to numerical values: very important = 5, moderately important = 4, slightly important = 3, cannot decide = 2, unimportant = 1.

| Behavior | Mean Rating |
|---|---|
| Enthusiasm | 4.8 |
| Communication skills | 4.8 |
| Self-confidence | 4.7 |
| Well groomed | 4.6 |
| Business attire | 4.3 |

| Behavior | Mean Rating |
|---|---|
| Politeness | 4.3 |
| Technical knowledge | 4.3 |
| Steady eye contact | 4.1 |
| Assertiveness | 4.1 |
| Decisiveness | 4.1 |
| Knowledge of employer | 4.1 |
| Firm handshake | 4.0 |
| Well-defined career goals | 4.0 |
| Good posture | 3.9 |
| Sense of humor | 3.8 |
| Other | .4 |

# Chapter 5

# Costuming for the Role

**In This Chapter**

▶ Wisdom of dressing to fit the role

▶ Avoid looking like an outsider

▶ Specific tips to look your best

▶ Dressing "business casual"

▶ Polishing images for aces and rookies

**1**n the film *Reality Bites*, two friends, Troy (**Ethan Hawke**) and Michael (**Ben Stiller**), tell Leliana (**Winona Ryder**) how she looks: "Like . . . a doily."

Fortunately Leliana wasn't going on a job interview. But you are, and you certainly don't want to look like a doily. How do you want to look?

The No. 1 guideline to follow in dressing for job interviews is simple:

> *Dress to fit the job and the job's culture.*

Companies and organizations are made of people working as a group to accomplish common goals. If your clothing or grooming sends a message that you are apart from them, you create an immediate, negative, nonteam player image. That's why you should strive to look as though you belong in the environment of your interview. Clothing is work-related costuming, not an outlet for self-expression.

Jack Stewart, director of career services at Abilene Christian University in Abilene, Texas, knows very well that an old theater adage holds true meaning for job interviews:

> *Look the part, and the part plays itself.*

During his years as a headhunter, Stewart's recruiting office accepted a search for an industrial sales rep from a new client. Stewart's firm began referring quality candidates, recommending to the candidates that they dress conservatively for their interviews, meaning business suits, stiff shirts, and silk ties.

Six interviews with different individuals brought the same response from the client, "Each candidate was basically qualified, but not what we're looking for."

Stewart's firm had a policy of re-evaluating a client's assignment if six candidates were referred and none received a job offer. A recruiter was sent to the client's offices to uncover the problem.

Imagine the recruiter's surprise when he entered an office filled with people dressed in very casual slacks and sport shirts sans ties. Well, the recruiter thought, these must be the foot soldiers. What does the captain wear? The recruiter found out soon enough when the sales manager arrived to greet him in a pair of black work shoes topped by white socks.

"From that day forward," Stewart explains, "we dressed down our candidates for their interviews with that client — but we couldn't bring ourselves to tell them to wear white socks — and finally, one of our referrals was hired. The experience is a good reminder for job interviewees — *When in Rome, wear a toga.*"

# *Keeping Up Appearances*

For years, virtually every job interviewing counselor has said that dressing conservatively is the safest route. That conventional wisdom is no longer universally and automatically correct. Artists, writers, and technical people, for example, may fit in better with potential associates when dressed like joggers out for a marathon run than dressed like buttoned-down briefcase toters.

A laid-back dressing trend creeping across the country has moved beyond workers who work alone or in creative groups. Sales and other professionals who interact with the public are dressing less business-correct in many areas of the country, particularly in the western states, than they were 15 years ago.

## Dressing up a notch

When you go job interviewing, the classic advice is, "Dress one step up from what you'd typically wear to work in that position." Other lines you may hear are "Dress 10 percent better than you ordinarily would," or "Dress for the position you'd like to have, not for the one you do have, so you'll be seen as promotable."

My take on upscaling for interview days is to "Dress the best you're ever going to look in the job you want."

So what's a job hunter to do? Subscribe to all the high fashion magazines? Nope! The only smart thing to do is to research the norm in your area, industry, and prospective company. You want to be on the team, and so you want to wear the team uniform — whatever that may be.

# Striking a Pose

A good beginning sets the stage for the *halo effect* — when the interviewer likes you right away, the interviewer may assume that if you excel in one area (image), you excel in others. The first impression you make on the interviewer sets the stage for what follows. Some potential employers make a subconscious hiring decision within seconds of meeting a candidate and spend the rest of the interview validating their initial impression. With this knowledge in mind, make your appearance a real curtain raiser.

 How can you look wonderful right off the bat? A discussion follows, but certain negatives are eternal and should be avoided.

## Smart idea: Interview in a team uniform

One of the problems faced by many strong personalities — especially rookies — in a job hunt is their desire to be distinctive in dress. They just don't get the message about how important projecting a professional image is.

Festooned in Ally McBeal skirts or athletic team shirts, they dig in their heels, tell counselors to let go of their ears, and insist that their clothing must reflect their personal style. This rebellious, anti-authority mind-set is, well, self-defeating.

I have the nerve to preach on this issue because when I was a rookie, I argued with supervisors about my proclivity to wear purple, sling-back, high heels to work. I thought they were wonderful and showed my cool taste. Honest to God. Finally, I gave the purple shoes to Goodwill when a supervisor got through to me with this remark: *"If you're not selling, why advertise?"*

If you see yourself on this page, I urge you to *forget about personal style until you get a job.* Insisting on doing your own kind of dressing marks you as immature, and immature kids don't get hired. If you really want to get off the beach, present yourself as one of "them." Who are "them"? Why, those people with whom you hope to work.

After you're on the job for a few months and discover how much personal style you can get away with in the workplace, you may choose to individualize your image. Of course, this advice presupposes you have little interest in being promoted. As unfair as it seems, people really are refused promotions because they do not dress to convey a managerial image.

For *women,* the checklist includes the following:

- ✔ No heavy makeup
- ✔ No makeup on the collar line
- ✔ No wearing a "coordinated" outfit with pieces that are near-misses
- ✔ No pastel overload (pink, baby blue) reminiscent of nurseries
- ✔ No provocative clothing (see-through, tight, slits, super-short skirts)
- ✔ No flashy jewelry, dangle earrings, or ankle bracelets
- ✔ No strappy shoes, sandals, or towering heels
- ✔ No big hair or elaborate styles
- ✔ No chipped or unusual color (blue, green) nail polish
- ✔ No hosiery runs or designer stockings

For *men,* the following checklist applies:

- ✔ No sagging coat lining
- ✔ No bulge in the pockets
- ✔ No battered briefcases
- ✔ No suspenders (or as the Brits say, "braces") worn with a belt or belt loops
- ✔ No five o'clock shadows
- ✔ No short or white socks
- ✔ No alligator shoes or sandals, or unshined or worn-down heels
- ✔ No mismatching belts and shoes (same color in leather)
- ✔ No ties too short or too long, or bowties
- ✔ No wrinkled or soiled clothing

For *everyone,* the checklist includes the following:

- ✔ No tinted glasses
- ✔ No joke or fad watches
- ✔ No disposable writing pens
- ✔ No visible body piercing or multiple earrings in one ear
- ✔ No visible body art; cover tattoos if possible
- ✔ No inconsistent look — no sneakers with suits

# Taking the Conservative Approach

Although Americans have been putting suits and ties in the back of their closets in recent years, most recruiters continue to agree that when you're not sure which way to dress, err on the conservative and professional side. For white-collar workers, here's what that means.

For *women*, the checklist includes the following:

- A two-piece suit: Women have a harder time than men being seriously. If you wear a dress, put a crisp jacket over it. Pantsuit? Yes, in a dark color. A pantsuit is especially appropriate if you're in a high-tech or youth-oriented industry. Accessorize it with a simple shell and silk scarf. But if you are interviewing with a traditionalist, stick to skirts.

- White, off-white, or neutral-colored blouse is good.

- Shoes: Closed-toe pumps with low or mid-heels show you're serious about working.

- Pull long hair back in a simple style.

For *men*, the following checklist applies:

- Two-piece, well-fitted suits are preferred. Trendsetters are wearing European-style three-button jackets, single-breasted, slimmer lapels.

- Shirt colors: White is first, light blue second. Long-sleeved oxford cloth is preferred.

- Dark ties are considered executive-like. Geometric patterns should be minuscule.

- No knit-shirt-and-khaki outfit for banking and other button-down industries.

For *everyone*, the checklist includes the following:

- The power suit colors are navy and other dark blues. Black is seen as somber — a charcoal gray is safer. The dark colors convey formality, conservatism, and authority.

- To show less authority, camel or beige are acceptable. Still less power is conveyed with a jacket and slacks, rather than a suit, and even a turtleneck on occasion.

# Choosing Business Casual

There's little doubt that the nation's workers are moving from Casual Friday to Casual Every Day. The most recent survey by the Society for Human Resource Management reports that 95 percent of responding companies allow weekly or daily casual dress policies; the number who allow casual dress every day is 42 percent.

For men and women, business casual dressing that's safe and appropriate for interviews consists of natural-fiber slacks in the $75 to $150 range, dressy casual shirts, a blazer or sweater, and quality loafers. If that's beyond your budget, scale down the costs but follow that pattern.

The quandary for job applicants is whether to dress in a suit even when you know everyone in the office will be informal. In a few cases, corporate blue suits can actually reduce your chances because you don't seem to "fit in" and haven't bothered to find out the dress code.

Advance research is the only way to be on sure footing. Assuming that you know what business casual means in your interview setting — or if you should dress in business casual — is risky. Research before stepping on stage.

# Getting Your Act Together

To sum up, dress to fit the role. When in doubt, scout it out. Before tackling a job interview, watch employees at the company, coming and going to work. Telephone and strike up a research conversation with whoever answers at the company. When an executive recruiter is running interference in your job search, ask the recruiter.

Plan that your first interview will go well and that you will be invited back for future meetings. By now you're "new friends" with the interviewer. The thought of relaxing your dress code is tempting. Big mistake! Maintain dress standards even if you have to wear the same suit with a different tie or blouse, or the same work clothes, washed and freshly pressed.

Your costuming can prove your qualification for the part before you even deliver your lines. Use every chance you can to win the audition — even if you have to wear a toga.

# Chapter 6

# Getting Psyched for the Screen Test

*In This Chapter*

▶ Fighting tests may be hazardous to your career

▶ Understanding the great testing controversy

▶ Meeting and beating the test types

▶ Preparing with sample test questions

After 30 tense minutes in a job interview, Dale Malone (not his real name) found himself sharpening a pencil for a three-hour pre-employment test. Two hours into the test, Malone jumped up from his chair and stormed out of the room thinking, *Some of the questions on this test are outrageous! They've got to be illegal!* Malone considered throwing in the towel because of these rude questions,[1] which were to be answered true or false:

*I have no difficulty starting or holding my urine.*

*I am very strongly attracted by members of my own sex.*

On the way out of the room, the thought hit Malone like a spray of cold water: *If I don't answer these questions, I probably won't get the job.* So Malone wrestled his temper under control, went back inside, and finished the test. After he arrived home, still seething over the indignity of some of the questions, Malone was riled enough to call his lawyer.

The lawyer's response surprised Malone: *There's no reward for confronting an employer about a test unless you can prove violation of your civil rights or discrimination against a disability.* Malone realized he might as well take his frustration to a punching bag.

---

[1] These two questions were among those that cost a prominent retailer $2 million in a class action settlement in 1993. The plaintiffs (who had been job applicants) said the psychological testing violated their privacy rights and the state's Labor Code, which bans questions about sexual orientation.

A number of test makers and their customers have been sued for discrimination — and lost. Those lawsuits were a wake-up call. Today the pre-employment test industry, a multibillion dollar effort, vigorously reviews tests for *100 percent relevance to job performance*. While no test is litigation-proof, mounting a successful legal challenge is much harder than it used to be.

Malone correctly sized up his situation — he had to take the test. If he didn't, he wouldn't have a prayer of getting the job. Malone's prospective employer, a security patrol company, immediately disqualifies anyone who refuses testing. Even though the tests struck Malone as invasive of his privacy, and frankly insulting, he had rent to pay and cats to feed — like millions of other job seekers. The moral of the story is

> *Fighting tests may be hazardous to your career.*

Tens of thousands of employers use tests as part of job interviews, not because the employers are test freaks, but because nobody has developed a more efficient method to sort large numbers of people into — or out of — positions.

If you don't want the job, don't take the test. Refusing to take a test implies that you're already refusing some part of the job.

# Understanding the Great Testing Controversy

I can't recall a single letter from a reader of my *Careers* column saying, *Oh wow, I can hardly wait to take another job test!* For a variety of reasons, people detest the tests. One basic argument effectively used against the concept of testing is that such elements as personality, learning capacity, and career goals are immeasurable without being tested by on-job performance.

By contrast, test makers and employers insist that their tests stick to questions that are 100 percent relevant to job performance.

Step into employers' shoes for 30 seconds:

- If you count expenses ranging from recruiting to the time period before the employee becomes productive, bringing a new employee onboard can cost thousands of dollars. Hiring mistakes are costly.

- Pre-employment testing usually costs less than hours of background checks on each applicant.

The debate over which is more important, testing accuracy or employers' wallets, will continue until someone designs a better applicant filter.

# Meeting and Beating the Test Types

Pre-employment tests are not like academic tests. The following types of tests are found in the workplace, but only the first three types are common for candidate evaluation. The last two types of tests are uncommon in pre-employment testing.

- **Personality tests** attempt to measure and compare your traits with those of other groups of people.

- **Integrity tests** (considered by some to be a type of personality test) rate your honesty, responsibility, and reliability for the job.

- **Skills tests** (also called *performance tests*) gauge your performance — not how fast you *may* be able to type, but how many words per minute you *do* type.

- **Aptitude tests** predict your potential for high performance in a given position. Scholastic aptitude tests measure your intelligence and learning ability.

- **Career interests inventories** match work activities with your personal preference (what you like to do), to see which occupations best fit your interests profile.

Examples of personality and integrity test questions appear later in this chapter. Skills testing varies by occupation. Aptitude tests and career interest inventories are more commonly found in academic settings.

# General Tips to Help You with Tests

Nonmanufacturing businesses, such as retailers, banks, utilities, insurance companies, and communications corporations, tend to use tests more than manufacturing industries. Tests are prevalent in jobs involving money, public safety, or merchandise. The following suggestions are useful anytime you're asked to test for a position.

## Questions you can ask before the test

Although you can't blow off the idea of taking employment tests, you can ask a few questions to put a little safety net under your candidacy. Try these questions:

> ✔ *I sometimes get uptight about tests. Can I take the test again if I don't do too well today, or is this take final?*
>
> ✔ *What kind of test(s) are you asking me to take? Personality, integrity, performance. . . ?*
>
> ✔ *Can I get any feedback regarding test results? How about areas I didn't do well in . . . at least I'll know what areas need improvement.*
>
> ✔ *Will I still be considered for the job if I don't do well on the test?*

Expect more "nos" than "yeses" to these questions, but they're worth a try. If the interviewer seems hard-nosed about your queries, at least you'll know the kind of company you're dealing with — if you think they're tough now, wait until you're hired and the honeymoon is over.

## Watch for combination tests

Many tests are combinations of several types of test questions. Even if the first ten questions ask about your personality traits, stay alert for questions about your aptitudes (such as potential for leadership or creativity) or your integrity (such as lying).

## Beware of absolutes

Watch out for absolutes like "always," "ever," and "never." For example, saying you *never* took more than your share of things in your life may paint you as a goody-two-shoes who can't be trusted.

## Leapfrog questions

Many tests have an uncomfortable time constraint. When taking a paper-and-pencil test, first answer only the questions to which you know the answers. Then answer the slightly difficult ones and set your own time limits for each (avoid persisting at a difficult question when you could be penciling in a sure thing). Save the toughest for last and if you have time, double-check your answers. Test experts claim the first answer is often the best answer.

## Computerize yourself

The new wave of technology computerizes many tests. At this time, most are academically oriented, such as college and graduate entrance program testing. But, undoubtedly, computerization will sweep through job testing as well. Be aware that in many testing platforms, you are not allowed to go back and forth between questions or change answers. Get the rules straight going in — and find out if you are penalized for guessing (when wrong answers count more against you than no answers do). Critics also point out that computerized tests may discriminate against individuals not experienced with computers. The solution? Get computer experience.

## Visualize high scores

Based on your own research of the company, imagine the ideal candidate — how would that individual think? When you hit a wall with a weird question, answer as the ideal candidate.

Position yourself as a person of moderation in the mainstream of contemporary thought. Interviewers see unconventional beliefs as potential trouble.

## Answer as the perfect employee

Obviously, "answering as the perfect employee" is not easy. You need to know what the perfect employee is like. How much and what kind of physical and mental abilities, specific knowledge, personality characteristics, and experience make for a better performance in the position for which you're testing?

No matter how much research you do, sometimes you cannot correctly guess the ideal profile, especially because some desired characteristics are not linear — in *assertiveness,* for instance, a moderate amount is best. When you're unsure, the best you can do is to call common sense to your rescue.

## Choose answers suggesting positive traits

Try to select answers that put you in the most positive light. Some favored characteristics include

- ✔ Achievement-oriented
- ✔ Agreeable
- ✔ Assertive
- ✔ Conscientious
- ✔ Dependable
- ✔ Emotionally stable
- ✔ Good talker

- Imaginative
- Intellectually curious
- Open to new experiences
- Optimistic
- Responsible
- Sociable
- Tolerant
- Trustworthy

## Avoid answers suggesting negative traits

Stay away from answers that show you in a less than stellar light. Some of the negative characteristics to avoid implying include

- Can't function under stressful conditions
- Dishonest
- Emotionally dysfunctional
- Not wrong to file fraudulent worker's compensation claim
- Not wrong to stir up legal trouble
- Poor impulse control
- Prone to interpersonal conflicts
- Prone to theft
- Prone to time theft (sick leave abuse, tardiness)
- Use drugs or other mind-altering substances
- Violence prone

## Suggest adaptability to stressful situations

Psychological tests award good marks for the capacity to work well in emergencies, under deadlines, with irate customers, and under heavy responsibilities. Studies say psychological tests identify stress-coping mechanisms that may limit satisfactory job performance, such as

- Disregard for rules
- Tendency to be tense or suspicious
- Oversensitivity to threats
- Perfectionism
- Rigidity
- Prejudice
- Negative interpersonal relationships

## Show confidence in yourself

A serious counterproductive trait in an employee is the lack of self-worth. Employers fear that low self-esteem types will merit discharge or will lack the motivation to stay on the job. For example, if asked (yes/no) *I am comfortable working with people,* say "yes," of course you are. The best worker is a happy worker.

### Special tips for salespeople

Any test administered for the sales industry probably measures characteristics like the following:

- Empathy — the capacity to identify or sympathize with another individual's feelings

- High energy — the force to stay with a challenge until met

- Achievement orientation — a drive for learning new abilities and impatiently accomplishing goals

- Intellect — qualities showing culture and imagination

- Self-control — a feeling of being in personal control of your destiny

- Self-efficacy — the belief that you can meet your expectations if you try hard enough

- Self-monitoring — the tendency to use social cues (not only your personal convictions) about what is expected

- Positive resilience — the ability to not take sales failure personally but also to bounce back for the next sales call

## Be alert to replayed questions

Some tests, particularly integrity tests, ask virtually the same question on page one, page three, and page ten. The test is trying to catch inconsistencies — figuring you'll forget a lie you told 30 questions ago. If possible, read through the test before you start. Consistency counts.

# Personality Tests

Some personality tests specifically ferret out specific traits. Following are a few tests with a brief indication of the factors they evaluate. This list is by no means comprehensive and is included here only to illustrate the types of tests you may encounter.

- **Personnel Decisions, Inc. (Employment Inventory)**

  Identifies applicants who are more dependable, stable, responsible, conscientious, and motivated; and less nonconforming and hostile

- **Business Personality Inventory**

  Tests for such traits as orientation to change, competitiveness, perfectionism, risk-taking, stamina, work orientation, and time management

- **Reliability Scale (Hogan Personnel Selection Series)**

  Looks for conscientiousness; measures hostility towards authority, confused vocational identity, and social insensitivity

- **The Wonderlic Personnel Test**

  Searches for a wide battery of traits, including a tendency to live for the moment and a general attitude toward challenge

- **Minnesota Multiphasic Personality Inventory or Inwald Personality Inventory**

  Scrutinizes behavioral patterns and personality characteristics relevant to job performance

# Integrity Tests

Personality based, these types of psychological tests typically have two sections:

✔ One section is designed to *measure your attitudes* about dishonesty and theft (such as your imagination about the ease of theft on the job, the extent of coworker theft, and any rationalized excuses for theft).

✔ The other section is designed to *detect a record of illegal activities or theft* (such as drug use or items stolen).

One way to beat these tests fair and square is to be sensitive to trick questions. For example, if you're asked to estimate the percentage of workers who steal from their employer, make a low guess. A high guess may be interpreted to mean you think employee theft is common, and therefore, acceptable.

Other tips to whiz through integrity tests

✔ **Think before answering.**

Use common sense in answering questions that you know if answered incorrectly will discredit you — questions like

*Circle the correct term for the following true statement:*

*I have thought of stealing (1) $0 (2) $5 (3) $100 in office supplies from my employer.*

✔ **Rate yourself high.**

Give yourself an above average score if asked to rate your honesty. Don't admit you have ever entertained the thought of cheating your employer.

✔ **Be a law-and-order hawk.**

Take a strong stand against theft and crooks to show you are upright. To advocate leniency may intimate that you are guilty of dishonesty.

✔ **Give the absolutely true answer.**

When a question asks for data the employer can easily access, such as your birth date, indulge yourself in no maybes or approximatelys. Answers that contradict the facts may cause the employer to suspect your honesty.

✔ **Anticipate common-sense employer objections.**

For instance, if applying to navigate a giant oil tanker headed for pristine waters and you're asked, *Have you ever drunk alcohol while on the job?*, you are under scrutiny for counterproductive behavior. A desirable employee would never risk an oil spill for a buzz.

# Sample Questions for Tests

Questions on all types of tests may require uncomfortable yes/no answers. (Following the questions, I explain their meaning in parentheses.) Here are some examples:

✔ *If you were sure that you would not get caught, would you sneak into a movie theater without paying?*

✔ *A coworker regularly borrows money from the cash register without permission and promises to return it at the end of the month, but never does; do you consider this person honest?*

✔ *Are you offended when criminals get off due to technicalities?*

(The previous questions are intended to discover if you rationalize dishonesty and theft.)

✔ *Do you believe that children or spouses are far more important than anything?*

(Will your family life interfere with your job?)

✔ *Do you exercise regularly?*

(Are you likely to be a high risk for health insurance?)

✔ *I feel there is only one true religion.*

(Are you too rigid to fit into a company culture?)

✔ *I am fascinated by fire.*

(Are you an arsonist or pyromaniac — will you burn down our building?)

✔ *I would like to be a florist.*

(Are your interests suited to this field?)

✔ *I still maintain close contact with friends from high school.*

(Do you get along with people for long periods of time?)

✔ *I have thought of trying to get even with someone who hurt me.*

(Are you vindictive, or can you put hurts behind you?)

Some questions require specific answers, rather than yes or no:

✔ *How often do you make your bed?*

(Do you clean up after yourself? Are you obsessive about it?)

✔ *On average, how often during the week do you go to parties?*

(Will you frequently come to work hungover?)

✔ *Describe how you see work.*

(Do you see work as mandatory or as a way to obtain rewards?)

# Concerned That You Didn't Do Well?

Our unhappy test taker, Dale Malone, called a week after the interview to ask how well he did on the test. The interviewer begged off, saying that test results are confidential. That typical answer did little to relieve Malone's anxiety about his test performance.

(In the United States, public sector test results are public information. If you, for instance, tested to become a law enforcement officer, you would be entitled to your civil service results.)

The stark truth is that unless you get an agreement to test more than once, you can't really do much about a test score when you flub up. Busy employers are focused on finding the right people to hire, not on helping those who are among the unchosen.

Even when you're worried that you didn't pass the test with flying colors, go all out on the follow-up strategies described in Chapter 22.

# Chapter 7

# Lining Up Your Credits

• • • • • • • • • • • • • • • • • • • • • • • • • • • • • • • • • • • • • • • • • • • • • •

## In This Chapter

▶ Reaching out for references

▶ Rehearsing your references

▶ Understanding legal knots

▶ Finding out who is saying what

• • • • • • • • • • • • • • • • • • • • • • • • • • • • • • • • • • • • • • • • • • • • • • •

*H*ere's why you should never take references lightly: You sell yourself at the job interview, but . . .

### *References verify your sales pitch.*

When references don't back up what you've said, you're written out of the show.

Reach out for good references. You want to make sure that your candidacy does not vaporize, because of references that are uninformed, lukewarm, or even hostile.

References are no problem if you've always given Oscar-winning performances, and everyone loves you. You no doubt have an outstanding list of rave reviews to flash at potential employers. But unless you live in a parallel universe, you've probably had a few box office flops at one time or another. If so, you have some work to do in dimming the spotlight on past mistakes.

Whatever your situation, take measures to ensure that you have the best references possible and that they will confirm what you say in your sales pitch. You will, of course, include your boss, direct reports, and coworkers; but if appropriate, you should also include clients, suppliers, and others with whom you have worked on a volunteer basis, such as other members of a professional society or community endeavor. Setting up your "reference package" also gets the word out that you're job shopping, in case anyone hears of an attractive opening.

Work up as large a list as possible so that you don't tire your references. Unless they're saints, your references will become annoyed with nonstop calls. They'll naturally be more enthusiastic the first couple of times they're contacted, but if the parade of reference checkers continues unabated, they may begin to wonder what's wrong with you. Why haven't you found a job yet?

Hand out your list of references — with names, titles, companies, and *correct* e-mail addresses and telephone numbers, including home numbers if possible — when the employer asks for them, not before. The longer the list, the better. A lengthy list suggests no skeletons or secrets — your life is an open book. Reference checkers probably won't call all of your references — they'll choose a few.

# Collect the Best Possible References

In addition to the key people you've worked with most recently, your references will have more clout if they have star power. If you know people at the top of your field who know your work and reputation, ask them for a reference. Their star power could be the trick to getting an employer's attention. If they're willing to praise you, the employer assumes you must be good.

The majority of your references should have direct knowledge of your job performance. The core of your reference package should include a supervisor, coworker, and someone you supervised with whom you have worked during the past three (and not more than five) years.

Try to choose references who will provide honest, objective information about you; experienced reference checkers can tell if someone's trying to puff up your past achievements.

## New graduates, be resourceful!

Even a rookie can construct a powerful reference package. Put down all your student job references, plus professors, academic advisors, and counselors. Did you tutor another student — that's a reference, too. Did you do volunteer or community work — list the people in charge of supervising you. Click through your memory banks — do you know any business owners, clergy, physicians, or bankers who can provide character references, if not actual work references? You have to be resourceful, but you can compile an impressive reference package.

# Maintaining Confidentiality

If you're currently employed and you don't want your immediate boss to know that you're searching, rely on a core reference package from earlier jobs or people who have recently left your present company, fleshed out with colleagues at other companies.

If you're dead sure that loyal coworkers, direct reports, or managers in other departments won't tell your boss your job bags are packed, you may recruit them for your reference package. Personally, I think this move is risky, but it's done.

Refusing to provide references from the company you currently work for is understandable and a definite option. One way of dealing with this issue is to say that after you are hired, the new company can check your present references; if your current boss and associates don't back up your sales pitch, the company can rescind the offer.

# Meet with References

Never leave anything to chance where references are concerned. Here's a good plan:

✔ **Get permission.**

Ask permission to provide references' names to employers. Never give out a reference whose endorsement you have not verified. You may regret the reference's memory loss or sabotage.

✔ **Recall accomplishments.**

Meet with each reference, in person if possible — or by telephone. Remember your golden moments with your reference.

✔ **Give a cue card.**

Write in linear style — one line, white space, another line, white space, and so on — the points you hope your reference will make. You are, in fact, orchestrating a coordinated response with a pool of people, each of whom is hammering home a variety of different comments. You certainly don't want these comments to sound staged, planned, or rehearsed — they merely indicate the "kind of thing" you hope will be said about you.

✔ **Give a resume.**

Along with the cue card, leave with each reference several copies of your resume; one to use as a cheat sheet for reference giving, the others in case your reference thinks of employers who may like to see your qualifications. (If your search is confidential, you probably won't want to leave extra resume copies.)

✔ **Check back.**

Touch base with your references periodically. Not only does the attention communicate to your references that you're still searching, but you also have an opportunity to re-inspire and remind references of your gratitude for their help. You'll also find out which employers are interested — companies do not audit references unless you're in the running for the job.

# When a Reference Can Kill You

Sliding by without identifying a present or former boss is almost impossible. Suppose that you and one of your supervisors tangled.

Leaving a job in a huff or telling your boss off on your last day of employment may feel great, but doing so can destroy your chances for a good reference later. If you've done something similar, or if you know you'll get a bad reference from someone, immediately start rehabilitating that reference.

Make an attempt to neutralize the expected bad reference by contacting the former boss and making a frank appeal for a decent reference. Thank your former boss for the informative experience you had while working there. Then ask your former boss to allow bygones to be bygones, adding that you have to earn a living. After the boss has cooled off, trying to keep you jobless may seem petty — and legally risky, as I mention later.

If the falling out was your fault or if you've only got one negative reference on the horizon, surrounded by plenty of good references, you are probably not in trouble. When you are certain a torpedo is heading your way, just say, *Except for Tom Jones, I've always hit it off with my bosses.* When the interviewer pursues your statement, asking for details, answer as briefly as possible and quickly steer the conversation to one of your strengths.

When you're in deep trouble and about to be fired for cause, immediately see an employment lawyer. Get advice on framing a statement — called a *reference statement* — that all parties agree will be the standard answer as to why you are out the door.

Managers and executives in a scary reference situation should read John Lucht's book, *Rites of Passage at $100,000+* (Viceroy/Holt).

Here are two resources for anyone in reference limbo. I have no direct knowledge of either firm.

- ✔ *Documented Reference Check* (www.badreferences.com) You can retain the firm's services if you suspect you're being hammered by a former employer and want to find out for sure. The site also offers free resources, including an attorney database and accessible law library links.

- ✔ *Job Reference* (www.jobreference.com) is another service that will find out for a price what a past employer is saying about you.

# Understanding Legal Knots

References are a complex issue for companies. To avoid legal exposure for libel and slander, savvy employers offer little information about previous employees. They'll confirm that "John worked here from [date] to [date]." They'll confirm the job title if the reference checker names it correctly but they may not offer a correction to an incorrect job title. Otherwise, very little reference information is forthcoming.

Reference checkers may find sidedoors to employment information, and not all employers realize their legal exposure when they say bad things about former employees. But employers who blast away at a former employee's reputation, especially if they do so with malicious intent, open themselves to lawsuits.

While these legal nooses may help you by silencing a negative reference, they can also hurt you. Companies that have a policy of silence may refuse to give any kind of reference. You may have been their star performer, but they'll never tell.

The other side of the reference coin is *negligent hiring*. Don't count on a say-nothing policy to clamp the lips of an earned bad reference. Legal precedents have established that a current employer can sue a former employer for withholding current information that may affect the company. For example, if you were fired for theft and your previous employer didn't provide that information, a lawsuit could follow, charging that the previous employer did harm by withholding important information. Remember, though, that any unsolicited information must be documented. If the theft was only suspected, not documented, the suspicion cannot be disclosed.

## More tips about writing a reference statement

If you're fired from a job and everyone applauds your departure, take quick action to minimize negative comments. Write a reference statement, no more than one page long, describing your performance in as positive a light as possible.

Ask your former boss to read it. If your former boss doesn't accept it, revise the statement until you come up with one you both feel comfortable with.

When your former boss does accept the statement, find two or three more references in the company, preferably ones who don't want to drop the curtain on your career.

Write more positive reference statements that they'll agree to support. Make sure that the statements are consistent.

# Find Out Who's Saying What

If you suspect you have a vindictive ex-boss trying to destroy you with bad reviews, make sure that's the real reason you're not connecting with a job. Find out for certain what is being said. Have a friend who knows the jargon of your field call your ex-boss and ask about you.

You may need to have your lawyer write a letter warning that the slander must stop — or else.

Pay serious attention to your references because that's how you validate your sales pitch.

## Dealing with a mum's-the-word policy

If you know that your employer has a strict say-nothing policy, ask for a letter of recommendation when you leave. A letter doesn't carry the weight of a reference, but it's better than

nothing. Compile a list of testimonials — short power statements about you and your performance. Gather these statements from job performance reviews, verbal praise, and letters.

# Part III

# Powerful Performance Prompters

The 5th Wave          By Rich Tennant

"I'm not saying my performance will be linked to my salary, but do you want the $30,000, $40,000, or $50,000 a year answer?"

# In this part . . .

You've researched and rehearsed — now move from slowtime to showtime! The first chapter in this part discusses typical scenarios to expect — from icebreaking remarks and finessing the right questions out of nervous interviewers to handling silence and overcoming objections.

Next up is the fine art of using questions as a self-marketing tool. You won't lead off with questions about salary or benefits, but instead you'll develop a set of questions to show your heart is in the right place — with the company.

Finally, the good part — the money. New graduates often say job satisfaction is what's important, not the money. Seasoned aces know better: It's job satisfaction and the money. Verbal negotiation secrets are laid bare.

# Chapter 8

# Scenarios to Expect

● ● ● ● ● ● ● ● ● ● ● ● ● ● ● ● ● ● ● ● ● ● ● ● ● ● ● ● ● ● ● ● ● ● ● ● ● ● ● ● ● ● ● ● ● ● ●

## In This Chapter

▶ A day in the life of an interview

▶ Drowning in interview flubs

▶ Sailing toward your highest expectations

● ● ● ● ● ● ● ● ● ● ● ● ● ● ● ● ● ● ● ● ● ● ● ● ● ● ● ● ● ● ● ● ● ● ● ● ● ● ● ● ● ● ● ● ● ● ●

*I*t's showtime! This chapter puts together all the information you've read so far — and hints at what's to come. The purpose is to walk you through a single interview, illustrating a typical flow of the interviewing mosaic.

For this tale of two job seekers, I've created a pair of characters, Cory and Chris. They illustrate the choices you have in interview scenarios.

Visualize Cory's inept interview tactics and Chris's spectacular moves. They aren't real people, but their experiences can be really instructional.

## The Day Before

The day before an important interview is the day to prepare. You have a choice. You can let the jitters send you into a tailspin, or you can take steps to turn your nervousness into excitement and energy.

### The ShowFlopper way

Cory's interview is set for ten o'clock the next morning. A nervous wreck the night before showtime, Cory decides a few drinks at the local bar would be calming. Tomorrow morning is soon enough to get the interviewing act together.

### The ShowStopper way

Chris begins the day before to prep for an interview at 11 o'clock the next morning. Chris stands outside the interview site and watches employees enter, noting how they dress. After getting a handle on the company's costuming culture, Chris decides on a charcoal suit and rushes it to the neighborhood cleaners for a quick press. Chris polishes black shoes and double-checks the requisite briefcase for five copies of the FirstRate resume that won the interview. (See my book, *Resumes For Dummies,* 3rd Edition.)

Then Chris verifies routing and parking directions. The last thing Chris does to prep is to carefully review lists of job-related questions to ask, lists of questions the interviewer could be expected to ask, and goes over how qualifications (including skills and accomplishments) could match job requirements. Finally, Chris gets a full night's sleep.

### Critic's review

To give yourself the best shot at a ShowStopper interview:

- ✔ Get everything ready the day before.

- ✔ Become familiar in advance with the route you will travel to the interview.

- ✔ As you travel to the interview, visualize yourself as someone about to be hired. As though you were starring in a movie, run interviewing images through your mind. Imagine the stories you'll tell and the impressed look on your interviewer's face as you ask your own questions and present your own commercial of qualifications — skills and accomplishments. Float pictures through your head about the scenario as you wish it to be.

- ✔ Imagine yourself being at ease, radiating sincerity, credibility, energy, enthusiasm, and competence. We act the way we think.

## Opening the Interview

As the actors find their places on the job interview scene, all the building blocks of the actor's preparation come together. Lights . . . camera . . . action!

## The ShowFlopper way

Cory scrambles into the office wearing a super trendy outfit topped by hair stiff with mousse. Conservative managers see Cory as being "too much" — "not one of us."

Arriving late after losing the way to the interview, an unsmiling Cory rushes to the receptionist's desk and, without bothering to greet the receptionist, asks for the interviewer. The receptionist hurries Cory to the interviewing office.

The interviewer glances up and calmly asks — *Do you know that you're 25 minutes late?* Nervously, Cory sits down, uninvited, and mutters — *Yeah, sorry. I got stuck in that stupid traffic jam that always happens on the bridge, and then I got totally lost. I guess I should have started earlier.*

The interviewer responds — *Uh-huh. Well, before we begin, I seem to have misplaced your resume — do you have an extra copy handy?* Flustered, Cory says — *Sorry, no. Because you already had a copy, I didn't think you'd need another.*

## The ShowStopper way

Chris arrives 10 minutes before showtime and makes polite small talk with the receptionist. The receptionist buzzes the interviewer, who comes to the lobby to greet Chris.

As they walk through a hallway toward the interviewer's office, Chris breaks the ice by saying nice things about the pictures on the wall.

Once inside the interviewer's office, Chris smiles and returns a firm handshake to the interviewer. Chris's eyes sweep the room, looking for some mutual interest (sports, colleges, or travel mementos) and spots a baseball picture of the Yankees on the wall. Chris doesn't sit until invited.

For a moment, Chris feels jittery. Then Chris thinks about Tom Brokaw and Barbara Walters, who always seem to have everything under control. Chris takes a deep breath and feels poise return.

The interviewer is distracted with Chris's resume, but to keep the momentum going, asks a few questions. Chris glides right into strong answers — stressing the good fit between Chris's skills and the job's requirements, making a mental note to repeat that information as soon as the interviewer's full spotlight is on Chris.

## Critic's review

When making your entrance, keep these tips in mind:

- Dress as though you belong where you're interviewing.
- Be friendly to all office staffers — they'll discuss you openly once you leave.
- Wait for the interviewer to initiate a handshake and then make your handshake a firm one.
- Make several copies of your resume in case you're asked for a copy. More likely, you'll be introduced to others who have a say in the hiring decision — leave one with each important person you meet.
- Stand until invited to sit.
- When you feel a sudden case of nerves, learn from the dramatic arts. Think of yourself as a favorite media personality who is cool, calm, collected, and confident.

# During the Interview

Research and rehearsal grow confidence in actors and job interviewers, ensuring they know their lines and moves — and recognize opportunities to charm — in fairly predictible auditions.

## The ShowFlopper way

After finding and studying Cory's resume while Cory sits quietly, the interviewer asks — *What can you tell me about yourself?*

Cory begins to ramble — *Um . . . I mean, like it says on my resume, I just got my degree from UTC . . . Um . . . I graduated summa cum laude . . . and . . . well, you know, I'm looking for a job. I was born in Louisiana, Missouri . . . but, my mother was in the Marines, and so we traveled a lot . . . I like tennis . . . I know I can do this job . . . what else would you like to know?*

Cory picks up a letter opener from the interviewer's desk and begins to fiddle with it.

# The ShowStopper way

As the busy interviewer skims Chris's resume, Chris comments on the Yankees' baseball picture — the interviewer and Chris are "alike," which results in a bonding experience.

Right away, the interviewer subliminally thinks — *I like this person! Let's see what else Chris has to offer.*

As soon as Chris has the interviewer's attention, Chris asks — *I wonder if you can confirm my understanding of this position. What are the job's most important duties, and what kind of person do you see as being best suited for it?*

The interviewer enters into the questioning portion of the interview with — *Could you tell me about yourself?* After a thinking pause, Chris skillfully mirrors the company's ideal employee for the target position (thanks to research) in a 60-second commercial of qualifications, focusing on skills and accomplishments.

Chris can smell a job offer coming when suddenly the interviewer falls deathly silent — the kind of silence that makes most people uncomfortable enough to blabber. But when Chris is satisfied with the information delivered, Chris falls silent, too, and waits for the interviewer to respond.

Finally, Chris asks — *Would you like me to tell you more about my skills in working with other people?*

Secretly impressed, the interviewer asks what Chris knows about the company's products and organization. The question session turns into a company-fact-trading workshop, and both participants feel good about the meeting.

# Critic's review

Use these tips to give an award-winning performance:

- Anticipate and rehearse challenging questions.
- Take note of the interviewer's personal items in the office as you try to establish rapport, but never touch anything.
- Ask the question that reveals the key to the entire interview — *What is the scope of the position and what are the qualifications of the ideal person for it?*
- Recognize that an interviewer's silence can move you to speak before you think. When things become too tense, ask a job-related question to parade your skills.

# Sizing Up Audience Reaction

If an actor is doing comedy, and no one is laughing, the actor needs to change the lines or change the delivery. Similarly, if you notice your audience (a potential employer) is disinterested, try to switch the subject and save the show.

How can you tell how your act is going over? Watch for obvious signs of inattention: The interviewer's eyes are glazed over, or the interviewer fiddles with desk objects, for example.

## The ShowFlopper way

Cory's interviewer spends a lot of time discussing the company and the job and asks very few questions — the interviewer is filling time until Cory can be decently dumped; the interviewer has already lost interest. There is still a slim chance that Cory can put the interview back on track, but Cory doesn't notice the warning signals of disinterest.

Cory misses nonverbal clues, too: When the bored interviewer begins tapping fingers on the desk, Cory does not say — *Would you rather hear more about my computer programming work or my international marketing studies?* Cory doesn't notice two more negative body-language signals when the interviewer crosses arms and leans back.

To top it off, Cory fails to observe how the interviewer is phrasing judgments, clearly implying that Cory is not under consideration. The interviewer says — *Many people have a problem handling all the travel required — frankly, the traveling is too heavy a burden.*

Cory nixes all chances at salvaging the job opportunity by agreeing — *Yeah, I'm really not much for travel. I like to stick around home with my friends and family.* Cory has never understood that once you're in a hole, it's time to stop digging.

## The ShowStopper way

Following the main question segment of the interview, Chris's interviewer lapses into lengthy praise of the company and the job. But, unlike Cory's experience, the body of the interview had gone wonderfully well, and Chris realizes that an offer is imminent. The interviewer isn't just filling time talking about the company — the interviewer is selling Chris!

Chris smiles and listens attentively.

The interviewer does have a few concerns — *Will Chris be able to handle the travel the job requires?* This job calls for about two days of travel a week, but the requirement is flexible. Will that be a problem?

Chris overcomes the concern by expressing a genuine interest in traveling and then recapsulates the other strengths that point toward a perfect job-applicant match. The interviewer's relief shows — *Then the commute won't be a problem for you?*

*Absolutely not!* Chris confirms.

## Critic's review

Follow these tips to keep your interviewer's attention:

- ✔ Pay close attention to your audience. Observe body language. Note subject matter and how comments are phrased.

- ✔ When you think the decision on you is thumbs down, try a last-chance statement — *Because I'm very interested in this job, I want to be sure that you have all the information you need to make a positive decision on my candidacy. Would you be interested in hearing more about my — ?*

- ✔ Note how interviewers ask touchy questions. The interviewers phrased the question about travel negatively in Cory's interview and positively in Chris's interview. The negative shading implied that Cory just didn't fit the job. Take a hint or move to overcome objections.

- ✔ Avoid money talk until a job is offered. Money wasn't a factor in the examples of Cory and Chris because the interviewer did not raise the issue. (See Chapter 10.)

# Ending the Interview

Put the finishing touches on your ShowStopper routine as the interview curtain begins to fall. Find out about the coming attractions of future contacts and prop open the stage door for your return.

## The ShowFlopper way

Cory tries to stretch the interview with small talk — chiefly personal information not related to the job — while the interviewer is making an obvious effort to leave by gathering papers, rising, and walking toward the door. Cory finally gets the picture and anxiously asks — *So, do I get the job?*

Cory's desperation adds to the interviewer's doubts. The interviewer decides to end the misery — *Sorry, you don't really fit the needs of this job.*

Hurt and offended, Cory demands to know why — *Hey, I've got the right college degree . . . what's wrong with me?*

## The ShowStopper way

Chris notices the interviewer glancing occasionally at the office clock before saying — *Thanks for coming in, I'll notify you when we make a decision.*

Chris refuses to fade into the sunset and grabs a chance for a follow-up interview — *I'm sure you have a busy schedule, and I appreciate your time. Thank you. But before we close today, could I make sure I understand what you're looking for?*

Chris wraps up with a superb 60-second recap of the job's description and requirements, matching them directly. The theme is "you want, I have." After this short monologue, Chris offers the interviewer the floor — *Do you see any gaps between what you need and what I'm offering?*

The interviewer mentions one deficiency in Chris's skills profile — a lack of supervisory experience. Chris immediately counters with two stories of managing huge special events for a church organization and a campus club, both of which required supervisory duties. Chris had not had paid supervisory experience, but the compensatory answer beat no answer at all.

As Chris and the interviewer shake hands good-bye, the interviewer implies that Chris is well-suited for the position, but that there is a pool of candidates yet to be interviewed. Chris asks — *When do you expect to make a decision or to schedule follow-up interviews?*

As the interviewer answers and shakes hands, Chris has a final question — *Can I get back to you to get an update on your timeline?*

*Feel free to call me,* the interviewer responds, thinking — *This candidate has plenty on the ball.*

## Critic's review

To end the interview on the right note, follow these tips:

✔ Interviewers get the message that a desperate candidate is a bottom-of-the-barrel candidate.

✔ Learn sales closing techniques; those who do not learn to close a sale — and make no mistake about it, you are selling yourself in an interview — do not get job offers.

✔ Watch the interviewer's body language closely for signs that the interview should end. Take the hint. Arguing wastes everyone's time.

✔ Expecting that an educational or experience credential is all you need to get the job is a mistake.

✔ Summarize your best-selling points one last time for the interviewer.

✔ Leave the door open for a follow-up contact.

# After the Interview

You get one last chance to make the interview memorable. Your follow-up work is an opportunity to write a happy ending to your job-search scenario.

## The ShowFlopper way

Cory promptly writes off the interviewing company as unfair and erases from memory all that happened during the interview.

Because Cory hasn't learned from these mistakes, Cory's other interviews won't go much better.

## The ShowStopper way

After leaving the interviewer's office, Chris immediately writes down everything that happened, including the main points Chris made, the interviewer's name, line of questioning, areas of interest, and the timelines of the hiring process.

Then Chris writes the interviewer a RedHot thank-you letter (see my book, *Cover Letters For Dummies,* 2nd Edition).

## Critic's review

To make the most of every interview, follow these tips:

- ✔ Turn every interview into a learning experience.

- ✔ Note what you learned in the interview (such as names and additional aspects of the company new to you) for your next contact with the interviewer.

- ✔ Note points discussed. Did you leave out significant selling points? Add them to your thank you letter.

# Pre-Interview Checklist

Do you want to be sure that you'll do everything you can to stop the show? Use this pre-interview checklist to get yourself prepped for a ShowStopper performance.

- ☐ Do you know how people dress where you're interviewing? (See Chapter 5.)

- ☐ Is your interviewing costume clean, pressed, and ready to go?

- ☐ Do you know where the interviewing site is located and how long it takes to get there?

- ☐ Did you research the position, company, and industry? (See Chapter 3.)

- ☐ Have you contacted and coached all your references? Have you neutralized any potentially damaging references? (See Chapter 7.)

- ☐ Have you memorized a short commercial to highlight your best-selling points? (See Chapters 1 and 14.)

- ☐ Have you rehearsed everything, from small talk to answering potentially dangerous questions? (See Chapter 4.)

- ☐ Have you practiced your answers to anticipated questions? (See Part V.)

- ☐ Have you prepared and memorized a list of questions to ask? (See Chapter 9.)

- ☐ Have you researched the market salary for the position? (See Chapter 10.)

- ☐ Did you gather everything you need? (Five copies of your resume, list of references, and samples of your work, if necessary.)

Once you knock each question off this checklist, stop cramming and relax. Otherwise, you'll suffer stage fright. Enter your interview with confidence. You've done ShowStopper preparation for a ShowStopper interview!

# Chapter 9

# Questions You Ask — and When

In This Chapter

▶ Asking work questions before the offer

▶ Asking personal questions after the offer

▶ Drawing out hidden objections

**S**o you just finished answering a seemingly endless line of questions about your work history and your education, and you're pretty confident that you held your own. Now the interviewer turns to you and asks, "Do *you* have any questions?" This question is your cue to ask how much money you're gonna make at this outfit anyway, right? Wrong!

The types of questions you ask and when you ask them are the least understood parts of the interview. Your questions offer major chances for garnering curtain calls or being booed off the stage. Sort your question opportunities into two categories:

✔ **Questions that sell you** — These kinds of questions help you get an offer; they're a way to sell without selling.

✔ **Questions that address your personal agenda** — These kinds of questions about pay, bennies (benefits), and other self-interest items should be asked *only* after you receive an offer — or at least a heavy hint of an offer.

## Selling Questions You Ask before the Offer

For all jobs, asking about anything other than work issues before a hiring offer comes your way is a serious strategic error. The interviewer, particularly a hiring manager who resents the time "diverted" to an interview, doesn't give two figs about your needs at this point.

What's important to the interviewer is solving the hiring problem. *First we decide, then we deal* — that's the thinking.

To talk about your needs before an offer turns the interviewer's mind to negative thoughts: *All you want is money, insurance, and a nice vacation on the company. You're not interested in doing the job.*

As a ShowStopper candidate, you're not going to make that mistake. Keep your focus on the employer's needs and how you can meet them. Sell yourself by asking questions that are

- ✔ work-focused

- ✔ task-focused

- ✔ function-focused

Ask about the position's duties and challenges. Ask what outcomes you're expected to produce. Ask how the position fits into the department and the department into the company. Ask about typical assignments.

Don't ask questions about information you can glean from research. And don't ask questions that could cause the interviewer to wonder when you were chipped from a glacier and thawed, such as quizzing an interviewer from Xerox — *Do you make anything other than copiers?*

Here are 15 sample work-related questions:

- ✔ **What would my key responsibilities be?**

- ✔ **How many and whom would I supervise? To whom would I report?**

- ✔ **Does the staff maintain a team spirit?**

- ✔ **Will on-job training be required for a new product?**

- ✔ **Can you describe a typical day?**

- ✔ **Was the last person in this job promoted? What is the potential for promotion?**

- ✔ **How would you describe the atmosphere here? Formal and traditional? Energetically informal?**

- ✔ **Where is the company headed? Merger? Growth?**

- ✔ **What would my first project be?**

- ✔ **What type of training would I receive?**

- ✔ **What resources would I have to do the job?**

- ✔ **How much travel, if any, is required?**

- ✔ **(If a contract job) Do you anticipate extensive overtime to finish the project on schedule?**

✔ **Where does this position fit into the company's organizational structure?**

✔ **What results would you expect from my efforts and on what timetable? What improvements need to be made on how the job has been done until now?**

How much time should you invest in asking selling questions? Five to ten minutes is not too much. Gregory J. Walling, a top executive recruiter in Alexandria, Virginia, says he's never heard an employer complain about a candidate being *too interested in work.*

# Questions to Ask after the Offer

Once you have the offer, you're ready to make the switch from giving to receiving information. I discuss negotiating salary and benefits in Chapter 10, but you'll also want to know about things like leave time, overtime, frequency of performance reviews, and (if it's a contract job) how long the job will last. Asking personal agenda questions in advance of an offer is dangerous, but after the offer, let fly with questions such as these seven examples:

✔ **Your company culture seems fairly unstructured. Is my impression correct?**

✔ **What problems might I face in this job?**

✔ **Is future relocation a possibility?**

✔ **Is employee parking included in the offer?**

✔ **Does management delegate decision-making to others, or does it micromanage — requiring approval of even the tiniest details?**

✔ **Where would I work in the building? Could I take a look at the location for a minute?**

✔ **Is the schedule fixed (such as 9 a.m. to 5 p.m.) or is it flexible (my choice of hours)?**

## Ask with confidence

Be aware of how you phrase questions. Ask "what would" questions that presume you'll be offered the job ("What would my key responsibilities be?" Not, "What are the job's key responsibilities?"). Presumption-phrasing shows self-confidence and subtly encourages the interviewer to visualize you in the position — an important step in getting the job offer.

Notice that the ratio of sample work to personal questions is about 2 to 1. That's a good guideline for your real interview.

# *Questions to Draw Out Hidden Objections*

Questions-you-ask have one more mission in the interview: They are a good way to bring concerns or objections to the table that the interviewer may not want to verbalize.

Why doesn't the interviewer want to raise certain issues?

Reasons employers hang back with unspoken anxieties are usually related to legal vulnerability (see Chapter 21 on inappropriate questions), or they may simply be uncomfortable asking about them.

Whatever the reason, silent concerns are hurdles standing in the way of your getting the job. Before the interview is over, you need to find a way to address the thorny issues and overcome them.

Good salespeople call techniques that do this *drawing out objections*. Once you know the issues you're dealing with, try to calm anxieties that keep you from being hired.

## Critics pan showoffs

*I noticed in subsection 3.a of the government defense contractor's manual I.2.A, concerning future plans, that you squared the round table, using your supercomputer's component play box, and found your sandbox is 95 percent superior to the market's; does this mean you plan to circle an outer galaxy and return to earth on Greenwich mean time?*

Huh? Research is essential, but guard against flaunting your newly found knowledge with questions that might give Einstein a little trouble. Interviewers interpret these questions as a transparent bid to look smart.

But, you ask, shouldn't you look "smart" at an interview? Yes, just don't cross the fine line that exists between being well researched and fully prepared for an interview, and trying to be a *nouveau omniscient*. (Don't you love that term? It means newly informed know-it-all.)

Showing off is a quality that causes otherwise charming, bright, gregarious, and attractive people to be turned down. It's just not a likable trait. If you don't have a good handle on what is and what isn't showing off, maybe a friend can help you work on that distinction.

Ask the interviewer questions to give the interviewer an opening to ask you questions the interviewer wants to know answers to but can't figure out how to bring up without getting hauled into the Equal Employment Opportunity Commission.

Here are a pair of examples of easing an interviewer's hidden concerns by bringing up a legally risky topic:

> *In your place, I'd probably be wondering how my children are cared for during the day. I may be concerned that I'd miss work should they become ill. Let me explain my very reliable child care arrangements to you . . .*

> *If I were you, seeing on my resume that I have spent a great deal of time in Paris, I may be questioning my legal residency and, green card or no green card, whether I plan to stay in Chicago long enough to complete this project. Let me assure you . . .*

As I see it, your basic choices are to allow an employer to make assumptions about you or to control the unspoken problem by telling the employer what you want known about the situation.

Once hidden objections see daylight, you've got a chance to clear away obstacles standing between you and a job offer.

# Questions to Ask Very Carefully

Questions to potential employers about their own performance should be handled with great tact — especially when you ask it of a boomer generation boss.

- ✔ **How would you describe your management style?**
- ✔ **Do your employees admire you as a boss?**

While you need as much information as possible to make good job choices, asking a potential boss these kinds of questions in the wrong tone of voice may make you seem way too audacious. Moreover, direct questions about personal characteristics and values tend to elicit pure topspin.

Instead, ask questions designed to draw out companywide anecdotal answers:

- ✔ **How did the company handle a recent downsizing?**
- ✔ **How did managers react to someone who took a stand on principle?**
- ✔ **Who are the company's heroes?**

This approach encourages conversation that can be very informative. One of the best ways to find out about a company you're considering is to track down former employees and get a debriefing. Ask a customer how the company responded when problems occurred. Go online: See Employee Message Boards in Chapter 3.

Questions are tools. Use them wisely.

# Chapter 10

# Getting Paid What You're Worth

• • • • • • • • • • • • • • • • • • • • • • • • • • • • • • • • • • • • • •

### In This Chapter

▶ Researching your market value

▶ Pacing the money talk

▶ Negotiating your best compensation

• • • • • • • • • • • • • • • • • • • • • • • • • • • • • • • • • • • • • •

*W*hat is the best single thing you can do to receive a higher pay offer when you're interviewing for a job?

> *Delay discussing salary until you're offered (or nearly offered) a specific position.*

The tip you just read headlines the purpose of this chapter — to share with you the staging that can help you get paid what you're worth. And maybe more.

Most people believe that pay and certain benefits are open to negotiation. The Society for Human Resource Management (SHRM) and careers.wsj.com, a free site from the Wall Street Journal Interactive Edition, polled 450 HR professionals and 500 job seekers. Eight out of ten HR professionals expect to receive counteroffers, and the equivalent number of job seekers believe that employers expect them to negotiate. Half or more HR professionals expect to negotiate relocation costs, vacation leave, and early performance reviews with the option for salary increases.

Although the word has spread that pay offers may not be dipped in concrete, many people still aren't aware that there could be room to negotiate compensation. Smaller companies without formal pay structures are easier to negotiate with than corporate titans.

But even at huge companies where pay scales are cut-and-dried, your potential boss may have the latitude to cut you a better deal. In fact, some interviewers see your negotiation attempts at improving your compensation as a favorable trait — yet another indicator that they've made the right choice. Their reasoning is as follows: *If you can look after your own best interests, you can look after ours.*

Job seekers who know that pay is often negotiable, approach salary discussions like buying a new car. Will they get the best deal, or will a more skilled negotiator talk them into accepting less than they're worth?

Most of us want to get the most we can in return for the parts of our lives that we sell:

> *Negotiating pay with skill and savvy can mean that you gain hundreds of thousands of extra dollars throughout your career.*

This chapter gives you a crash course on the key points of pay negotiation: "Where do I start, and what do I say?" But to gain the confidence of a natural-born negotiator, I suggest you enroll in pay negotiation workshops (sometimes available in continuing education classes) and read entire books on the subject.

The best of the bunch is Jack Chapman's *How to Make $1,000 a Minute — Negotiating Your Salaries and Raises*, Ten Speed Press.

Jack Chapman, who is a highly respected counselor in Wilmette, Illinois, (members.aol.com/payraises/index.html; 773-4-SALARY) also offers excellent salary telecoaching services, and PinPoint Salary Service, which customizes pay research to your specific situation. Readers of my newspaper column, *Careers,* continue to tell me that Chapman has been instrumental in helping them achieve huge salary increases.

# Background on the Bucks

Start by looking at trends and buzzwords for new ways to think about pay.

**The way things were:** With the exception of people in sales, most white-collar job seekers limited negotiations to one specific compensation figure — base salary. If they didn't get as much money starting as they wanted, they bargained for the future — a quick review and a raise in three to six months. Extras like employee benefits came automatically. The cushy perks — bonuses, stock options, relocation payments, company cars, and club memberships — were available only to high-level managers.

**The way things are:** The new pay concept is *total compensation* — base pay, variable pay, and indirect pay.

*Base pay* is the money you get on a regular basis (weekly, biweekly, or monthly) rain or shine, economically speaking.

*Variable pay* equates to a bonus system, now attainable by lower levels of employees as well as by managers. Generally linked to performance, variable pay is available to most white-collar personnel. Stock options and certain other big-ticket items (like club memberships, skybox season tickets to sporting events, and professional conventions in Hawaii) are usually offered only to managerial personnel.

*Indirect pay* (a.k.a. employee fringe benefits) now commonly comprises about one-third of your base pay and includes items like vacations, health insurance, and retirement funds, plus government-mandated fringes such as Social Security.

# Those Big Little Extras

Stock options aren't just for Internet wizards and top executives anymore. Now managers and engineers and delivery drivers are supplementing their take-home pay with perks and benefits once only dreamed of.

Studies reporting what's typical and what's wanted in variable and indirect pay packages vary. Health benefits and retirement promises are high on everyone's list, as are generous vacation leave and flextime opportunities. Tuition reimbursement is gaining in popularity as more people realize that keeping their knowledge and skills up to date is the best way to thrive in changing times. Health club membership and a company car are two more extras job seekers prize.

Little things count, too. The promise of free food and beverages on the job make the list of top corporate perks, says Ceridian Employer Services, a Minneapolis-based human resource service. The Ceridian online poll of 129 companies also reports that the opportunity to come to work in casual dress is another big attraction.

Even in a tight labor market, some job seeker requests are judged to be unreasonable. IT (information technology) professionals — lords of the universe in the job market — are reported to have asked for vacation leaves spanning an entire summer. Hiring managers passed on that one, suggesting that the candidates instead seek careers in consulting.

Many national career sites, such as CareerBuilder (`careerbuilder.com`), offer employee benefits reports. See Chapter 3.

# Discovering the Going Rate for Your Kind of Work

Where's the new, easy place to find out what your work is worth in the marketplace?

> *The Internet. Close seconds are salary studies in printed publications.*

Knowing your fair market value is the centerpiece for negotiating the compensation you deserve. *Market value* is the going rate for people in your industry with skills and a job description similar to yours. Most people guard their income figures like gold at Fort Knox, but a smooth talker like you may be able to pry loose pay figures by promising to trade earnings information once you find a job.

In gathering salary data from surveys, the mouse has become mightier than the pen.

## Where to find salary information online

A new world is opening in salary data that you can obtain on the Internet to discover the market rate for the kind of work you do. Here are three ways to attack your search for salary information by using the Internet:

- ✔ Research on JobStar.org (jobstar.org), a California site that offers more than 300 national and local salary studies in a multitude of fields.

- ✔ Visit national career sites; most offer some type of salary survey collection. See Chapter 3.

- ✔ Use search engines to find earnings data. Search on "salary studies." DirectHit (directhit.com) and Google (google.com) are good places to start. More search engines are noted in Chapter 3.

## Where to find salary information in print

For printed information about salaries, try a library for career and reference books with pay figures, and for magazines such as *U.S. News & World Report,* *Working Woman,* and *Parade*, which annually report on salaries.

Read recruitment advertisements, looking for earnings data. Check for civil service postings at public job service offices and libraries — pay may be similar to comparable jobs in private industry.

## Sometimes you can "just ask"

To make certain your salary research is on target, network in professional groups. At association meetings, speak to people in a position to hire you. Work the conversation around to asking a question: "What could someone with my skill set expect to earn in your organization?"

Read the trade press. For instance, *Chemical Engineering & News* publishes salary surveys for chemical engineers. *The Scientist* does stories about median annual salaries of scientists.

Most professional societies and trade associations conduct salary studies among members. The information may or may not be available to non-members. If you don't belong to the appropriate organization, consider joining. Look them up in *The Encyclopedia of Associations* in a library.

# Timing Is Everything

*How much money are you looking for?* Just when the interview is starting to take wings, bam! — the interviewer lets go with this dangerous question that could clip them. Should you name your price right now?

As I said in Chapter 1, *no — not until they give you an offer* (or a near-offer). Until you have the offer, the employer holds all the weight. Once you have the offer, the scales shift. You have something the employer wants, and you become equals negotiating a business proposition.

Learning to deflect salary questions until the timing is right can greatly influence the amount of money that you take from the bargaining table.

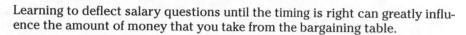

## How to avoid negotiating pay

"The best way to negotiate is to avoid having to do much negotiating at all," says John Lucht in *Rites of Passage at $100,000 Plus.* Present the prospective employer with a line-by-line summary of your current compensation, Lucht strategizes. For an executive position, such a summary may include base salary, bonus, short-term cash incentive, long-term deferred incentive, annualized value of stock options, child's tuition scholarship, and other indirect pay perks. Lucht's reasoning: If the prospective employer knows what you're already getting, you're more likely to get an offer you *can't* refuse rather than one you *can* refuse.

Some interviewers know exactly what they're doing by front-loading the salary question. They are trying to instantly determine your professional level or slyly probing to see if you'll be happy with the low side of an offer.

Others ask the salary question just to shop around — they may not even have an idea of the position's market value and are shopping candidates to simplify budgeting. Still others are open to paying whatever is necessary to get the right person. Whatever the motivation, until the job offer, salary disclosures put too much power in the employer's hands.

As a West Coast director of human resources is reported to have said: "While I may request salary histories from others, I never comply with that demand when I'm in the job market. Why not? I know a guillotine when I see one — I design them."

A salary request too low devalues your abilities; a salary request too high looks like you're too big for the company budget. Both bids leave you out of luck. Be aware that some employers have already budgeted for the position, and the first offer is their best offer. They ask what you want merely to confirm that the money's enough to interest you in the job.

So what should you do when the salary question comes at you too soon? What can you gracefully say to hold off a premature discussion? The following pages give you a number of lines to use in response to premature questions about your salary expectations. They are followed by lines to use in sidestepping a salary history so low that it will damage your chances of stepping up in the world.

# What to Say to Stall Money Talk

When an interviewer presses salary negotiation before you've established your value, don't let a frog clog your throat; answer along these lines:

*I'm sure that money will be no problem once I'm able to show you how my qualifications can work to your advantage.*

*My salary requirements are open to discussion. Your company has a reputation of being fair with employees, and I trust you would do the same in my case. My focus is on finding the right opportunity, and I'll be open to any fair offer when that happens.*

*I'm aware of the general range for my kind of work, but I'd feel better talking about pay once we've established what the job calls for.*

*I'd be kidding if I said money isn't important to me — sure it is! But the job itself and the work environment are (equally or far more) important to me. I wonder if we can hold the pay issue for a bit?*

*I'm a great believer in matching pay with performance, so I can't speak with any certainty about the kind of money I'm looking for until I know what you need.*

*Money is not my only priority; I'd really like to discuss my contributions to the company first — if we could.*

*I'm a lot more interested in getting started in (type of work) here at (name of company) than I am in the amount of beginning pay.*

*The amount of my starting compensation is not as much of an issue to me as how satisfying my filling the position will be for both of us. Can we talk more about what the position entails?*

*Before we get into the compensation issue, can you tell me more about the kind of skills and the type of individual you're looking for to help you reach your goals?*

*All I want is fair market value for the job's demands, which I'm sure you'll pay, so is it okay if we talk about the details of the job first?*

*As far as I can tell, the position seems like a perfect fit for me. So as long as you pay in the industry ballpark, I'm sure that we won't have a problem coming up with a figure we're both happy with.*

*Before we can come to an agreement, I need to know more about your strategy for compensation, as well as confirm my understanding of the results you're looking for. Can we hold that question for a bit?*

*Since pay includes so many possibilities for compensation, I'd like to first know more about your compensation plan overall and how it relates to the position.*

*I'm sure that you have a fair salary structure, and if I'm the best candidate for the position, we can work something out that we'll all like.*

*I'm not used to talking money before a job offer; are you making me an offer?*

*I will consider any reasonable offer. Should we talk about it after we've wrapped up the details of the job, and I've been able to show you what I bring to your company?*

*I'm paid roughly the market value of a (occupational title) with (number of years') experience and the ability to (manage, or do something special). If you're competitive with the market, there won't be a problem with salary.*

# What to Say to Downplay Your Salary History

Disclosing an undermarket salary history can jeopardize your negotiating power. Try out these lines to lessen the impact of having worked for too little money.

**Use the job's market value as the measuring stick, not your salary history.**

*I'm uncertain how my salary history will help you, because salaries are affected by geography, benefits packages, and company priorities. Maybe I'm wrong, but it seems to me that the going market value for the position will be more useful. According to my research, that's a range of $000 to $000.*

*(A biting-the-bullet answer) My salary history won't bring us to any conclusive figures. I've been working under market, and that's one more reason I want to make a change. This job seems perfect for me. I wonder if we could value the position on the basis of its worth to you?*

*I don't feel comfortable limiting the discussion to my salary history because a large portion of my compensation has been in variable and indirect pay. I've received bonuses regularly based on my performance. What I think you're really asking is how I plan to do the job you need done — can we talk about that?*

*If we discuss my salary history, can I say up front that I view this position as a new challenge that will require higher performance than my last? I'd like to think I'm worth more to you than to previous employers.*

# Tips to Get Your Worth's Money

Oh happy day. Your interviewer looks you straight in the eye and says, "We'd like you to join our team; I'm offering you a job, but before we go any further, we should talk about how you'd like to be paid."

The moment of truth has arrived. You've got the offer. No more dodging the money issue.

The novice interviewee will cave in and ask the interviewer to suggest a salary based on what the company would like to spend. But after all your research on your market value and on the company, you'll realize that this cop-out won't bring home top dollars.

*You can't be sure that a company is bidding its best offer with the first offer — unless you ask.*

You can do better by following the guidelines contained in the sections that follow.

## Find a home in the range

Most experienced job changers know by now that expressing their salary requirements in ranges based on the going rate for the job is a good idea: *I'd be expecting compensation in the range of ($000 to $000).* A range gives you haggling room and shows that you're economically aware.

But what part of the employer's range should you target when you can get the employer to name the price spread? Opinions vary.

No one suggests asking for the bottom of the range unless you're a rookie. Even then, if you've worked while in college, ask for a two-striped corporal's pay rather than a one-striped private's. You're positioning yourself as a top rookie candidate.

A conservative school of thought recommends that experienced people ask for a pay point just above mid-range — not only to show you're above average, but also that you understand the need to leave room for raises.

More daring candidates head toward the top of the company's projected range.

## Tell recruiters your salary history

Should you ever disclose your salary history or salary expectations before a job offer? Yes. When you are asked by third-party employment specialists — chiefly executive recruiters and employment consultants who find people for jobs — tell all. Why?

These professionals are specialists at their work, like lawyers and physicians, and are paid for their time, either on a retained or contingency basis. They get paid to find good talent, and so they won't let salary deter them from presenting you when your skills are a match for a job opening. Recruiters are far too busy with the matchmaking task to waste time with you if you make their work difficult. Time is money.

My recommendation for seasoned aces who are prime candidates is to head for the top 15 percent of the range, and if your qualifications will support it, the absolute top or even above.

If you're hired as a supervisor, you'll soon know what the people who report to you directly (your direct reports) are earning. If you come in at too low a figure, within a few months you can ask your boss to put more dollars between you and those you supervise.

## Plot your salary history carefully

When your salary history lists you at the top or above the range of market value, you can afford to discuss that history.

You can try John Lucht's approach (described in the sidebar "How to avoid negotiating pay" earlier in this chapter), or you can be less specific. You can state your figures in wide ranges so that you're more likely to stay in the game for positions for which you're qualified. Include figures slightly above and below the market value to cover all your bases. For example, *For the past three years, I have earned between ($000 and $000) for my work in this field.*

Some job seekers feel they should inflate their salary history. That's a risky idea — the odds of discovery are stacked in the employer's favor. Instead, try this:

- ✔ Show compensation modules. List base pay and variable pay in one figure; give another figure for indirect pay; then add the figures together for the total compensation package.
- ✔ At executive levels, list compensation items line by line.

Decide in advance what you will do should your interviewer ask you for proof of your salary — tax forms or pay stubs. The request is not illegal, but you should anticipate whether you will comply.

## Stonewalled? Try to upgrade the job

**Warning:** This gambit is not for the faint of heart. Once you've established what the position entails and you're told you've received the best offer and that the job isn't worth more, try to make the position more important in the scheme of things.

Point out how the job requires more than the standard duties suggested by the job title — how it fits in a job description that merits a higher pay bracket. Clarify how you plan to minimize company costs through your performance. Explain how you'll pay for yourself. By using this tactic, you establish your worth to the company and your performance-based reason for asking a higher price.

I once became one of the highest paid managers in an organization by combining two positions and creating a new job title.

When you're told the pay offer was designed by compensation specialists and your chances of improving it are nil because "everybody starts at that pay level" and we can't violate "our policy," try this ploy: Say you'll be glad to start at the lower figure, provided you receive a raise the second week. Smile. Don't expect it to happen, but you'll have put your new boss on notice that you expect an early review and raise.

## Use dramatic silences

What should you do when the interviewer offers you a salary near the floor of the salary range for the position? Keep quiet!

As the interviewer finishes the offer and waits for your reply, let the interviewer wait for enough time to notice your silence. Everyone has trouble out-waiting 30 seconds of silence. Look at the floor. Keep your face glum.

These moments of nonverbal communication show your dissatisfaction with the offer, without a word to incriminate you as overly hungry for money. The interviewer may feel compelled by this uncomfortable silence to improve the offer. Or at least open a dialogue in which you can campaign for other kinds of rewards.

## No flexibility? Make creative suggestions

In negotiating with a small company, for instance, you are less likely to encounter fixed pay policies, permitting you to get creative about your comp package. If a small company can't afford you on a cash basis, what else do you want?

You have a wide range of options from asking for a company car, stock options, extra generous mileage reimbursement, parking privileges, additional paid vacations, and a sign-on bonus. If you're negotiating for a job that pays below $30,000 and you know the company's salary cap can't be raised, try to get a shorter work week or flexible work hours, and take a second job to keep a roof over your head. If your spouse can cover you with health benefits, maybe you can trade insurance for cash.

## How's your imagination?

Of course, you know about the movie *Star Wars*. Do you remember the part where Han Solo **(Harrison Ford)** asks Luke Skywalker **(Mark Hamill)** how much the reward would be to rescue rich Princess Leia **(Carrie Fisher)**? Luke tells him it would be more wealth than he could imagine. Han's answer: "I don't know, I can imagine quite a bit!"

**Ask:** *Is there any flexibility in the salary portion of the offer?* When the answer is no, get creative and begin talking about alternatives. (Of course, you have anticipated imaginative options before talking money, right?)

# The Magic of Market Value

You research to find out the fair market value of your work before negotiating a price. Slip those exact words into the discussion whenever you can — *fair* and *market value* are terms that people like. Remember, too, that you can always come down on your price — but coming up is almost impossible after you name a low figure.

# Part IV
# Technology Makes an Entrance

The 5th Wave          By Rich Tennant

"Very good answer! Now, let me ask you another question..."

## In this part . . .

Technology is the big job interviewing news as the third millenium unrolls. Love high tech or hate it, geek days are here.

The first of three technology chapters tells you smart ways to handle telephone interviewing, which seems to be growing as rapidly as cell phones.

Next comes the mind-bending technology of virtual interviews where you may be thousands of miles away from the interviewer — or just across town. Analysts expect videoconference interviewing to spread quickly within the next few years.

Finally in this part, suggestions are offered to help you handle video online interviews like a pro.

# Chapter 11

# Telephone Interviewing: A Growth Industry

- - - - - - - - - - - - - - - - - - - - - - - - - - - - - - - - - - - - -

### In This Chapter

▶ Landing in-person interviews via phone interviews

▶ Scheduling telephone interviews

▶ Preparing: tips on being ready

- - - - - - - - - - - - - - - - - - - - - - - - - - - - - - - - - - - - -

*L*ike a universe-creating Big Bang, the technology explosion is racing across the world's jobscape. Not all of the technology is cyberspace-bound, but all of the technology is used to save time and money.

This chapter looks at how telephones are being used in job interviews, which changes the way you market yourself.

## Tougher Than Face-to-Face Talking

Jean Yale was primed to turn in a winning interview: her resume and supporting materials, pen, paper, and glass of water — all were at the ready on a table by the telephone, waiting for the call that could change Yale's life. This story happened a decade ago, long before telephone interviews became popular.

One of six finalists for the director's position at a displaced homemakers center several states away, Yale was interviewed by telephone, with the understanding that a tape of the interview would be played for the organization's board of directors. Seated before the interview work table, Yale included lots of examples (storytelling) to back up her qualifications. The interview rolled out like 16 yards of premium satin. It couldn't have gone smoother. Or so the candidate thought.

The telephone rang again. The tape recorder had malfunctioned, the interviewer said apologetically: *Can we run through the interview again?*

Round Two went as well as the first. The telephone jingled yet again. This time the interviewer was mortified — he had forgotten to turn on the tape recorder. *Once more?*

Yale says that by now she was totally relaxed: *Starting the same question sequence over, I curled up on my bed talking as though I were chatting with my best friend. Several times I had the memory of mentioning a point and so moved quickly to the next question.*

After hanging up, Yale realized the first two interviews had lasted 30 minutes each, but the third version only 15 minutes. Realization struck: *The points I remembered making in shortcutting the third interview were made during the first two interviews!*

Yale wasn't taped for the final interview round, but by then she didn't care — she dined out for months on her true story of technology run amok. Today, Jean Yale directs career services at Texas Woman's University in Denton and is a superb coach when students ask for tips on telephone interviewing.

## Calling your shots

Telephone interviews are no longer rare and are expected to be used with increasing frequency as interview costs continue to rise.

Calling someone long-distance is much cheaper than flying that person to another state. That's why, in this age of downsizing and corporate cutbacks, employers are relying more and more on telephone interviewing to screen job candidates. Notice I said *screen job candidates.*

> **Rarely will you be able to win the job on the telephone. You work hard during the telephone interview to land an in-person interview.**

Even at companies with fewer than 1,000 employees, recruiters pick up the telephone and try to identify skills of candidates who will be strong performers in a high-growth, fast-paced environment. Often the recruiting task is outsourced to a private firm specializing in telephone interviews.

The interviews may be brief or lengthy. That is, they can be quick fact-finding calls to announce your presence is requested, or they can be an in-depth third-degree determining whether you should be invited at all. Telephone interviews serve two purposes:

- Recruiters use them as preliminary evaluations to round up a pool of candidates for jobs that their clients want to fill. The interviews are probably scripted. Recruiters must cover all the bases in confirming that you can indeed perform the specific objectives of the position before they include you in the candidate pool.

- Recruiters use them to narrow down a pool of applicants to a few finalists.

In looking for reasons to rule you out, recruiters will hone in on your possible lack of appropriate credentials or education, your inconvenient geography, and whether your financial requirement is too low or too high for the job's predetermined range.

Because most people don't prepare for screening telephone interviews as rigorously as they prepare for face-to-face meetings, the casualty toll is heavy. When the caller is trying to reduce the list to a few finalists, getting knocked out of the running is very easy if the call doesn't go well.

Why aren't job seekers rigorously prepared? Because recruiters may purposely try to catch job seekers off guard, hoping surprise strips away the outer layers of preparation, exposing genuine, unrehearsed thoughts and feelings. Recruiters also see unanticipated calls as useful for measuring the job seekers' ability to think on their feet. Remember these stage directions:

- View any telephone interview as an opportunity to win an in-person interview.

- Behave as though you expect the call to be the overture to an in-person meeting.

- Win an invitation to meet face-to-face, or you are wiped out in the first act of the job play.

If you don't like surprises, follow these preparation suggestions to reap applause for your telephone performance.

## *Keep your telephone well stocked*

Keep one telephone stocked with all your interview essentials. Must-haves include

- Current resumes

- A list of answers to anticipated key questions

- A list of points, such as specific skills and achievements, that you want to mention

- A calendar, with all scheduled commitments

✔ A folder for each company you've applied to — put any correspondence in this folder

✔ A notepad, pen, and calculator

## Make telephone appointments

Whenever possible, don't answer questions when the call comes in, but schedule an appointment for your telephone interview so that you can be ultra-prepared — you have to take your child to Little League, you're repainting your apartment, or something. Find a reason to be the one who calls back. Conventional wisdom says that the person on the calling end has an advantage over the one on the receiving end — use this knowledge to your benefit. Simply say: *Thank you for calling. I appreciate your interest. I'm quite interested in speaking with you about my qualifications. Unfortunately, this is not a good time for me. Can I call you tomorrow? Or is there another time you'd prefer?*

If a recruiter insists on calling you back, do what you would do for any other interview: Be ready early. This may sound surprising, but as a reminder to interview as a professional, change out of your jeans and into the type of dress you'd wear in a face-to-face business meeting.

## How do you sound?

Recruiters rely on your telephone presence in deciding whether to call you in for a face-to-face, so make the most of your vocal graces:

✔ Speak loudly enough that you can be easily heard.

✔ Use correct grammar.

✔ Use complete sentences.

✔ Avoid pauses.

✔ If your voice is high-pitched, try to lower it a bit.

Most importantly, *put warmth in your voice.* Smile. You should sound energetic and enthusiastic. A few rounds with a tape recorder will help finesse your vocal performance.

BASICS

## Telephone interviewing when you're at work

If your current employer doesn't know that you're looking for a new job, close the door and speak to the interviewer for only a couple of minutes, asking the caller if you can set up an in-person interview right then — or if you can talk in the evening when you're at home.

## *The screening script*

When the oh-so-important call comes, follow these tips to get yourself off the telephone and into the interviewer's office:

✔ **If you have a home office, use it because it's businesslike** — You may find it helpful to face a blank wall to eliminate distractions of gazing out a window or spotting a smudge on your favorite painting.

✔ **Gather essential information** — At the start of the conversation, get the caller's name, title, company, address, and telephone number. Read back the spelling.

✔ **Be a champion listener** — Prove that you're paying attention by feeding back what the interviewer says: *In other words, you feel that expansion is needed in the blue division.*

✔ **Expect challenges** — Some telephone interviewers ask candidates to join them in an improvisation.

The interviewer sets up a job-related scenario for a role-play. The interviewer may, for example, play a boss asking why a deadline was not met, a vendor trying to change the terms of a contract, or a disgruntled customer; your challenge is to try your hand at acting out the situations in the pretend problem. Interviewers say they're looking for creativity and a cheerful spirit. They downscore you if you run out of talk early in the exercise or refuse to go along with the game.

Your dialogue in the role-play isn't as important as showing how your mind works — how fast you think and what thinking processes you use to solve the problem. **Tip:** Avoid giving long-winded, detailed responses.

✔ **Be coachable** — If the interviewer criticizes one of your role-play answers, don't get defensive. The interviewer is testing you. Instead, recognize the objection and try to understand it. Once you get a handle on your weakness, revise your answer to show that you understand and that you're willing to take direction.

✔ **Provide feedback and ask for it in return** — After making a statement, inquire, *Is this the kind of information you're seeking?* or *Have I sufficiently answered your question about my managerial experience?* Be sure that the interviewer is listening and that you say things the interviewer wants to hear.

✔ **Don't rush** — You may feel pressure on long-distance calls to rush through the interview, aware of dollars ticking away. But make a heroic effort to feel relaxed and speak exactly as you would in an interviewer's office.

✔ **Divert important questions** — Tickle interviewers' interest by answering most of their questions. Then, when they ask a particularly important question, give them a reason to see you in person. Tell the interviewer that you can better answer that question in person: *That's an important question — with my skills (experience) in _____, it's one that I feel I can't answer adequately over the telephone. Can we set up a meeting so that I can better explain my qualifications? I'm free on Tuesday morning — is that a good time for you?*

Decide beforehand which questions can best be put off. You can use this tactic two or three times in the same conversation.

✔ **Push for a meeting** — As the call winds to a close, tell the interviewer, *As we talk, I'm thinking we can better discuss my qualifications for (position title) in person. I can be at your office Thursday morning. Is 9:30 good, or is there a better time for you?* Remember, what you want is an in-person meeting. Assume you'll get it and give the interviewer a choice as to the time.

✔ **Say thanks** — Remember to express your appreciation for the time spent with you.

✔ **Remember to write a thank-you letter** — Just because the interview was via telephone doesn't negate the wisdom of putting your thanks in writing (fax, postal mail, or e-mail).

Remember, telephone interviews can screen you out of the running in the first leg of the race. Avoid getting skunked by stating only the positive and eliminating the negative.

## The salary question

Telephone screeners often ask you to name an expected salary. Play dodge ball on this one. You don't know how much money you want yet because you don't know what the job is worth. If the interviewer persists, flip the coin and ask the interviewer to identify the range for the job for someone with your qualifications. If pushed to the wall, give an estimated salary range with a spread between $15,000 and $20,000. Techniques to avoid premature salary discussion are outlined in Chapter 10.

JUDGMENT CALL

## Should you pay your own way?

Traditionally, employers have paid every dime of a candidate's travel expenses to the interview. In these budget-pinching times, an employer may give you a choice between paying your own travel expenses or undergoing a telephone interview. Should you cough up the money to travel? I wouldn't — unless you're desperate, have a bundle of frequent flyer miles, or it's the job of the century.

Try this instead: Ask for an initial telephone interview. Use that opportunity to turn the tables, interviewing the interviewer. Find out as much as you can about the position, the responsibilities, and your potential boss.

When you decide the job is right for you, you may decide to gamble with the expense of traveling to the interview. A face-to-face meeting obviously gives you an advantage in the selection process.

# *Psychological Readiness Carries the Day*

Are you psychologically ready to work a telephone interview as effectively as you would an in-person discussion? You have the same challenge to establish a rapport with the caller and communicate effectively.

Be ready to use stories, examples, and anecdotes to prove your skills and sound believable about the contributions you can make. Have a list of your own questions ready to ask the recruiter. Preparation makes the difference in whether you're invited to take the next step in the selection process.

# Chapter 12

# Say Hello to Video Online Interviews

### In This Chapter

▶ Seeing-and-hearing interview technology is getting hot

▶ Q&A about video online interviews

▶ Glancing at other kinds of computerized interviews

*F*irst, about terms in this chapter:

A *video online interview* (VOI) is what I call the interactive electronic transmission of pictures and sound between an employer and a candidate. I use this term to include interviews transmitted by both commercial and consumer videoconferencing methods, whether

✔ By modem or over a network

✔ By high-speed commercial connectivity or by lower-speed home connectivity

What is the purpose of a video online interview? The VOI replaces an in-person interview. The point of a VOI is to allow the employer and the candidate to look at each other and talk with each other at the same time — to pass pictures and sound back and forth as though both parties were in the same room. "Everything but the handshake," is how videoconference professionals explain it.

In my review of the literature and interviews with videoconferencing experts, I discovered a lack of agreement about what to call the video online interview.

Suggestions of terms from videoconferencing insiders ranged from "video-conference interview" to "video interview." To hit on a single term the recruiting industry could use, I checked with several recruiters. *Which term do you prefer?* I asked.

"Video interview" was discarded because it carries the baggage of the old videotaped interviews of the 1970s, which never really caught on. "Videoconference interview" was deemed more appropriate as a term for an intercompany business conference than for a structured employment interview.

So *video online interview* it is. By any handle, in the near future, you may find yourself on-camera interacting with someone (or some people) who think you're a possible hire or they wouldn't be interviewing you.

The term video online interview does not refer to other types of computerized interviews, such as interactive text interviews driven by keyboards where you type in your answers to interview questions. Those interviews — whether conducted at kiosks in malls or on your home computer — are not video online interviews because they are text- and graphics-based and do not include moving pictures and sound. I touch on computerized interviews at the end of this chapter.

# Interviewing Live . . . From Anywhere to Anywhere

Have you ever seen an old silent **Charlie Chaplin** film that was an exercise in serial jerking? "Jerky" is how many people think of consumer videoconferencing.

Commercial videoconferencing systems, while of television quality and vastly superior to consumer systems, were expensive and sometimes tagged as not being cost effective when telephone line charges and the cost of staff to handle the equipment were added in.

So despite nearly a decade of effort, for reasons of quality and price, video online interviewing never became popular.

And with the exception of interviews conducted by executive search firms, VOIs still are not commonly used for job interviews. Not yet. But heavy-duty researchers foresee that picture changing rapidly.

Optimistic observers anticipate that only a few years will pass before VOIs are commonplace; more conservative forecasters don't expect VOI mainstreaming to become a reality for five to ten years. What they all agree on is that video online interviewing is up and running now, and there's no looking back. A shortfall in bandwidth is the big hang-up.

Bandwidth is the amount of data that can be transmitted in a fixed amount of time. For our purposes here, bandwidth is expressed in thousands of bits per second (kbps). The greater the bandwidth, the greater the information-carrying capacity of the medium and the smoother the moving picture. The minimum for fluid transmission is 384 kbps.

The other number to keep in mind for good picture performance is a sustained speed of 30 fps (frames per second), which generally is achieved at 384 kbps, and is equivalent to television. Anything less than a sustained 30 fps will be jerky.

What does sustained mean? Think of taking a shower with a pleasant, steady stream of water when the yard sprinklers activate suddenly. Your shower's flow of water slows to a trickle. Your water system didn't sustain the pressure. Similarly, the flow of pictures must be sustained at a minimum of 30 fps for a natural, television-like effect.

Only about 10 percent of the United States has plenty of bandwidth, but capacity is expanding as you read these words. Bandwidth capacity is mushrooming on cable, DSL (digital subscriber lines) telephone lines, and satellites.

When bandwidth is widely available, job interviews will spring from settings everywhere — offices and homes, schools and libraries, employment service offices and social service facilities, as well as corporate offices, commercial recruitment centers, and videoconference centers.

# Here's Looking at You, Kid

As **Humphrey Bogart's** character, Rick, might have intoned (but didn't) in the classic *Casablanca,* you're in or you're out, kid. The video online interview is typically used to screen candidates, to weed out the nonqualifieds. But not always.

Some companies report they've hired personnel right from video. Employers who face the expense of flying candidates in for interviews often use the 1-2-3 pass-along system: If you do well in a "phoner" interview, you are invited to a second-round meeting, a video online interview; if you do well on a VOI, you're flown in for an in-person meeting.

Companies are gravitating toward VOIs for various reasons, including saving money. These include the opportunity for multicast interviews, allowing more than one person to interview a candidate at the same time from different locations. And a video meeting permits a company to tape the interview, giving decision-makers the option of reviewing the tape or showing it to others who were unavailable during the live video.

# *What You Should Know about Video Online Interviews*

Because the technology used for video online interviews is unfamiliar to many, here are some basic questions and answers that should help you get a grip on the way they work.

**For what kinds of jobs are VOIs used today?**

The VOI is used primarily for managerial, professional, and executive jobs, plus positions in high-tech industries. Video online interviews tend to be for high-level or technically specific jobs at this time.

**How fast must the system be so my image isn't distorted?**

If your VOI travels at anything less than 30 fps, you won't look your best. Right now, you might not want to do a VOI for a professional job using a consumer video system. If a company won't pay for your high-speed interview on a commercial video system, the company may pinch pennies in other areas as well. If you are willing to do an interview on a slower-speed system, you'll just have to do the best you can: Maximize your chances by reading the performance tips in Chapter 13.

**What's wrong with VOIs?**

As the candidate, you can't yet control the process. The quality depends on the lowest common denominator. For example, a connection at Kinko's, using 30 fps technology, to a PC, using only 5 fps, will result in a picture display at the rate of 5 fps. If a candidate is overly active in a virtual interview with low-end technology, the candidate will come across "all wrong," experts say.

**How has videoconferencing equipment improved?**

The equipment is significantly easier to use these days — like a TV remote, point and click. Earlier equipment required training to use the control panel.

Audio and video are much improved as well. Advances in compression technology have sharpened the video quality at lower bandwidth. And prices have dropped dramatically. You can get a pretty good consumer desktop system for $1,000 or less. Commercial videoconferencing equipment that cost $40,000 to $60,000 per site in 1997 now runs about $12,000 to $35,000. Prices went down, quality went up.

**Are videophones likely to be used for VOIs?**

Probably not. The screen sizes on videophones are about three to four inches, whereas videoconferencing monitors are much larger, often 31 inches. Employers prefer seeing people on a big screen, especially when offering substantial salaries for important jobs.

**Where can I find a commercial videoconferencing center?**

Employers and recruiters choose and pay for the videoconferencing center. They decide from where the interview will originate on your end. When you interview at a videoconferencing center, all you need to take with you is the contact information for the employer who has set up the interview. Typically, commercial videoconferencing systems are found at

- ✔ Campus career centers
- ✔ Commercial conference centers (Televideo Conferencenters)
- ✔ Airport lounges
- ✔ Hotels (Radisson)
- ✔ Office service firms (Kinko's)
- ✔ Staffing firms (Manpower)
- ✔ Executive recruiters
- ✔ Job fairs
- ✔ Corporation offices (Citibank)

**Tip:** As a job candidate, never pay for the costs of a video online interview.

**When will consumer system video online interviews become routine?**

That all depends on how quickly bandwidth saturates our nation and world.

# Computer Online Interviewing: Pushing the Right Buttons

In addition to video online interviewing, you may encounter a range of other new-breed interviewing technologies.

## Outsourced service

The automation used by *InterviewNow.com* (`interviewnow.com`) illustrates the cutting-edge approach several service firms are taking.

You are referred to the Net-based InterviewNow.com by employers; maybe you saw a job ad in a paper or online, or you made direct application. You log on to the InterviewNow site and move through a series of questions that will determine your suitability and compatibility with the target job opening.

From combinations of yes/no, to multiple choice, to self-evaluation queries, you provide the employer with an in-depth assessment of your skills, temperament, and the intangibles you offer.

Working from this online package, InterviewNow's proprietary software ranks you as a candidate for the job.

If you're not qualified, you're screened out immediately. You get an automatic "Thanks but no interest" note by e-mail.

Because InterviewNow launched at the same time this book went to press, specific sample questions and estimates of how long it will take you to pre-qualify aren't available. Look for instructions on the InterviewNow Web site.

## Company direct

Companies also use prescreening computer online interviews directly on their own Web sites.

Tech companies in particular are using pre-assessment techniques. Tech Watch syndicated newspaper columnist Bob Weinstein says a good example is the information services company EDS's Web site at `www.eds-imagineit.com`.

In some cases, the prescreener is a combination test and resume. You're required to answer 45 minutes' worth of questions on such topics as

- Would you rather have structure or flexibility in your job?
- How often do you forget important details?
- In the past, what approach have you chosen to solve difficult problems?

Weinstein reports that experts say your best tact is to tell it like it is, rather than what you think the company wants to hear. On the last question, for instance, you could choose from these answers:

1. **I have thoroughly investigated all aspects of the job.**
2. **I have felt overwhelmed and asked someone for help.**
3. **I have requested guidance from my supervisor or professor to find the solution.**
4. **I have given up and moved on to a new task.**
5. **I don't know.**

Most people would pick "1" for the right answer. But, as Weinstein reports, that may be the wrong answer, depending on the job. If the objective in a particular job is to get the problem solved as quickly as possible and move on to the next problem, the employer wants someone who can ask for help and not spend five weeks on a five-minute task.

More examples: Companies plagued with high turnover in the United States, such as the food service and retail industries, are turning to PC-based recruiting systems and voice-activated telephone screening tools to cut hiring costs. Burger King, Wendy's, McDonald's, and Chili's Grill & Bar are using these new-age recruiting methods. So is Macy's, the New York-based department store.

## Who's in charge?

Computers should never make the final hiring decision, but are certain to be increasingly used to help a human interviewer ask the right questions to gain additional facts about areas of interest or to flag concerns. Or to find out if a face-to-face meeting is pointless.

# Big Time Cyber-time Ahead

Just as the movies emerged from black-and-white, silent **Charlie Chaplin** stuff, to full-color epics with sound to buy earplugs by, the video online interview is coming of age.

Several stars of old didn't make the cut from silent to sound — **Rudolph Valentino** and **Clara Bow** come to mind. You don't want to be left behind. So, as Chicago technology speaker/consultant Bill Metcalf (www.technoshift.com) and Scott Darling of Zydacron Corporation advise, pay attention to the tips in the next chapter. When you find a few extra minutes, work in a little sneak-preview practice. You may be glad you did. Perhaps sooner than you think.

# Chapter 13

# Special Tips for Camera Closeups

- - - - - - - - - - - - - - - - - - - - - - - - - - - - - - - - - - - - - - - - - -

### In This Chapter

▶ Discovering the culture of virtual interviewing

▶ Choosing your wardrobe to face the cameras

▶ Respecting technology limitations

- - - - - - - - - - - - - - - - - - - - - - - - - - - - - - - - - - - - - - - - - -

*T*he red light on the camera and I did not enjoy our partnership. It happened a half-dozen years ago when I flew to Los Angeles to tape a national TV morning show segment publicizing one of my books. At the studio, I was shocked to discover that the usual accoutrements of major-league TV — makeup artist, well-lighted studio, and human interviewer — were missing.

Instead, I was ushered into a TV producer's small office to face a machine — that camera with its red light burning, like an unrelenting laser, into my very mind. An earphone was embedded in my ear with the instructions to "Just listen to the questions and reply to the camera." Hah!

If I hadn't known before that day that I was far from flameproof at human-free interviewing, I knew it then. I muttered, stuttered, and froze like a deer in headlights talking about topics I knew as well as my own name.

For all the performance-improving feedback I was getting, I may as well have been standing alone at the Pacific Ocean, talking to the waves. Thrown for a loop, I gave a series of ditsy, half-baked answers.

When the taping event was over, I was not smiling. By allowing the technology and the lack of a human in the interviewing room to intimidate me, I had blown a nice opportunity to spread the word about the electronic revolution in the job market. Fortunately, the show's New York producer heavily edited the segment, and the result was better than I had any right to expect.

My introduction to new media potholes continued the following week when I taped another TV show interview that featured a similar setup, except this time I did the interview from a Denver station's news-anchor desk. These questions, too, came from an earplug, but this time I could see the interviewer on a screen buried in the desktop. The interviewer was working in another studio across town.

Each time the interviewer called my name prefacing a question — "Joyce, what do you think about. . . ?" — my reflex action was to look down into the desktop screen, which the audience could not see. For each response, I jerked my head back up to speak to the red-eyed camera. When I saw a tape of that interview, all I could think of was a puppet on a fast-forward setting bobbing for apples. My face was as red as the camera's light.

I had much to learn about handling myself with new kinds of pictures-and-sound technology. And in an era of emerging video online interviewing, you probably do, too. If you are asked to participate in an interactive video online interview (see Chapter 12), you'll want to consciously consider what you wear and how you act.

Here is a screenplay summary of tips I have collected (chiefly from Bill Metcalf and Scott Darling; see Chapter 12) to help you learn the culture of virtual interviewing.

# *Watch Your Look*

To succeed in video online interviewing, should you consult a makeup specialist and fashion consultant? Not necessarily, but you should pay plenty of attention to how you look:

- **Mirror:** Both men and women should bring a compact with a mirror to check last-minute looks. Delete shine by using a tissue to mop your perspiring face or oily brow. Ditch even more shine with a touch of powder on the old schnozz.

- **Face:** Men: Make sure you are close shaven and trim any wild eyebrows and nose hairs.

- **Cosmetics:** Women and men, wear special camera-friendly makeup only if you first practice and see how it looks on a home videocamera. You can benefit by getting instructions from a professional makeup artist at a makeup center who understands video appearance; expect to pay between $50 and $75.

  Dark makeup minimizes double chins. Concealer makeup hides dark circles under your eyes. Matte finish makeup tones down a shiny bald dome. Women: Choose brownish tones of lipstick rather than bright red. Wear a tiny bit of foundation makeup to hide blemishes.

- **Facial expression:** Choose full-face camera angles (not profile or three quarters).

In an interview when you are really concentrating, you may knit your brow or purse your lips, thinking this "earnest look" portrays you as truly listening. But cameras tend to project a sullen-looking face even if you are neutral. Boost the energy to your face: Smile more than you might in real life. You don't want to be a toothpaste ad, causing viewers to wonder what you're smiling about, but remember that the camera zooms into your face and whatever it sees will be magnified.

✔ **Big head:** Sit 3 to 4 feet away from the camera. You don't want a big head filling the screen (Hi, Godzilla!). You want a good upper body shot. For an illustration of this tip, study how your favorite TV news anchors are framed in the screen.

✔ **Eye focus:** The avoidance of darting eyes is important. They look sneaky. Suppose that the interviewer asks you a potentially threatening question, such as "How's your credit history?" Make sure that you address the camera directly when answering. If your eyes dart off, the interviewer may take your response as an evasion or lie.

✔ **Eye contact:** In an in-person interview, you normally would look the interviewer in the eyes (or bridge of the nose, which is equivalent). During a virtual interview, pretend the camera lens is the interviewer's eyes.

The mistake some beginners make is to look at the monitor (on which the interviewer's face appears) instead of at the camera. Looking at the monitor makes it appear that you are not looking your interviewer in the eyes.

✔ **Clothing:** Solid colors are safest. The color of the room in which you're interviewing is a factor. You want to contrast a little (darker clothing on light fields, lighter clothing on dark fields), with your background, but don't go to extremes. Medium tones are best. Too much white, and the camera can't adjust properly for your face. Too much black, and your nice suit will look like a big lump. A medium-toned suit with a blue, off-white, or light pink shirt or blouse will almost always look good.

What about other colors and patterns? Reds in big doses tend to streak and trail color, which is why TV newscasters don't wear lots of red, but do wear little touches of red in accessories such as ties. Avoid plaid or stark white clothing. Stripes or busy patterns may vibrate on screen. Perhaps you've noticed how team pinstriped uniforms sometimes vibrate on TV baseball games.

✔ **Jewelry:** Avoid clanking bracelets or bright jewelry. Noise from a clanking bracelet carries over the microphone and could possibly drown out your voice — plus the noise is irritating. Flashy, bright jewelry — metal necklaces and earrings, for instance — can be very distracting.

# Watch Your Setting

Like a frame around a picture, the background surrounding your image makes a statement about you. These suggestions can help:

✔ **Lighting:** The lighting in your interview setting affects your appearance. If you have deep-set eyes, the lights can cause shadows. A trick to prevent that from happening: While you are talking, slightly tilt your head up to avoid the reflection.

Another trick: If there is overhead lighting, place a white legal pad on the table in front of you. You can "bounce" the light onto your face to help reduce the shadows. You may have to prop up the pad with a pencil to get the right angle. If the white-legal-pad trick helps you, you'll see it in the monitor when you check yourself out before the interview begins.

✔ **Background:** If you're working with a consumer videoconference system at home, be aware of the background. You don't want the interviewer to be distracted by your mess. Make sure the camera isn't pointing directly to your cluttered bookshelves or damaged wall. If necessary, hang a sheet to cover the bookshelves or wall. The best color for the sheet is a medium blue.

# Watch Your Performance

Presenting yourself in a virtual interview differs in some respects from how you participate in an in-person meeting. For best results, heed these recommendations:

✔ **Timely arrival:** When you are using a videoconference center or corporation location, arrive 30 minutes early to allow for time consumed in setup arrangements and familiarize yourself with the environment, much as a platform speaker checks out the room in advance of speaking. At commercial facilities, testing of the interview video connection is usually scheduled 30 minutes before your interview begins.

✔ **Posture:** Sit up straight. The camera isn't kind to a slouch. Don't lean forward when you speak. If you do, your head will look too big.

✔ **Hyperactivity:** Be careful about what you do with your hands. The eyes go right to your hands if they are fidgeting with paperclips or pens. Fold your hands in front of you on the table or desk.

Consciously avoid being hyperactive. Don't wave your hands around. Any extraneous movement on camera doesn't help you communicate and may distract. Of course, you don't want to look frozen in time, but when you move, try to move with a purpose. Watch your favorite news anchors, and you'll see how they "work" a camera to appear animated but move very little.

✔ **Nervousness:** Nervousness shows at an in-person interview, but it shows double on a video online interview. Nervousness cannot be commanded away, but lots of practice can reduce it. A good way to overcome nervousness is to focus on something other than yourself. Really focus on the employer. Concentrate on hearing what the employer says. You will relax and appear friendly and interesting.

✔ **Pausing for effect:** Although your pauses should not drag into eternity, when you are asked a significant question, such as "Tell me about your-self" or "How do you handle disappointment?" feel free to pause a split second. Then smile, look the employer in the eye (camera lens), and answer the question.

✔ **Self-viewing:** If the equipment you are using contains a picture-in-picture (PIP) feature, turn it off if you are uncomfortable looking at yourself while interviewing. But do check yourself out before turning it off. See how far you can move left and right or up and down and still remain in the frame. You might turn the PIP on and off again if you need assurance that you haven't smeared your lipstick or deposited a sneeze residue on your face.

✔ **Delay-time:** Only the top-of-the-line videoconference equipment is free of delay time. Before the interview, ask about the approximate frame rate and about the delay inherent in the equipment you'll use. If the equipment handles 30 fps (frames per second), you won't get much, if any, delay. At the interview, doublecheck by asking, *How's the transmission going today? Is there much delay?* Then you'll know if you should slow down.

✔ **Speech-speed:** The faster the connection, the fewer problems you will have with dialogue. Generally, employers on the other end will be able to hear you just fine, and you can hear them as well. But remember, because there is a delay in transmission, it becomes harder to interrupt each other. Be certain you give the employer a chance to speak. When you are finished making a statement or asking a question, hush up! Stop speaking. Give the employer a chance to talk. If you keep "filling the void," the employer may feel you have grabbed control of the interview and not like it.

You cannot make adjustments if your lips are out of synch with the sound. Don't try. The situation is beyond your control.

Instead, concentrate on the camera lens (which makes it seem as through you are looking into the eyes of the employer) and the lack of synch will be less noticeable. Perhaps you've seen old movies on TV with out-of-synch sound. The actor's lips move but the sound comes out a split second later. If you like the movie enough to put up with the annoyance, you'll begin to pay more attention to the actor's eyes. Which is what happens in video online interviewing.

✔ **Readiness:** Don't try to wing a video online interview. Every time you are caught unprepared will stick out like a sore thumb. Be ready with interviewing essentials.

If you're a rookie, have at hand your college overall and major grade point averages, undergraduate and graduate aptitude test scores, key facts about your accomplishments, and job history including addresses and references if asked.

But don't waste time fumbling with paper looking up answers and don't try to give addresses and other numbers during your interview. Say that you will follow up by sending the requested information immediately by e-mail. In fact, that's a good way to follow up even if you're not asked: Write a thank-you e-mail and include information you think will strengthen your chances of being chosen for hire.

Aces should follow a similar path but adjust the information appropriately.

Prepare for an online interview as ardently as you would an in-person interview. At the very least, study the employer's Web page.

✔ **Resume display:** Ask if the employer would like a nicely formatted version of your resume to be e-mailed as an attachment or sent by fax prior to the video online interview. In most cases, that's all you'll have to do other than prepare for the interview itself.

Some advisers suggest that you show your resume onscreen during portions of the video online interview. You do this by hooking up a PC to the videoconference equipment. Resume display really doesn't add much to the interview and can backfire: A typo on your resume may go unnoticed on an 8.5 x 11-inch piece of paper but it becomes unmissable when blown up on a big screen.

If you're technologically savvy, you might like to know that some of the newer videoconference systems have a wide range of integrated presentation tools, including PowerPoint software and Internet browsers. You should consider using these presentation tools during the interview only if the employer would like you to do so.

Always ask for the employer's preference when you agree to face the camera. It's a big mistake to assume that presentation bells and whistles are wanted and to spring them unannounced during the video online interview.

✔ **System control:** If you are working at home with a consumer video-conference system, you should be thoroughly familiar with your equipment. To be otherwise is like planning a driving trip across country and learning to drive the night before your trip begins. You've got to be at ease. Some people find that having a technologically skilled friend on hand for the first couple of interviews is a big help in feeling relaxed and not worrying if a system glitch occurs.

Do a few dry runs to a friend using the equipment. Record the video-conference trials. Be your own worst critic.

## *Looking on the Bright Side*

There's an upside to the growing use of video online interviews: You and the employer don't shake hands. That's one way of getting through an interview without worrying whether your palms are sweaty or whether your breath is sweet and fresh.

After the debacle at the Denver TV station when I kept bobbing my head down to see the screen buried in the desk each time the interviewer addressed me by name, I figured out what to do to prevent that from happening again. My answer: Cover the screen with a pile of papers and never look down. It works. At least, I think so.

# Part V

# Rave Answers to Interview Questions

The 5th Wave          By Rich Tennant

@RICHTENNANT

"All my interviews are second interviews.
One second and I'm out."

# In this part . . .

*I*f you've gotten as far as the interview, chalk one up for your side. You're doing a good job of finding a job! Now comes the clincher. You have to prove to an interviewer that you're the best person for the job, and the key to doing that is giving the best answers to questions lobbed at you.

But how can you prepare when you don't know what the questions will be? Unless you're a star improviser, you're likely to stumble through your answers. Use this part to practice your answers to actual questions.

This part helps you prepare for and answer specific questions — from evaluating yourself, to explaining why you were fired, to describing your skills, to describing your weaknesses — all aspects of the interview process that can make even interview veterans cringe when they're not expecting them. I even give you suggestions on wriggling gracefully out of inappropriate questions.

# Chapter 14

# Now, Tell Me about Yourself

*In This Chapter*

▶ Star-studded approach to answering questions

▶ Describing yourself and looking good

▶ Preparing a commercial — about yourself

▶ Some possible questions, decoded

*Q*uestions and answers are the storylines of job interviews. Their variations seem endless. Questions about you and your psychological makeup are the topic of this chapter.

Some job-change experts say that no matter how many different ways they are expressed, only a few basic questions are asked — infinite variations on a few themes. Most of the questions relate either to your ability to do the job (skills, education, and experience) or to examine the kind of person you are.

✔ **Questioners want to know what's right with you:** Are you the sort of individual who will be cheerful about pitching in and getting a project done even when doing so is not in your job description?

✔ **Questioners want to know what's wrong with you:** Are you creative about finding reasons not to do the work, or do you upset others on your team?

The matriarch of all self-revealing questions is often a statement instead of a question:

> *Tell me a little about yourself.*

No matter how this request is phrased, the *tell-me-about-yourself* question is the big bazooka of the interviewer's arsenal. Why? The TMAY question comes early in an interview — a time when the initial impression is forming. A weak first impact may color the interviewer's perceptions about all that follows. If your debut is unimpressive, you can't count on recouping with strong responses later.

When you start to tell about yourself, focus on aspects of your life that illustrate your values as a person as well as an employee admirably suited to the job.

Employers want to get to know you so that they can feel confident that, as I've said earlier, you're the sort of person who not only can do a job, but also will do it and will get along with others while you're getting the job done.

Employers want to know how well you accept management direction. They want to know whether you are expecting to get too comfortable on the job. They want to know whether, despite their lack of long-term commitment to you, you will jump ship at an inconvenient time if another employer dangles more money before your eyes.

When answering the TMAY question, bear this thought in mind:

> ***Focus on the Best You.***

In sticking to the Best-You theme, you may ask, "But isn't that kind of like lying?" No. I would never tell you to lie. Lying is a time bomb that can come back and blow away your job.

(I know a woman who did not inflate her previous salary — she lowered it because she didn't want to be considered overqualified for the job she wanted. After 11 months she was fired for lying when her reference checks finally caught up with her. Just the week before that she had been offered a promotion!)

Always be honest — about the wonderful parts of you. Just don't blurt out anything that could make you look like a poor hiring choice. Neither should you watch your nose grow by wildly exaggerating your best traits.

# More Telling about Yourself

A competent questioner focuses not only on *what* you say in response to the TMAY question, but also on *how* you respond.

- ✔ Do you focus on your skills or your education as they relate to the job? The interviewer may think you're work-oriented.
- ✔ Do you focus on your hobbies? The interviewer may decide that you're more interested in your leisure hours.
- ✔ Do you focus on your present job? The employer may think that you're not ready to move on.

The Tell-Me-About-Yourself question

- ✔ Tells employers what you consider important
- ✔ Gives employers insight into your values
- ✔ Tells employers what you've accomplished
- ✔ Tells employers if you're organized, self-motivated, and focused
- ✔ Helps employers determine how well you'd fit into the company culture

# Narrow the Question

You can jump right in and give your pitch, or you can ask for prompts:

> *I can tell you about experience and accomplishments in this industry or the education and training that qualify me for this position or about my personal history. Where shall I start?*

Employers typically answer that they want to hear about either your work-relevant background — or a little bit of everything.

# Write a Commercial — about You

The key to handling a request to tell about yourself is to memorize — literally memorize — a one- to two-minute commercial about yourself.

Think about what a commercial does. It focuses on selling a product in a minuscule amount of time. It grabs your attention immediately with information of interest to you. Then it tells why you should buy the product.

That's exactly what your commercial should do. Grab employers' interest with a confident statement about yourself and then support that statement with specific facts. Concentrate on selling your strong points; tell employers exactly why they should hire you instead of someone else.

The better you know your commercial, the more confident you'll feel — and look. Memorize your commercial and practice it until it sounds natural. Just like an actor, you need to learn your script and deliver it in character.

What if you sound canned? Even if you do sound slightly stilted, that's better than sounding as though you have no idea who you are and what you bring to the job. The information in your commercial is too important to leave anything out, so make sure that you know it backwards and forwards.

Your commercial can include any of the following information:

- ✔ Your job title or position for which you're applying
- ✔ Your academic degree
- ✔ Positions of leadership
- ✔ Specific skills applicable to the job
- ✔ Specific job training
- ✔ Date of expected graduation (if applicable)
- ✔ Honors or achievements
- ✔ Goals (not long-term or covetous of the interviewer's job)
- ✔ Business philosophy (not pretentious or preachy)

# Sample Commercials

Here's a commercial for a prospective new graduate:

> *I have always found the journalist's world both exciting and challenging. That's why I chose to study journalism, and although I've discovered that the work is much harder than I ever imagined, I've also found I love it even more because of that. I can't wait to start working as a newspaper reporter.*
>
> *I will graduate in May from the University of Kansas with a Bachelor of Arts in Journalism. I was a feature writer on the school's newspaper. I would have been named editor, but I worked throughout my education to pay for 80 percent of my school expenses. At the same time, I managed to maintain a high GPA, so I expect to graduate cum laude.*
>
> *Working and attending school full time taught me to organize and prioritize for superior time management skills — I wouldn't have succeeded without these skills. Considering the demand of deadlines, I see these skills as especially important in a journalism career.*

Notice that the prospective new grad starts with an enthusiastic statement of interest in journalism. So that the grad doesn't come across as a dreamer, the grad lets the interviewer know that the hard work of journalism is one of its attractions. The grad continues by pointing to achievements and how they relate to the position. This new grad sounds focused, enthusiastic, and mature.

Here's another, shorter example:

> *I'll graduate in June from the University of Arizona with a major in marketing. I was on the track team. Through a series of student jobs, I managed to earn half my college expenses. But I also found time to participate in campus activities — for instance, I was elected vice president of the student marketing club.*
>
> *Usually I have an upbeat outlook about life. I don't have any trouble digging in and getting started on a project. I like working with people — and I especially like doing my best to persuade people.*

A seasoned ace highlights experience and accomplishments. For example:

> *I am an experienced line manager with extensive knowledge in team-building that ranges from organizing project teams to informally encouraging people to work together. I've developed solid skills in hiring and retaining employees.*
>
> *I also have experience in smoothly incorporating technological advances into a company where such advances require a significant amount of employee retraining.*
>
> *My track record is substantial in major presentations to clients, which has led to as much as an 87 percent increase in sales.*

This ace focuses on concrete skills and experience related to the job, showing technological savvy and a positive attitude toward implementing change.

You may wish to prepare one all-purpose commercial and edit it on your feet. If an employer only wants to know about your skills managing a budget and training staff, for instance, you need to cut-and-paste on the spot to discuss only those topics.

If you're not too good at instant editing, prepare several different commercials. You stand a better chance of being prepared if you can reach into your bag of commercials and pull out the one that delivers a succinct account of the information that the employer wants to hear.

For both approaches, remember to tailor your commercials to the jobs for which you're interviewing. Use your commercial to showcase why you are the best person for the job. And don't make employers guess what makes you star stuff — be your own press agent.

Now try writing your own commercial. Start with your position or field of interest and describe your experience and skills relevant to the position you want. Make the information interesting and remember to sell yourself. You don't have time to be modest; show employers what you've got and why they should want it.

## Your roadshow commercial

Your commercial is one that you can take with you wherever you go. You don't have to save it just for formal interviews.

Use a shortened version of your commercial at parties, group presentations, seminars — anywhere you're meeting new people and are asked to introduce yourself. Using your spiel can make you feel more confident and get the conversational ball rolling. Your commercial can even help you to network your way to a job. Consider this example, which in real life would likely be punctuated with responses from your listener:

*Hi. My name is Shari Bright, and I teach U.S. history at Martingale High School. I also have a strong background in literature, and I've been studying recently how to teach history through literature.*

*My goal is to give students a broader perspective of the world we live in. Additionally, I work on our school's literacy committee. Not only do we work toward reducing illiteracy in the school, but we also place students in community literacy programs where they teach reading and writing to adults.*

# *The Questions*

Some employers disguise the tell-me-about-yourself question with different words or a different focus. Following are common variations. For each variation, I give tips for **ShowStopper** answers (things to do), followed by tips for **ShowFlopper** answers (things **not** to do).

**Q** **What is your most memorable accomplishment?**

*For a ShowStopper answer*

✔ Choose a recent career-related accomplishment.

- Give details about that accomplishment, as if you're telling a story.
- Explain why this accomplishment is important to you.
- Give results.
- Relate the accomplishment directly to the job for which you're interviewing.

✔ Reply confidently and immediately.

*For a ShowFlopper answer*

- ✔ Give a vague or unfocused answer.
- ✔ Discuss an accomplishment with no connection to the job you want.
- ✔ Discuss responsibilities instead of results.

**Where do you see yourself five years from now?**
**How does this position fit with your long-term career objectives?**

*For a ShowStopper answer*

- ✔ Answer realistically; in a changed business world where a long-term job may mean three years, speak of lifelong education to keep abreast of changes in the field and self-reliance for your own career.
- ✔ Describe short-term, achievable goals and discuss how they will help you reach your long-term goals.
- ✔ Explain how the position you want will help you to reach your goals.
- ✔ Strive to look ambitious, but not too much so.

*For a ShowFlopper answer*

- ✔ Say that you want the interviewer's job.
- ✔ Describe unrealistic goals.
- ✔ State goals that aren't consistent with the company's needs.

**What is your greatest strength? Greatest weakness?**
**What key assets can you offer in this job?**
**What are three things I should know about you?**

*For a ShowStopper answer*

- ✔ Prepare three to five strengths to discuss.
- ✔ Discuss strengths necessary to the position you want.
- ✔ Use specific examples to illustrate your strengths.
- ✔ Mention team-building, leadership, and people skills.
- ✔ Cite a positive trait in disguise — you tend to expect everyone to work as hard as you do. If you cite a true but negative trait, minimize it by re-directing the conversation to actions you've taken toward improvement.

*For a ShowFlopper answer*

- ✔ Discuss strengths unrelated to the job you want.

**What are your outside interests?**
**Do you have any hobbies?**
**Do you participate in any sports?**
**What books have you read recently?**
**What movies have you seen recently?**

*For a ShowStopper answer*

- ✔ Be enthusiastic.

- ✔ Tell why you enjoy the activities you mention.

- ✔ Focus on team-oriented, active activities — sports over reading.

- ✔ If possible, show how your hobbies or reading materials help you in your work.

- ✔ Focus on movies or books that relate to personal growth.

*For a ShowFlopper answer*

- ✔ Say that you don't have any outside interests.

- ✔ Discuss ultra-competitive solo sports, unless applicable to the job you want.

- ✔ Mention fiction books or horror movies.

**Would you rather work with others or alone?**
**Are you a follower or a leader?**
**What is your experience working with teams?**

*For a ShowStopper answer*

- ✔ Discuss your adaptability and flexibility in working with others or alone, as a leader or a follower.

- ✔ Give concrete examples.

- ✔ Mention the importance of every team member's contribution.

*For a ShowFlopper answer*

- ✔ Label yourself as a loner or a follower, but not a leader.

- ✔ Let the interviewer think that you're willing to carry the load of team members who don't contribute.

- ✔ Say you don't like to work on teams.

**Describe your ideal job.**

*For a ShowStopper answer*

✔ Show how the position that you're interviewing for relates to your ideal job.

✔ Give examples showing why this position is your ideal job.

*For a ShowFlopper answer*

✔ Describe a job in a different career field.

✔ Give a generic, vague answer.

✔ Describe the interviewer's job, unless that's the position that you're interviewing for.

**What would you like to change about yourself?**
**If you could change any past decisions, what would they be?**

*For a ShowStopper answer*

✔ Focus on what you could change to improve what you already do well. Keep it positive.

✔ Discuss why you would like to make the changes you mention.

*For a ShowFlopper answer*

✔ Say that you wouldn't change anything.

✔ Volunteer negative information.

**What is your definition of success? Of failure?**
**How do you describe your success?**
**Why have you been successful?**

*For a ShowStopper answer*

✔ Use specific examples as illustration.

✔ Show that your success is balanced between your professional and personal lives.

✔ Relate success to the position you want.

✔ If you have to talk about failure, do so positively. Show how you turned a failure into a success or discuss how and what you learned from the failure. (See Chapters 18 and 19 for more information.)

✔ You're a happy person. The world is more good than bad.

*For a ShowFlopper answer*

- ✔ Spend a great deal of time talking about failure.
- ✔ Say that you've never failed.
- ✔ Discuss success as a fast-track shot to the top.

**How do you handle stressful situations?**
**How do you work under pressure?**

*For a ShowStopper answer*

- ✔ Give examples of how you've dealt with on-the-job stress in the past.
- ✔ Discuss what you do to relax and refresh.
- ✔ Give positive illustrations of how job stress or pressure makes you work harder or more efficiently.
- ✔ Illustrate your problem-solving skills and decision-making process through an example.

*For a ShowFlopper answer*

- ✔ Say that you avoid stress.
- ✔ Imply that stress is usually the result of lack of preparation or knowledge.

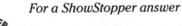

**Why should I hire you over the other candidates?**
**What can you tell me about yourself that will make me remember you?**

*For a ShowStopper answer*

- ✔ Even if the interviewer doesn't ask you this question, make sure that you answer it.
- ✔ Prepare *at least* three key reasons to roll off your tongue that show how you're better than the other candidates.
- ✔ Use specific examples to illustrate your reasons.
- ✔ Tell something unusual or unique about you that will make the interviewer remember you.

*For a ShowFlopper answer*

- ✔ Leave without addressing this question.
- ✔ Be humble.

**Describe the process you go through to make a decision.**
**Tell me how you deal with unexpected problems.**
**How do you set goals?**
**How do you go about achieving your goals?**

*For a ShowStopper answer*

- ✔ Illustrate how you go about seeking, prioritizing, and organizing information to make a decision.

- ✔ Discuss how you stay focused when pursuing a goal or making a decision.

- ✔ Give specific examples of how you've confronted and solved a challenge.

- ✔ Give examples showing your flexibility in the face of unexpected problems or situations.

- ✔ Research to find out if the company values gut decisions or head decisions; give examples compatible with the company's values.

*For a ShowFlopper answer*

- ✔ Imply that you have no system for making decisions.
- ✔ Imply that you prefer to follow others' leads.

**Is there anything else I should know about you?**

*For a ShowStopper answer*

- ✔ Discuss any selling points the interview failed to uncover and relate those selling points to the job you want.

- ✔ Repeat the selling points you've already discussed and remind the interviewer why you're the best candidate for the job.

*For a ShowFlopper answer*

- ✔ Say "No."

# In Getting to Know You, Storytelling Counts

As you may have noticed, you benefit from using specific examples — storytelling — to illustrate your answers to any questions. As I say in Chapter 2, use true stories to "prove" your answer and interest the employer with concrete facts. Storytelling is an indispensable prop in a critically acclaimed performance. And remember: Put *everything* in a positive light.

# Chapter 15

# Questions about the Job and the Company

• • • • • • • • • • • • • • • • • • • • • • • • • • • • • • • • • • • • • • •

### In This Chapter

▶ Proving that you understand the job

▶ Showing savvy about the company

▶ Confirming that you know the industry

▶ Answering sample questions for practice

• • • • • • • • • • • • • • • • • • • • • • • • • • • • • • • • • • • • • • •

*I*f you're aiming for a professional or managerial job, expect a number of questions testing your knowledge of the position, company, and industry to be fired across the footlights.

## Know the Job and the Industry

Employers figure that if you're who you say you are — a leading man or a leading woman — you grasp what the job entails and how that job fits into the big company picture. You'll have looked into the company — what it does and where it stands in the industry. You'll have a shrewd knowledge of whether the industry is going up, down, or sideways.

The interviewer may come out with questions like this:

> *Where would you rank this company in the marketplace and why?*

This kind of question requires you to go into some detail about the company's place in the scheme of things — its products, profitability, industry position, goals, and so forth.

An interviewer may not look at your answers for definitive details, but he or she will be interested in how you arrived at your conclusions. You could say:

> *You ranked second in the industry in total earnings last year, so that's a positive. Your level of debt is a little high, but that was the result of tooling up for your next line of products due out in June. If the new line is as successful as forecast, then most of the rest of the company debt will be wiped out by new sales, leaving the company with a shot at being the most financially secure in the industry. Plus, you still enjoy an enormous potential for growth in the near future.*

If you mention problems in the company's performance, offer general solutions. Otherwise you appear clueless, or as some interviewers may say: *Nice cage, no bird.* Or, *all foam, no beer.* Or, *clogged chimney, no fire.* Well, you get the idea.

Give specifics. If you have ideas about improving the company's performance, prove that you're doing more than just guessing. Cite statistics and figures to back up the problems you note and your bright ideas to fix them.

Avoid barging in to solve problems that have eluded company managers. Chances are that there are hidden facts you don't have. Don't overreach in such a way the interviewer is tempted to think: *I'd like to buy this guy for what he's worth and sell him for what he thinks he's worth.*

# *The Questions*

Look at the following questions and the strategies you can use to answer them as you gear up to show harmony between yourself, the job, and the company.

**What do you know about this position?**

*For a ShowStopper answer*

✔ From your research, discuss how the position fits into the company structure and how you would fit into that position.

✔ Mention how you can help the company along toward its goals.

✔ Confirm your understanding of the broad responsibilities of the position. Ask if you missed any key points (thereby setting up your qualifications matching for the remainder of the interview).

*For a ShowFlopper answer*

■ ✔ Ask what the company makes.

### What do you know about our competition?

*For a ShowStopper answer*

> ✔ From your research, discuss the current climate of the industry and how competitors are affected.
>
> ✔ Add details showing that you truly understand the industry and the competition.

*For a ShowFlopper answer*

> ✔ Say you know very little about the competition.
>
> ✔ Admit you recently interviewed with the competition.
>
> ✔ Reveal trade secrets from current employer.

### What are your opinions about some of the challenges facing our company?

*For a ShowStopper answer*

> ✔ Show the depth of your research by discussing some of the company's upcoming projects.
>
> ✔ Mention possible solutions to potential problems the company may be facing.

*For a ShowFlopper answer*

> ✔ Say you don't know of any challenges, but you're all ears.
>
> ✔ Mention problems but add no possible solutions.

### What do you see as the direction of this company?

*For a ShowStopper answer*

> ✔ Give a detailed answer, displaying a solid grasp of the company's movement in the industry and adding how you can help.
>
> ✔ Support your answer with facts and figures.

*For a ShowFlopper answer*

> ✔ Make guesses because you haven't a clue.
>
> ✔ Offer no data to back up your comments.

**How would you predict the market performance of our new product?**

*For a ShowStopper answer*

- ✔ Explain how you work — organize, gather, and interpret data and then make decisions.
- ✔ Discuss your development of multiple models, which includes anticipating contingencies.

*For a ShowFlopper answer*

- ✔ Discuss only one strategy. Seem like one who flies by the seat of his pants.

**Why did you apply with this company?**

*For a ShowStopper answer*

- ✔ The position is a dynamite opportunity and the company a place where your qualifications can make a difference. Explain why.

*For a ShowFlopper answer*

- ✔ The company is in an industry you've always wanted to try.

**Our company has a mission statement; do you have a personal mission statement — or personal vision?**

*For a ShowStopper answer*

- ✔ In one or two sentences, give examples of your values (customer service, ethics, and so on) that are compatible with the company's.

*For a ShowFlopper answer*

- ✔ Ask what a mission statement is.

**How will you help our company?**

*For a ShowStopper answer*

- ✔ Summarize how your key skills can help the company toward its goals.
- ✔ Describe what intangibles you can bring to the company.

*For a ShowFlopper answer*

- ✔ Give a short answer with no specifics.

# Chapter 16

# Questions about Skills

. . . . . . . . . . . . . . . . . . . . . . . . . . . . . . . . . . . . . . . . . . .

*In This Chapter*

▶ Spotting skills questions

▶ Responding to skills questions

▶ Sample questions for practice

. . . . . . . . . . . . . . . . . . . . . . . . . . . . . . . . . . . . . . . . . . .

**W**ith job security in today's market going the way of the ozone layer, the operative word is *skills*.

What skills do you have to do a bang-up job?

Here's where you gear up for interview questions that reveal your own mono-grammed package of skills. Talk skills every chance you get — skills you gained from previous jobs, skills from school, skills from hobbies, and skills your ancestors gave you.

## Recognizing Questions about Your Skills

Accomplishments, like some wines, don't travel well. You catch an employer's eye with accomplishments, but when you change jobs, you leave your accomplishments behind.

What you do pack along with you are the skills that allowed you to achieve those accomplishments: ability to learn, meet deadlines, and surf the Internet; vision, persuasive skills, and other skills that make you a winner.

Savvy interviewers move past the citations of what you did to discover how you did it — the essence of your skills.

Interviewers may be straightforward in trying to determine your skills through questions about specific work experiences — *Tell me about a time that a supervisor gave you a new project when you were racing the clock to complete an earlier-assigned project.*

Or you may be tossed a pretend workplace scenario and asked how you'd handle the situation — *You're monitoring and integrating control feedback in a petrochemical processing facility to maintain production flow when the system suddenly goes down; what do you do?*

Other questions are less direct, going in a conversational side door to see how you react — *How would you deal with a difficult boss?*

To pull off a ShowStopper interview, learn to recognize questions that spotlight the skills you bring to a job stage.

# Answering Questions about Your Skills

Use storytelling (see Chapter 2) to comprehensively answer skills questions. Remember, too, that social, or soft, skills (people skills) play a significant role in determining the winning candidate. Take pains to convince the interviewer that you're a pleasant individual who gets along with people.

Take that earlier question on this page about how you'd deal with the difficult boss. Here's an answer, underscored with storytelling, that makes you look like a reasonable and conscientious person:

> *I would first try to make sure that the difficulty isn't walking around in my shoes. Then I'd read a few books on how to interact with difficult people. I've never had a boss I didn't like, but I have had to use tact on occasion.*
>
> *On my last job, my boss and I didn't see eye to eye on the best software for an office application. I researched the issue in detail and wrote a short, fact-filled report for my boss. Based on this new information, my boss then bought the software I recommended.*

This answer centers around research skills, but also highlights patience and acceptance of supervision.

## Soft skills needed in technical jobs

"Dealing with other people" and "adapting to new environments" are two soft skills that technical people working on contract assignments should cultivate, says Jack Brumbelow, a technical recruiter in Dallas, Texas.

The recruiter notes that once the candidate's technical qualifications are established, technical contract people should remember to sell the interviewers on their personality, attitude, and ability to seamlessly join an existing team where organization, cooperation, and communication ease are essential.

# *The Questions*

These sample skills questions are generalized for wider application, although in an interview you should expect skills questions that relate to your career field.

Note that questions in this chapter may seem to be close relatives of the questions in Chapter 14. The difference is that those in Chapter 14 are intended to draw out your qualities as a human being; those in this chapter go after your skills. Is it a big goof if you mix them up? Not at all. Both are reminders to keep your sales pitch up and running.

**What is the toughest job problem you've ever faced?**

*For a ShowStopper answer*

- ✔ Recall an accomplishment, the skills you used to deal with it, and the successful results.
- ✔ Apply those skills to the prospective job.

*For a ShowFlopper answer*

- ✔ Recall a problem, but not an accomplishment or skill related to it.

**What do you like least about researching?**

*For a ShowStopper answer*

- ✔ Comment that wanting to do a first-rate job, you're never quite sure when you've compiled enough research to quit.

*For a ShowFlopper answer*

- ✔ You don't like research, or if the topic doesn't interest you, the project's a bore.

**How good are you at making oral presentations?**

*For a ShowStopper answer*

- ✔ Discuss how you prepare. Name presentation skills. Mention specific instances where you've given a good show.

*For a ShowFlopper answer*

- ✔ Say that you never do them because you're terrified of speaking in front of large crowds.

**How would you rate your writing skills in comparison to your verbal skills?**

*For a ShowStopper answer*

> ✔ Discuss how both skills are important in the business world, and that while (one or the other) may be your strong suit, you're working to become strongly proficient at both speaking and writing.

*For a ShowFlopper answer*

> ✔ Rate your skill in one area as better than the other and hush up.

**How do you deal with unexpected events on the job?**

*For a ShowStopper answer*

> ✔ Discuss how you must immediately reprioritize your assignments.
> ✔ Mention specific instances where you were able to complete a project (or projects) on time despite unforeseen complications.

*For a ShowFlopper answer*

> ✔ Tell how you just keep doing what you were doing until you're finished.
> ✔ Discuss an instance when an unexpected event resulted in disaster.

**How do you organize your time?**

*For a ShowStopper answer*

> ✔ Write things down. Make lists. Mention specific instances where you completed multiple tasks on time.
> ✔ Discuss the typical day on one of your previous jobs and how you would go through the day.

*For a ShowFlopper answer*

> ✔ Say that you don't usually handle more than one task at a time, or that you manage time but just take crises as they come.

**How do you delegate responsibility?**

*For a ShowStopper answer*

> ✔ Discuss how you involve everyone in the overall picture.
> ✔ Discuss specific projects that were successful because of your team effort.

*For a ShowFlopper answer*

- ✔ Reveal your micromanagement tendencies in every project.
- ✔ Mention that your coworkers on the project let you down.

**What's been your experience with group projects?**

*For a ShowStopper answer*

- ✔ Mention a specific project, including the group goals and your specific responsibilities.
- ✔ Discuss your positive relationship with the project supervisor. Compliment coworkers.

*For a ShowFlopper answer*

- ✔ Don't identify your responsibilities. Rip your coworkers.

**Why should I hire you?**

*For a ShowStopper answer*

- ✔ Review your research into the company, industry, and position.
- ✔ Summarize why your skills match the job's requirements, plus any competitive edge you enjoy.
- ✔ Include accomplishments and the skills that facilitated those accomplishments, plus relevant experience and training.
- ✔ Be sure of yourself and enthusiastic.

*For a ShowFlopper answer*

- ✔ Indicate that you've done no advance research and fail to make the "perfect match" connection.
- ✔ Project yourself as a commodity candidate with a wooden personality who lacks self-confidence and who has no good answer.

# Chapter 17

# Questions about Experience

. . . . . . . . . . . . . . . . . . . . . . . . . . . . . . . . . . . . . . . . . .

## In This Chapter

▶ Recognizing questions that target experience

▶ Focusing your answers on the employer's needs

▶ Sample questions for practice

. . . . . . . . . . . . . . . . . . . . . . . . . . . . . . . . . . . . . . . . . .

*I*n the landmark adventure film *Raiders of the Lost Ark*, **Karen Allen** (playing Marion Ravenwood) hasn't seen **Harrison Ford** (playing Indiana Jones) for awhile when she comments that he's not the same man she knew ten years ago. Ford's Indiana Jones has a great comeback:

> *It's not the years, honey, it's the mileage.*

And so it goes with experience. You can have ten years of skill-building experience — or you can have one year's experience with nine years of reruns. Solid experience is yet one more confirmation of your ability to do a job.

## *Make Your Experience Relevant*

Simply reciting your experience and successes isn't going to wow an employer. You have to make the connection — to show exactly how you achieved your accomplishments and how your experience and those accomplishments work together to make you the perfect candidate for the job opening.

What if you don't have any experience?

✔ The usual response when you lack experience is to try to convince employers that you have the determination, the willingness to work hard, and the quick-learning skills to make up for any lack of experience.

✔ A better way to handle the experience issue is to show that you *do* have the experience needed to do the job. The experience may come from part-time jobs, internships, cooperative education, involvement in campus groups or other nonprofit organizations, or school projects. Learn to speak about transferable or portable skills. (See my book *Cover Letters For Dummies,* 2nd Edition, for more on the skills issue.)

### When you're technically great, but quiet and shy

Some people, including those who have technical talents, are sometimes very shy at interviews, appearing introverted and timid. Is that you?

Here's a trick around that problem from Martin Yate, author of *Knock 'em Dead* and other bestselling job search books. Yate says that if you reach across the desk to hand the interviewer papers, graphs, and reports from your portfolio of work samples, the interviewer will ask you questions about the samples. Your answers will keep the flow of conversation going — and you'll answer the questions and won't come across as, well, bashful.

Whether you've got a lot or a little experience, employers want to hire people who will continue to learn and grow in the atmosphere of their company. So as you answer the experience questions, focus not only on your experience, but also on how your experience changed in adapting to the changing needs of the companies for which you've worked.

If you can show how you've adapted in the past, you'll be more likely to convince employers that you have what it takes to adapt your experience to their workplaces.

Always give specific illustrations of your experience and accomplishments. Employers are convinced by results, not by a laundry list of responsibilities.

What if you don't understand a question? Don't be shy. Ask for clarification — *I'm not sure I understand your question, and I don't want to give you an irrelevant or incorrect answer.*

## *The Questions*

Following are some questions you may be asked about your work experience, along with suggested answering techniques and definite mistakes.

**What kind of experience do you have for this job?**

*For a ShowStopper answer*

✔ Gather information before answering. Ask what projects you would be working on in the first six months. Apply your experience to those projects, detailing exactly how you would go about working on them.

✔ Give specific examples of your success in dealing with similar projects in the past, focusing on results.

✔ Show how transferable skills drawn from even seemingly nonrelated experience (waiting tables or planning club functions) apply to this project. You learned the value of being reliable, of coordinating efforts, of organization, and so forth.

*For a ShowFlopper answer*

✔ Say you have no experience and clam up.

✔ Show that your experience overreaches this particular job, unless you know that's a plus.

**Q** **How do you see the broad responsibilities of the (job title you held)? In what ways has your job changed since you got into this field?**

*For a ShowStopper answer*

✔ Mention that since job titles vary according to the company, you'll describe your concept of the job based on experience with that particular title.

✔ Match the individual responsibilities of the job title to the employer's need for efficiency and profit.

✔ With brief, broad brush strokes, sketch changes in your line of work over the years. The point is to show that you recognize epic change.

✔ Ask if you failed to cover any key responsibilities, in case the job description between your present employer and your prospective employer is different. If there's a gap, show how you've handled missing responsibilities, perhaps in other positions.

*For a ShowFlopper answer*

✔ Leave out important functions. You'll look like you need too much retraining.

**Q** **How long would it take you to make a contribution to our company?**

*For a ShowStopper answer*

✔ Ask the interviewer to explain which areas need the greatest contribution, perhaps focusing on a specific project.

✔ Show step by step how long it would take you to get settled and get working — the quicker, the better.

✔ Detail how you would go about working on the particular project, showing how much time each step would take. Be realistic, yet optimistic, in your time estimation.

*For a ShowFlopper answer*

- ✔ Say you'll make a contribution the very first day, unless you can support it with facts.

- ✔ Estimate that you won't become productive for at least four months (unless you're headed for an incredibly complex job in which a settling-in period lasting beyond three months is normal).

**What are your qualifications?**

*For a ShowStopper answer*

- ✔ Clarify the question; ask if you should focus on academic and training or job-related qualifications.

- ✔ Ask what specific projects or problems you may be expected to deal with.

- ✔ Discuss your related skills, whether academic or professional, and identify the projects you've accomplished in the past that qualify you to work successfully on the project mentioned.

*For a ShowFlopper answer*

- ✔ Assume you know what the interviewer wants to hear about and plunge right in.

**Describe a difficult problem with which you've had to deal. Have you ever had to discipline a problem employee? Describe how you resolved a tense situation with a coworker. Have you ever had to fire someone?**

*For a ShowStopper answer*

- ✔ Discuss your analytical process for solving any problem.

- ✔ Show how you go about collecting information before making a decision.

- ✔ Give a specific example of a difficulty that you've dealt with (conflict resolution, discipline, termination), focusing on how you used your analytical skills to effectively solve the problem.

- ✔ Show that you follow company policy and that you're tactful in dealing with employee problems.

*For a ShowFlopper answer*

- ✔ Discuss an example where you made a hasty or impulsive decision.

- ✔ Focus on how horrible the problem or employee was.

**Give a specific example of a time that you had to put your needs aside to help a coworker.**

*For a ShowStopper answer*

- ✔ Mention teamwork and the importance of coworkers being able to rely on each other.

- ✔ Give a specific example, showing that the reliance was not one-sided.

- ✔ Show either how your efforts contributed to getting the work done or how the help you gave did not cause problems with your own work. (If you can honestly show both, then go for it.)

*For a ShowFlopper answer*

- ✔ Say it happens all the time and leave it at that.

**How do you go about preparing for speeches or presentations?**

*For a ShowStopper answer*

- ✔ Discuss your system of preparation, step by step.

- ✔ Give a specific example.

- ✔ Discuss the positive results of your speech or presentation.

If you've never given a speech or presentation, think of a time you wanted to persuade your coworkers or boss to do something. Discuss how you prepared and presented by using good communication skills.

*For a ShowFlopper answer*

- ✔ Say you've never given a speech or presentation.

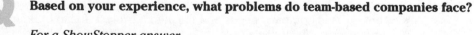

**Based on your experience, what problems do team-based companies face?**

*For a ShowStopper answer*

- ✔ Show, with storytelling, that your experience includes being a leader or member of teams.

- ✔ Discuss teams as an overall positive addition to the work world of the 1990s.

- ✔ Discuss a minor negative aspect of teams and show how that negative aspect can be overcome. (Magazine articles and books about teamwork are helpful to develop teamwork language skills.)

*For a ShowFlopper answer*

✔ Say that you've always preferred to work alone or to let the people who report to you handle the grunts down the line.

**Your experience doesn't exactly match our needs right now, does it?**

*For a ShowStopper answer*

✔ Yes, it does (if true). Your skills are cross-functional. Speak the language of transferable skills and focus on how you can transfer your experience in other areas to learning this new job more easily.

✔ Stress that you are dedicated to learning the new job quickly. Gee, are you quick to catch on!

✔ Say you don't have any bad habits to unlearn and discuss your good work habits that will help you get the job done efficiently and well.

*For a ShowFlopper answer*

✔ Agree, smile, and say nothing to compensate for the mismatch — unless, of course, you don't want the job.

**Describe a time that you had to work without direct supervision. Have you ever had to make department decisions when your supervisor was not available?**

*For a ShowStopper answer*

✔ Discuss your decision-making process. You don't rattle easily.

✔ Show that you are self-directed and self-motivated, but still willing to follow others' directions or to ask for assistance when needed.

✔ Storytell: Discuss a specific example of a time you had to make a decision without supervision. Preferably, discuss a time that you anticipated company needs and finished a project ahead of time or made a beneficial decision.

*For a ShowFlopper answer*

✔ Whine about being forced into a decision that turned sour.

**Have you ever misjudged something? How could you have prevented the mistake?**

*For a ShowStopper answer*

✔ Briefly discuss a specific — but minor — example.

✔ Briefly discuss what the mistake taught you and how it led you to improve your system for making decisions or solving problems.

✔ Then, refocus the discussion to your accomplishments.

*For a ShowFlopper answer*

✔ Discuss a mistake that cost your employer plenty of time and money.

✔ Pass the blame to someone else.

✔ Say you've never misjudged anything.

 **Has a supervisor ever challenged one of your decisions? How did you respond?**

*For a ShowStopper answer*

✔ Discuss an example where you supported your decision with research or analytical data.

✔ Show that even though you supported your decision, you were open to suggestions or comments.

✔ Show that your decisions are flexible.

*For a ShowFlopper answer*

✔ Blame your supervisor.

✔ Stubbornly declare that you were right.

# Chapter 18

# Questions about Your Education and Training

● ● ● ● ● ● ● ● ● ● ● ● ● ● ● ● ● ● ● ● ● ● ● ● ● ● ● ● ● ● ● ● ● ● ● ● ● ● ● ● ● ● ●

### In This Chapter

▶ Focusing aces on adaptability and updated education

▶ Focusing rookies on educational experience

▶ Applying educational skills to your job interview

● ● ● ● ● ● ● ● ● ● ● ● ● ● ● ● ● ● ● ● ● ● ● ● ● ● ● ● ● ● ● ● ● ● ● ● ● ● ● ● ● ● ●

*W*e live in a new economy built on knowledge and skills — making *education* and *training* words that you'd better be able to back up in a job interview.

At some point, an employer is going to ask you straightforward questions about your learning background, questions that probe behind the scenes.

More is gleaned from your answers than just the facts. What you say reveals your decision-making processes, your values, your ability to keep up with the times, and your willingness to adapt to a rapidly changing technological world. An increasingly skill-oriented, global economy has profound significance for all.

## Aces: High on Adaptability

If you graduated before computers took over the world, interviewers will probably focus on your work experience — but you should still expect them to ask about your education or training. They want to know if you're rusted out — or ready to keep up with your industry by making the effort to learn new skills.

Education and training come in many forms. In addition to colleges and universities, vocational-technical institutions, and other career-related schools, discuss

- ✔ Company training programs you've participated in, telling prospective employers what you learned in those training programs
- ✔ Trade or professional journals that you read regularly
- ✔ Professional conferences or seminars that you've attended recently (or plan to attend soon)
- ✔ Computer training you've had, are taking, or expect to take; use computer jargon during your interviews

However you address employers' questions about education and training, your posture should be that, although you're focused, you're flexible about the way you get the work done. You do not expect to do a job the same way tomorrow that you did yesterday. You have continued to learn new trends and developments in your field throughout your career — and you certainly are always willing to learn more.

# If You Are Degree-less

Never claim to have education or training that you don't actually have; studies continue to show that people who claim degrees they don't have frequently get caught.

This fact doesn't mean that you should raise the issue that you have less education than required. If you must address your lack of education, discuss your experience and skills as education. Speak of *experience-based skills,* for instance, and redirect the conversation to your self-teaching efforts. Assure that your degree-less state does not affect your ability to do the job well. Use specific examples from your experience to prove this point.

Using experience as education will not change anyone's mind when the education requirement is rigid — such as in health fields. But it may keep your candidacy afloat when an educational requirement is simply a convenient screening device.

You can, of course, begin to correct any educational deficiencies that are blocking your way to the job you want. If you enroll in a degree program, be sure to mention this fact when explaining that you don't have a sheepskin now but you are pursuing a degree.

*My experience in the point-of-sale industry more than compensates for my present lack of a marketing degree. (Cite several examples showing you know what you're talking about.) However, I can see that a degree is important to you, and I want to mention that I'm enrolled in a degree program now, with expected graduation in 20XX. So you have the best of both worlds with me — heavy-duty experience, plus current academic knowledge.*

What can you do when these ideas don't pull you through and the lack of a degree continues to shut you out? Choose from among three basic solutions:

- ✔ **Persevere.** Continue job hunting at companies too small to operate a human resource department. HR staffers are paid to exclude applicants who miss their criteria, including education. A smaller company also is more likely to handle hiring without using computer automation, which incorporates a college degree as a keyword for search and retrieval. Without that education keyword, your resume won't surface for consideration.

- ✔ **Work short-term.** Seek staffing firms that will send you on temporary or contract assignments so that employers can see how good you are and offer you a regular status job.

- ✔ **Get a degree.** Keep the day job you find but eliminate the credential barrier. Use distance education to earn a college degree.

# Hot-Wiring the Ivory Tower

Taking college courses or even getting an entire degree is something you can do from home — and still keep your day job.

Private and public colleges around the world are moving into cyberspace to serve working adults and to accommodate millions of upcoming Generation Y students expected to swamp campuses over the next ten years.

How many students are hitting the cyberbooks? Researchers estimate that some 1 million students are taking online courses, and that number is expected to more than double within a couple of years. Distance education, primarily over the Internet, has moved from novelty to mainstream status, co-existing with bricks-and-mortar schooling.

Much of the online scholarship doesn't come cheap, so it will pay you to shop around. (Web search engines and distance education books will help you go online to sharpen your skills.)

The issue of concern to you in your role of job seeker is the marketability of your online degree. Will someone perceive online learning as inferior to on-site learning? In particular, that answer depends on the institution or program you choose. In general, online courses may be of inconsistent quality at first as colleges edge into a new world of learning. But the online trend is unstoppable: Quality will level out, and employers will become accustomed to candidates who are credentialed by online study.

# *Aces: Updated Education Is Marketable*

Once we thought that you went to college or career training, got out, and went on with your life. Now we know that lifelong employability and enjoyability come with the price tag of constant vigilance in keeping your skills up to date.

# *The Questions*

**What do you do to keep up to date in your job? How do you improve yourself professionally?**

*For a ShowStopper answer*

- ✔ Describe your participation in professional associations, seminars, meetings and activities, and Internet professional discussion groups.

- ✔ Say you study professional magazines, look for technical breakthroughs, and seek certifications that document your continued skill-building (describe certifications).

- ✔ Discuss classes and programs in which you are enrolled.

*For a ShowFlopper answer*

- ✔ Be nonspecific in saying you keep your radar up.

- ✔ Look uncomfortable and mumble that you plan to start back to school soon.

**Of what value do you consider academic degrees?**

*For a ShowStopper answer*

- ✔ Comment that when matched with solid experience, the degrees are excellent.

- ✔ Remark that degrees are essential, but you must continue to learn throughout your life.

- ✔ (When you have no degree) Assert that human traits and skills are as important as education and that your record shows you have the background to succeed in this position.

- ✔ Reply that you will let your work achievements and interpersonal skills speak for you.

*For a ShowFlopper answer*

■ ✔ Knock the value of formal education. Say it's overrated.

**Q** **I see you have been attending a training program online. Do you believe it is as beneficial as sitting in a classroom?**

*For a ShowStopper answer*

✔ Be positive, responding that *what* you know is the important issue — not where you learned it.

✔ Identify the institution's accreditation. Say that your study was designed by the best minds in the field. Mention any honors accorded your online program.

✔ Be confident, noting that some educators think online students are more committed than campus students — that their motivation is stronger. Say from personal perseverance, you agree.

✔ Say the experience immensely improved your computer skills.

*For a ShowFlopper answer*

✔ Apologize, lamenting that distance education was the only way you could manage to work and learn.

# Rookies: High on Education, Low on Experience

Education is magnificent, but education isn't everything.

You have to look focused. You have to look *passionate* about what you want to do. You have to show how your education has prepared you for the job you target.

Whenever possible, present your education as work experience.

If that seems like a reach, think of it this way:

✔ You have experience working with deadlines and with applying skills that you've learned throughout the years to various projects.

✔ You've probably given at least one presentation, so you've had experience preparing it, and you have experience communicating to a group of people.

✔ To get through school without killing yourself, you probably had to develop some type of time schedule, so you have valuable experience in organizing your time for greatest efficiency.

Don't neglect any of these important experiences.

# The Questions

Following are some of the questions you may be asked related to education and training.

**Why did you attend (name of school)? What factors influenced your choice of school?**

*For a ShowStopper answer*

✔ Describe the process that you went through to determine which school you wanted to attend, such as matching the schools to your career plans, visiting the schools, and talking to faculty.

✔ Discuss at least four specific reasons why you chose your school, focusing on career-related programs and academic considerations such as distinguished faculty, research opportunities, student government programs, leadership opportunities in campus organizations, or school reputation.

*For a ShowFlopper answer*

✔ Say you chose your school because of its great social life or because your best friend went there.

✔ Say you made a mistake in choosing your school.

## The new grad who spoke up and won out

A career counselor told me this story about her own son (the name is changed):

Denton's GPA dropped to less than 3.0 (the magic number for many corporate recruiters) because he was working his way through school. Wanting to find an engineering job in a specific company, Denton noticed that its recruiter would be on campus to interview those with a 3.0 and above GPA. Denton signed up anyway, slotting himself into the last interview so that the recruiter wouldn't try to hurry him out for the next waiting student.

Denton was just waiting for the recruiter to comment on his low GPA. After responding that he worked 40 hours a week, Denton described the rich range of experiences he'd acquired. The recruiter was impressed, saying that he, too, had worked his way through college and understood how tough it was. Denton was hired and remains with that company 15 years later.

**How or why did you choose your major? What factors led to your decision to choose your major?**

*For a ShowStopper answer*

- ✔ Show that you took a systematic approach in choosing your major, focusing on future career goals.

- ✔ Liberal arts: You sought to learn how to reason, research, and communicate as well as "do." Plus you put meat on academic bones with practical, career-oriented courses, seminars, internships, co-op education programs, and extracurricular activities.

- ✔ Discuss the courses you've taken that are most job-related and show how they can help you meet the challenges of the job.

- ✔ Show that your choice was logical considering your interests and skills.

*For a ShowFlopper answer*

- ✔ Ramble or give vague answers.

- ✔ Complain about your education.

**How has your education prepared you for working as a (targeted job)? How has your education benefited you? What specific work-related courses have you taken? How has your education helped with your current job?**

*For a ShowStopper answer*

- ✔ Storytell: Give specific examples of how the skills and abilities you learned in school can be transferred to the job.

- ✔ Emphasize that your education has not only provided you with job skills, but has also prepared you to learn new skills throughout your career.

- ✔ Discuss the computer skills you learned at school.

- ✔ Discuss your leadership activities and how that leadership experience transfers to the job.

- ✔ Discuss experience you have with teamwork and how that will help you on the job.

- ✔ Discuss how your education has expanded your mind, opening you up to new ideas or perspectives.

- ✔ Discuss specific examples of career-related problems you solved or results you have achieved.

- ✔ Show your enthusiasm for your education and future career.

*For a ShowFlopper answer*

✔ Give vague answers.

✔ Recite a list of the courses you took (unless asked to do so).

**What was your GPA? (grade point average) Are your grades a good reflection of your performance in school? Why didn't you get a better GPA? Do you think that your GPA indicates how successful you will be in this position?**

*For a ShowStopper answer*

✔ Give positive reasons for a poor or marginal GPA. You had to work to pay for your school and living expenses. For jobs working with people, you devoted much time to "real life" experiences, such as leadership positions in campus organizations.

✔ Emphasize that your grades within your major are excellent or that they improved dramatically the last two years. Cite reasons why your grades improved.

✔ If you have an impressive GPA, emphasize that your education extends beyond the classroom. Discuss extracurricular activities and what you learned from them that you can apply to the job.

✔ Emphasize that success in academics and in the job requires more than a high GPA. Discuss the skills you learned outside of your course work that can contribute to your success.

✔ Discuss how your GPA gradually rose as you learned better study habits and say you wish you had learned them sooner.

✔ Answer the question and quickly redirect the discussion to your skills and how you can apply those skills to the job.

✔ Give specific examples of your success in job-related pursuits, outside of your GPA.

✔ Explain the factors that are common between a high GPA and success on the job, such as organizing, prioritizing, and commitment to goals.

*For a ShowFlopper answer*

✔ Blame other people for your low GPA.

✔ Say you don't know why you got a low GPA.

✔ Confess any weaknesses, unless you can show how you have overcome them.

✔ Offer alibis for poor grades.

✔ Assert that grades aren't important or be defensively arrogant.

**What extracurricular activities did you participate in? What leadership positions did you hold? Why didn't you participate in more extracurricular activities?**

*For a ShowStopper answer*

- ✔ Emphasize goal-oriented activities or groups over "fun" ones. About sororities and fraternities — carefully mention only leadership and doing good works, not the social aspect; otherwise, nonmembers may think "party animal" and write you off.

- ✔ Discuss all leadership roles, teamwork, and self-motivation; explain how those experiences will help you in the job.

- ✔ Discuss skills you learned from the activities or groups and how those skills apply to the job.

- ✔ You had to work so many hours that being active in campus groups would have left you with too little time for your course work.

- ✔ If you didn't join campus organizations until later in your education, say you wish you had joined them sooner, emphasizing what those organizations taught you.

- ✔ Mention all elected offices you held.

*For a ShowFlopper answer*

- ✔ Present yourself as a professional activist (who may stir up trouble on the job).

- ✔ Dwell on membership in political or religious groups; it's okay to mention what the membership taught you of value in relationship to a job, but don't go any farther than that.

**If you could do it over again, would you change your university/major? What didn't you like about school?**

*For a ShowStopper answer*

- ✔ Say you made the right choice and discuss why.

- ✔ Discuss education as more than just courses and college life; it's a broad base for learning and a training ground for meeting challenges.

- ✔ You liked everything about your school — except maybe the high cost of tuition. You have a little loan money to pay back and look forward to working hard at a job to do so.

*For a ShowFlopper answer*

> ✔ Be negative about the school or faculty.
>
> ✔ Admit that you made a poor decision.

**In what areas could your education have better prepared you for your career?**

*For a ShowStopper answer*

> ✔ Your academic studies did not include hands-on experience, but all-around, your education prepared you superbly.
>
> ✔ Show how you made up for lack of experience with student jobs, co-op education, internships, or unpaid work with campus organizations or nonprofit organizations.

*For a ShowFlopper answer*

> ✔ Insist that you're totally prepared for your career — you could be vice president of Microsoft tomorrow.

**Academically, what were your best and worst courses? What courses did you like best and least?**

*For a ShowStopper answer*

> ✔ For best courses, choose ones that you got the best grades in that were most related to the job.
>
> ✔ For worst courses, choose ones least related to the job and avoid mentioning courses you did poorly in.
>
> ✔ Discuss course content or presentation as reasons for liking or not liking a course.

*For a ShowFlopper answer*

> ✔ Discuss courses you did poorly in.
>
> ✔ Cite poor academic performance as a reason for not liking a course.

# Chapter 19

# Questions about Your Age

● ● ● ● ● ● ● ● ● ● ● ● ● ● ● ● ● ● ● ● ● ● ● ● ● ● ● ● ● ● ● ● ● ● ● ● ● ● ● ● ● ● ●

### In This Chapter

▶ Fighting fictions; bearing benefits

▶ Looking good at any age

▶ Avoiding age stereotyping

▶ Ducking hidden age queries

● ● ● ● ● ● ● ● ● ● ● ● ● ● ● ● ● ● ● ● ● ● ● ● ● ● ● ● ● ● ● ● ● ● ● ● ● ● ● ● ● ● ●

*Y*oung, old, green, or gray — age haunts our culture. The fashion model is described as "aging" at 38, while the 42-year-old senator is called "boyish."

People in the middle of the working age spectrum — say 25 to 50 — have few tight interview moments that are age related. But for everyone else, a familiar observation characterizes problems of perceptions:

> *If youth only knew, if age only could.*

Although employers should not pose questions about your age, some employers believe that age is a legitimate concern and will do anything they can to ferret out the number of your birthdays. Sure, this policy is unfair. But if you're a recent graduate or a near retiree, you have to deal with it.

## Boos and Hisses

Your interviewing behavior need not be as age-sensitive when you're young and the interviewer is also young; the interviewer already believes that youth rules. To a lesser extent, the same is true of an older you and an older interviewer.

But, as mentioned in Chapter 1, when generational dynamics are involved, the age issue is usually under the surface of a job interview, often clustered around these basic myths.

### Myths about younger workers

- They're too inexperienced to get the job done right.
- They're not willing to start at the bottom.
- They're not committed to their jobs.
- They don't have any real skills, just book smarts.

### Myths about older workers

- They're less productive than younger workers.
- They're absent more often than the norm.
- They're uncompromising and inflexible.
- They're stuck with old skills and can't learn new ones.
- They have less motivation than younger employees.
- They can't learn new technology, new ways of doing business.

# Emphasizing the Positive

If you're a raw new graduate or a late prime-of-lifer, make the right moves to push these negatives way into the background.

Begin with your first appearance before the camera in the interviewer's mind. State your answer to their age question with an image that is professional, alert, and confident. (Review the costuming tips in Chapter 5.)

When you think an interviewer's judgment could be hindered by age concerns, emphasize the positive aspects of your age in your behavior and conversation.

Review the following lists of age-benefits to spark your own positive age spinning.

### Benefits of younger workers

- No bad work habits to break
- Easily trained — quick productivity
- College experience has taught them how to learn
- Will work for less money than experienced candidates
- Fresh ideas — updated education

- ✔ Adaptability — can be molded
- ✔ Usually comfortable with current technology and computers
- ✔ Enthusiasm — no been-there-done-that syndrome
- ✔ Will work less convenient hours
- ✔ Will tackle less desirable tasks

How do you know when an interviewer thinks you may be too young for the job? Listen for questions that seem concerned about your "real world" experience, your maturity, your stability, or your career expectations.

Answer those concerns with positive examples of your potential contribution to the employer. Use storytelling (see Chapter 2) to illustrate past accomplishments that highlight your potential worth as an employee.

Above all, don't think of your youth as a drawback; instead, highlight your fresh approach, your abundant energy, and your understanding of a younger market — anything that uses your youth to the employer's advantage.

**Benefits of older workers**

- ✔ Commitment to a career — not clock watchers
- ✔ Hands-on experience and specific skills
- ✔ Proven success — verifiable track records
- ✔ Dependable — maturity develops reliability
- ✔ Stable — understand what work ethic means
- ✔ Not likely to voluntarily change jobs soon
- ✔ Need little or no training
- ✔ Lower turnover and absenteeism rates, according to surveys
- ✔ Realistic expectations — know the work score
- ✔ Appreciative — glad to be working

If you're an over-50 job seeker, think about ways to prove to the interviewer that these benefits apply to you. Use storytelling techniques (see Chapter 2) to underscore your claims. Above all, project yourself as cheerful and flexible, and back up that beaming personality with concrete proof of your skills and success. Remember, a new broom sweeps well, but an old one is best for the corners. If you forget that, recall what **President Ronald Reagan** said on a campaign stop when running for president at age 73: "I believe Moses was 80 when God first commissioned him for public service."

# Avoiding the Trapdoors

No matter how positively you pose your answers, the following rookie and ace traps brand you as a youngster or an oldster right away. Read and be warned.

Rookie traps include

- ✔ **Trying to answer every question as quickly as possible** — Slow down. Think before you answer and don't be afraid to ask for clarification. If you don't know the answer to a question, either admit it or ask to return to that question later.

- ✔ **Downplaying internships and student jobs** — Working part-time or summers while going through school indicates maturity to employers. Make sure that you give examples of transferable skills, such as time management.

- ✔ **Describing student jobs negatively** — Don't knock your student jobs because they were boring drudge work. Most entry-level jobs (the ones you're applying for) consist of boring, routine tasks, the ones that nobody else wants to do. If you complain about being treated as an extra in your student job role, you may miss your chance at a speaking part in a new production.

- ✔ **Wanting too much too soon** — If you're applying for an entry-level position, understand that although, as this book goes to press, the market for new college graduates is very healthy with salaries ranging from $30,000 to $46,000, don't expect that overnight you'll become a director of Sun Microsystems. If you're asked to describe your career goals, use research to keep them realistic. Don't mention "management" as a career goal unless you really mean it and you know what management is and how to do it.

Seasoned ace traps include

- ✔ **Appearing surprised at the interviewer** — Looking at the interviewer with wonderment when the person is a woman, minority, or someone younger than you is old-fud territory. Be prepared to face any race, sex, or age sitting across the desk from you and deal with it.

- ✔ **Apologizing for your age** — Your age doesn't matter if you have the qualifications, so don't mention your age as a liability.

- ✔ **Using age-revealing language** — Avoid the following:
  - Referring to women as *girls* or *gals*
  - Referring to *when I was younger* or *when I was just starting out*
  - Referring to *the good old days* or *back then* or *back when*

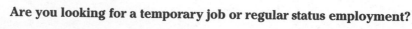

# The Questions for Rookies

Age-revealing questions don't have to be blatant. Often they're indirect, as these queries suggest.

**Are you looking for a temporary job or regular status employment?**

*For a ShowStopper answer*

✔ Answer regular status employment and explain why. (The interviewer may be concerned that you're going back to school and just want to work a couple of months, wasting the company's training costs.)

✔ Ask if the job you're interviewing for is regular status employment or temporary.

*For a ShowFlopper answer*

✔ Lie.

✔ Answer "Temporary" when applying for a position that is regular status employment.

**How did you pay for college?**

*For a ShowStopper answer*

✔ Explain how you worked part-time and took out loans to pay for your own education. (You're committed! And you're grown up!)

✔ Relate that while your parents paid all or most of your expenses, you maximized your college experience by participating in school organizations, team sports, tutoring other students, or any activity indicating that you took your role of student seriously.

*For a ShowFlopper answer*

✔ Say that your parents paid for it, adding nothing to suggest your commitment to work.

**Do you like routine tasks, regular hours?**

*For a ShowStopper answer*

✔ Explain that you understand the importance of routine tasks and regular hours.

✔ Explain how doing a good job with those routine tasks will move you forward in your career direction.

*For a ShowFlopper answer*

- ✔ Say "Yes." (Are you so immature that you can't say more than one word?)
- ✔ Say "No."

## What type of position are you interested in?

*For a ShowStopper answer*

- ✔ Describe the position for which you're interviewing.
- ✔ Explain how that position will help you reach your career goals.

*For a ShowFlopper answer*

- ✔ Describe a position well beyond your skills and experience.

## How do you think you would like this type of work? Can you explain how this industry works?

*For a ShowStopper answer*

- ✔ Research the company, position, and industry.
- ✔ Indicate through your answer that you thoroughly understand the position and the company's expectations and that they sound great.

*For a ShowFlopper answer*

- ✔ Say you won't like the work or aren't sure.
- ✔ Guess at whether you would like it.

## What do you think determines progress in a good company? How do you think people get ahead here?

*For a ShowStopper answer*

- ✔ Explain that a combination of skills and constant growth of skills, resourcefulness, flexibility, results, and the like will contribute to progress and advancement.
- ✔ Include all the positive personality traits you've used to describe yourself.

*For a ShowFlopper answer*

- ✔ Display an entitlement mentality: Discuss progress and promotions as if they're expected and deserved after a certain amount of time.

**If you had the chance to do college over again, what courses would you take and why?**

*For a ShowStopper answer*

 ✔ Show that you have gained judgment over the past school years. Briefly mention the courses you would take that would make you a better candidate for the job you're discussing. Java programming? Statistics? Accounting? Then switch to a discussion of how seemingly unrelated courses you did take helped you to develop maturity.

*For a ShowFlopper answer*

▌ ✔ Mention courses unrelated to the job.

# The Questions for Aces

The questions for seasoned aces can be as indirect as those thrown out to rookies. Following are some sample questions an ace may hear.

 **Aren't you overqualified for this position? Do you think you have too much experience to be happy in this position?**

*For a ShowStopper answer*

 ✔ Clarify the interviewer's concerns. Find out if the interviewer really thinks that you're overqualified — or just overaged — and that you'll want to earn too much money or be bored by the position.

✔ Enthusiastically address the interviewer's concerns, emphasizing the positive.

✔ Explain how you can grow in this position.

✔ Show how you can use your experience to benefit the company in solving long-term problems, building profit, or assisting in other departments.

✔ Make sure that the interviewer understands your qualifications.

✔ If you'll be working in a sea of young people, explain how you are an anchor — experienced, calm, stable, reliable, and can provide day-to-day continuity.

✔ Tactfully ask in a pleasant tone: "What do you mean by overqualified?" or "Specifically, why do you believe I am overqualified?" or "Is it my resume that gives you this perception?" Use the question to draw objections and then overcome them.

✔ Say you are confident you have many productive contributions to offer the company. Name a couple.

*For a ShowFlopper answer*

✔ Agree that you're overqualified. (Maybe you really are too good for this job and should forget about it.)

✔ Assume you understand the objection and address the wrong concern.

### How old are you? When did you graduate?

*For a ShowStopper answer*

✔ Use Chapter 21 to find out how to sidestep these questions.

*For a ShowFlopper answer*

✔ Hit the interviewer with your pocketbook or ivory-handled cane for asking an inappropriate question.

### Can you work overtime and on weekends?

*For a ShowStopper answer*

✔ Discuss your commitment to the job and the extra time you're willing to put into it.

✔ Use terms that proclaim your motivation and energy.

✔ Provide an example of how you've worked long hours recently in dedication to a project.

*For a ShowFlopper answer*

✔ Say "No."

### Why are you looking for a job after being retired for three years?

*For a ShowStopper answer*

✔ Retire? Who retired? Explain that you didn't actually do the R-word. Discuss your positive reasons for taking time off. Everyone needs to refresh and refill from time to time.

✔ Discuss work positively and show that you're all set and raring to get back to it.

✔ Show how you can contribute to the company.

*For a ShowFlopper answer*

✔ Say you need the money.

✔ Say you were bored and leave it at that.

# Pensions and health-care costs are career culprits

A reader writes: "Joyce, I've searched high and low, and it has become nearly impossible to find a job. Even though I am 62, I am not brain dead. I do need to work to subsist. There are a lot of us in that boat."

Another reader writes: "This may be the best economy in world history, but it is really hard to find a job when you're 63. I once was my community's small-businessman-of-the-year, until my company went under. Help, I'm drowning."

Pension and health-care costs are the biggest reasons that late prime-of-lifers find themselves uninvited to job interviews. What you can do for the company may not receive the priority it deserves when all managers can think of is company money flying out the window on wings feathered by pension and health-care costs.

Unless Washington (which underwrites the current pension system with large tax breaks) changes the rules and devises health-care insurance that doesn't penalize age, job-seeking late primers can't compete with younger workers on a level field.

**Demographics may help**

But as in the old Western movies, simple demographics is the cavalry that is riding to the rescue of seniors suffering hostility in the workplace. America is graying. In this decade, baby-boomers will be leaving the workplace in droves, but far too few young workers are available to fill the gap. Despite immigration and productivity increases, a talent shortage looms.

Because the boomer generation is so huge, its members have always had an impact on society. Their movement into the 50 to 65 age bracket this decade is another reminder of their generational clout. Boomers have had their say on everything else in the last century as they progressed through their lifetimes: from a tidal wave demanding more college slots to a frenzy for a huge expansion of housing. Their immense numbers, as an obvious labor pool, prodded by a talent shortage, will force employers to rethink antiquated policies that devalue and discard late primers.

**Check out temp jobs**

But like the frustrations of medical breakthroughs down the road that never seem to arrive in time to do you and me any good, an impending talent shortage doesn't help many of you right now. One immediate answer to closed doors is staffing companies (temporary, employee leasing, contract firms), which may not offer health or retirement benefits. A number of these agencies operate as nonprofit organizations and specialize in senior workers. Ask at a public employment service office or library to be referred to an age-specialty staffing agency in your locale.

# Chapter 20

# Questions about Special Issues

● ● ● ● ● ● ● ● ● ● ● ● ● ● ● ● ● ● ● ● ● ● ● ● ● ● ● ● ● ● ● ● ● ● ● ● ● ● ● ● ● ● ● ● ● ●

## In This Chapter

▶ Handling potential ShowFloppers

▶ Putting out the fire in firings

▶ Dealing with sexual-orientation bias

▶ Respecting people in substance recovery

● ● ● ● ● ● ● ● ● ● ● ● ● ● ● ● ● ● ● ● ● ● ● ● ● ● ● ● ● ● ● ● ● ● ● ● ● ● ● ● ● ● ● ● ● ●

The job of the interviewer is to ferret out information about you — even if you're not anxious to talk about a particular topic.

Perhaps you've been in the same job too long without promotion, and you appear to be unmotivated. You have employment gaps or too many jobs hanging around your neck. You're battling bias against a disability or sexual orientation. Or you're a woman who knows an underlying concern may be parental absenteeism — or whether you can supervise men. Or you're in alcohol or drug recovery and running into brick walls. Or you were fired for cause or demoted. Or you've been convicted of a crime and don't know what to say.

Interview questions that target concerns like these can melt the courage of the bravest job hunters. But if you don't do anything to address these special issues, you lower your chances of getting the job offer you want.

Think carefully before discussing special issues. Even a question that seems innocent may cause you to reveal things you didn't mean to tell. For non-sensitive questions, asking for more time to think about your answer is okay.

***But for special issue answers, you'll seem more straightforward and sure of yourself if you anticipate the question and are ready with a good answer.***

This chapter provides comments and response strategies to help with your special issue.

# *When You've Been in the Same Job Forever*

What could be considered stability by some is seen as fossilization by others. Your chief strategy is to look industrious, ready to take on any challenge that comes your way, and adaptable to new ideas.

 **Because you've been with your last employer for so long, do you think you may have a hard time adjusting to a new company's way of working?**

*For a ShowStopper Answer*

✔ Not at all. Give examples of how you've already learned to be adaptable — how your previous job was dynamic, provided a constantly changing environment, and shared common links with the new company. Note parallels of budget, business philosophy, and work ethics. You plan to take up mountain climbing and sky diving when you're 80 — figuratively speaking.

✔ Emphasize your commitment to your previous company as one of many assets you bring with you to the new position — and name more assets.

*For a ShowFlopper Answer*

✔ Discuss your relief at escaping that old rat-trap job — at last!

✔ Say you're ready to try something new.

 **You've been in your previous position an unusually long period of time — why haven't you been promoted?**

*For a ShowStopper Answer*

✔ Present the old job in modules (by clusters of skills you developed instead of by your periods of employment), and concentrate on all increases in responsibility (to show upward mobility within the position) and on relevant accomplishments. Note raises.

✔ Say that you're interested in this new job precisely because of the inertia of your previous position. Mention any lifestyle changes (grown kids, second family income) freeing you to make a move at this time.

✔ Agree that your career hasn't progressed much, but note that many good people are forced to root or to take lateral moves because few upwardly mobile job slots are available. Say your career plateau gave you time to reflect, lighting a fire under your motivation.

✔ Explain that you had reached the highest position the company offered individuals in your specialty.

*For a ShowFlopper Answer*

> ✔ Complain about office politics keeping you down.
>
> ✔ Say you were happy where you were and ask why fix what isn't broken.

# When You've Served Prison Time

The key to dealing with prison time is to make the experience as positive as possible. Work double-time to outshine the other candidates with your positive outlook and qualifications for the job.

Your prison administrator or parole officer should know of guidebooks with specialized details for ex-inmate job hunting and have the contact information for nonprofit organizations that specialize in helping former inmates survive the job search process. Many of these programs offer classes that teach you what questions to expect in an interview and how to deal with them.

If you were under 21 when you were sentenced or your offense was not a violent felony (substance abuse, for example), in some states you may be able to obtain what is called an *expungement*. An expungement means your conviction record is legally sealed, except to law enforcement and certain other government agencies, and is not available to potential employers or their sleuths.

You probably need a private defense lawyer or your previous public defender to get your record expunged. Expungement is a difficult do-it-yourself project. A private defense lawyer typically charges between $500 and $1,000 to process the flood of paperwork required. The enormous advantage you gain by obtaining an expungement is that you can legally answer "no" to the question of "Have you ever been convicted of a crime?"

Use Internet search engines (see Chapter 3) to find out more about this plausible solution to your job finding problem. Search on "legal expungement." Getting their records sealed has given a second beginning to many who needed another chance in life.

 **Tell me about your incarceration.**

*For a ShowStopper Answer*

> ✔ Discribe how it was one of the best learning experiences you've ever had. Explain the cross-functional (transferable) skills and education you acquired in prison.

*For a ShowFlopper Answer*

✔ Lie about your conviction, figuring no one will learn about it until after you've been hired. (Why risk a firing on top of your criminal record?)

# When You're Shoved out the Door

The No. 1 rule in explaining why you were fired is *to keep it brief, keep it honest, and keep on moving.* Say what you need to say and redirect the conversation to your qualifications. As for what you should say, you have two core options.

**Were you fired from your last job?**

*For a ShowStopper Answer*

✔ **If it wasn't your fault:**

Explain the firing as a result of downsizing, mergers, company closure, or some other act beyond your control. Sometimes firing happens several times in a row to good people who figuratively happen to be standing on the wrong street corner when the wrong bus comes along. So many people have been on that bus these days that being terminated is no longer a big deal. Being let go wasn't your fault, so you have no reason to feel guilty. Go on with the interview.

✔ **If it was your fault:**

Say you learned an enormous lesson during the experience. You messed up, but you know better now, and you won't make the same mistakes again. Explain briefly how you benefited from this learning experience. Then quickly turn the interview back to the better you and go on to explain how you're the best candidate for the job.

*For a ShowFlopper Answer*

✔ Give interviewers the impression that you're hiding something — that you're not being absolutely honest and open with them.

✔ Bad-mouth your former boss. (See Chapter 7 for suggestions on handling an expected horrible reference from your old boss.)

✔ Tell the interviewer that you've had personality conflicts with more than one boss. That admission sets off blaring sirens warning that you're a troublemaker.

## Sidelining a series of firings

If you've been fired from a significant number of jobs, few employers will be willing to give you a second chance; understandably, they don't want to deal with the same problems your previous employers did.

The best course for you to take in this situation is to call on a third party's help. Appeal to your family and friends to step in and recommend you to people they know personally who can hire you. Make sure that the people with hiring power are aware of your past mistakes and assure them (honestly) that you've learned from the experiences and have reformed your wicked ways.

Your other most likely options are to obtain additional education or training for a fresh start or consider self-employment.

**Have you ever been asked to resign? Why?**

*For a ShowStopper Answer*

✔ Being allowed to resign (a gentler process than being fired for cause) suggests that you may be able to work out a mutually agreeable rationale with your former employer. Do so and stick to that rationale.

✔ When you have no rationale, admit your mistake and say it was a painful lesson that caused a change in your work habits.

*For a ShowFlopper Answer*

✔ Lie or give excuses to justify why you should not have been treated so unfairly.

✔ Rip on your ex-bosses or coworkers for forcing you out.

✔ Give multiple examples of your interpersonal conflicts.

# When Sexual Orientation Is Up for Discussion

Sexual orientation is a nonissue with some employers, but it can bring out the worst of biases in others. For gays and lesbians, avoiding the truth during the interview may mean living a lie in the business world. On the other hand, revealing same-sex orientation during the interview may set candidates up for discriminatory rejection.

If you're gay, you have some judgment calls to make. Although you won't be asked directly about your sexual orientation, an interviewer may nibble around the edges with inappropriate personal questions.

For example, a male candidate may be asked: *Is there a special woman in your life?* Or *How's your marriage?*

> A nonanswer: *I consider a number of women special in my life* (meaning your mother, your sister, and your aunt), or *I'm not married yet.*

> A confirming but neutral answer: *You asked about women in my life. I'm gay. I am in a stable relationship. My sexual orientation bears no relationship to my work. It's not a problem for me. I hope it isn't a problem for you.*

Some job seekers with same-sex orientation reject out of hand the notion of working for companies where they can't be open about their sexual orientation.

But sometimes the need for employment takes over. When you can't find a workplace where your sexual orientation won't be used against you, and you have rent to pay, you may choose not to disclose.

Thoroughly research the company's culture and civil rights policies before the interview. Look for companies that proclaim a nondiscriminatory policy on sexual orientation — and mean it. How can you tell if the policy is real or window dressing? Ask members of gay support networks what they know about a company where you're supposed to interview.

# When You've Worked Everywhere

In a time of contract workers and just-in-time temporary hirings, hearing employers allude to "job hopping" is almost amusing. Still, you may need to deal with this issue on an upbeat note.

 **You've changed jobs more frequently than is usual — why is that?**

*For a ShowStopper Answer*

✔ Give acceptable, verifiable reasons why you changed jobs so frequently — project-oriented work, downsizing, dead-end positions, company sold out, or the department shut down.

✔ Say that you've become more selective lately, and you hadn't been able to find the right job until this opportunity came along — explain your employment travels as a quest for a fulfilling job.

✔ If this move is a career change for you, show how your experience and skills support this change and how the position fits your revised career goals.

✔ If your positions were for temporary agencies, cluster them by responsibility and recast them as evidence of your use of cross-functional skills in many situations.

✔ Ask if this is regular status employment. If so, admit you've lacked some commitment in the past, but now you're ready to settle down with a good company such as this one. If not, say a temporary job is just what you have in mind to keep your skills refreshed with experiences gained at various companies.

*For a ShowFlopper Answer*

✔ Complain about what was wrong with each of your ex-employers that made you quit.

✔ Show a lack of focus — you just couldn't get into your jobs.

✔ Say you're looking for something that pays more.

# When Gaps Shred Your History

Employers may rush to judgment when gaps are found in your job history.

If your job history has as many gaps as a hockey player's teeth, try to find growth experiences (self-directed study or broadening travel). If you must blame your jobless patches on sick leave, emphasize that you have recovered and are in excellent health. If personal problems take the hit (ill parent or sick child), again follow up with facts that indicate the personal problems are history.

When your record is spotty beyond belief, try to get on with a temporary job and then prove by your work record that you've turned over a new leaf.

Sometimes the gaps in your record are of recent vintage — you've been looking for employment without success for a very long time. In current periods of unemployment, your posture is commitment — you throw yourself heart and soul into your work and you want to be very sure to find a good fit. Explain your waiting period as a quest for a fulfilling job.

**How long have you been job hunting? Wow! That's a long time — what's the problem? Why haven't you had any job offers yet?**

*For a ShowStopper Answer*

- ✔ Say you've become more selective lately, and you hadn't been able to find the right job until this opportunity came along.

- ✔ If you were given a sizable severance package, explain how it financially allowed you to take your time searching for the perfect next move.

- ✔ Admit your career hasn't progressed as much as you'd like, but the good news is you've had time to think through your life direction, you've re-assessed your career, and you feel focused now. You're fueled up and ready to go!

- ✔ Explain that while you're good at building consensus (through compromise) with others, you haven't been willing to settle for a job that doesn't maximize your skills and qualifications. And that low-end jobs are all that's turned up in this market. Clarify that you've taken your time to find the perfect job fit because the position is very important to you.

*For a ShowFlopper Answer*

- ✔ Say you don't know what the problem is.

- ✔ Admit how many opportunities you've missed out on.

- ✔ Look depressed and admit you're becoming discouraged.

# When You're Demoted a Notch

Oddly, demotion carries more negative weight than does firing today. Demotion suggests personal failure; firing doesn't, unless you're fired for cause.

**Do I read this resume right — were you demoted?**

*For a ShowStopper Answer*

- ✔ Your best move is to deal with demotions before you reach the interview. Ask your demoting boss for a positive reference (see my book, *Resumes For Dummies,* 3rd Edition) and come to an agreement favorable to you on what happened.

- ✔ Explain honestly and as positively as possible the reasons for your send-down.

> ✔ You weren't ready for the responsibility at that time, but now you are. Describe the actions you have taken to grow professionally (school courses in deficient areas, management seminars, management books, and introspection).
>
> ✔ You're looking for a good place to put your new and improved management skills to use, and you hope that place is where you are interviewing. Quickly remind interviewers that you are qualified for the job you're interviewing for, and back that up with examples of your skills and quantified achievements.

*For a ShowFlopper Answer*

> ✔ Lie or try to shift the blame to ABY (anybody but you).

# When People in Recovery Interview

A head-on question in the job interview — *Do you abuse alcohol?* or *Do you use drugs?* is unlikely to be asked. But what if you are directly or indirectly questioned?

If you are in recovery — say, you're in a 12-step or another program and have been substance-free for a year — your answer is

> *No, I don't use drugs (alcohol). I'm very healthy, clear-thinking, and reliable.*

Or

> *I have no health problems that would prevent me from giving you 100-percent effort on every assignment.*

Networking is the way many people in recovery get job interviews, with the result that the referring party often has revealed your background to the interviewer.

When you're sure that the interviewer is well aware of your substance history, find a way to introduce the topic on your terms.

Emphasize that you are a tested, proven individual who has survived a crucible, taken control of your life, and grown into a stronger person. Try not to become mired in interminable details of your recovery, but stick to your main theme of being a well-qualified applicant who overcame an illness and is now better equipped to meet new challenges.

As soon as you think you have tapped into the interviewer's sense of fairness, redirect the conversation to reasons that you should be hired. But until you calm the interviewer's anxiety about your recovery, the interviewer won't truly hear anything you say about your strengths and qualifications.

Laws regulating drug abuse in the workplace are a mixture springing from the Americans with Disabilities Act, state laws, and court decisions. Employers can test new applicants for traces of drugs if all applicants for the same job are tested by a state-certified laboratory, you've been told in advance (often via a statement on a job application form), and been offered the job. Refusing to submit to the test takes you out of the running for the job.

If you are victimized by a drug test's false positive, you may want to offer to pay for a second test yourself, at a mutually agreed upon laboratory. Get agreement from the interviewer that you will be hired and reimbursed for the cost of the second test when the test results come back negative for drug usage.

# When Women Are Put on the Spot

Young women of child-bearing age battle questions about family matters.

Standard responses to the subtle (or not so subtle) probes about the patter of little feet: Kids are way, way in the future because (say why); the lifestyle you'd like to grow accustomed to requires a two-income family; you have super reliable child care (explain).

The best way to deal with the mommy issue is to research before you apply. You're looking for companies with expressed family-friendly policies. Women's magazines regularly run stories on companies that treat women fairly; read them to stay up with the state of corporate generosity in policies that support new parents — from parental leave to child care.

When you have small fry and you choose to stay home with them but you still need the pay, think of alternatives: working part-time, pairing up with another person to do the same job (job sharing), taking your work home (telecommuting), and rearranging work schedules without cutting productive hours (flextime).

As readers of my *Careers* column tell me loud and clear, moving your work home as a valued employee is much easier than starting from scratch with a new employer. Don't bother trying unless you have terrific skills, because your job talk must tackle the employer's bottom-line concern.

Women established in their careers trying to work their way to the top battle a variety of interviewing threats beyond the family concerns, as these illustrative questions show.

**What are your career plans?**

*For a ShowStopper Answer*

✔ This job meets your immediate career plan. It allows you to be a solid producer, yet build on your already strong skills. You plan to work hard at this job to prove yourself and accept greater responsibility as it is offered. You're reasonably ambitious. You don't plan to relocate. Making career plans five years out is not realistic in today's changed job market.

*For a ShowFlopper Answer*

✔ You expect a promotion within a year (suggesting that you'll be unhappy if you don't quickly rise through the ranks).

**What is your management style?**

*For a ShowStopper Answer*

✔ Explain how your management style is compatible with the company culture (you researched the company culture). Incorporate contemporary management style language (you read books on it). State how you handle insubordination, motivation, serious mistakes, and other supervisory issues.

✔ Explain that just because you're a woman, you don't flinch at making tough decisions and implementing them. But you're not a bully or a screamer. Storytell: Give examples of how you've handled past supervisory problems.

*For a ShowFlopper Answer*

✔ Give a vague answer on management style revealing your naiveté.

✔ Outmacho a male interviewer or seem to be too lightweight for the job.

# When Disabilities Are Up for Disclosure

The Americans with Disabilities Act severely limits what interviewers can ask people with disabilities prior to offering a job. If you have a visible disability, you may benefit by giving an explanation of how you are able to do the job.

**Even though you say you can do the job, I'm wondering how you can with your disability. Can you explain more?**

*For a ShowStopper Answer*

- ✔ If practical, ask to give a demonstration — if practical, bring your own equipment.

- ✔ If a demonstration is impractical, pull an example from your last job (paid or volunteer) or educational experience. Storytell a tale of will-do-because-I-have-done.

- ✔ Anticipate essentials to job performance (anything in the job description) the interviewer may be worried about — such as physical mobility, safety, and motor coordination. If you have vision or hearing impairment, expect some concerns that you'll miss visual or aural cues essential to job performance. Explain how you've adapted in these areas or will overcome obstacles.

- ✔ Suggest a few references (previous teachers, counselors, employers, or coworkers) who can testify to your abilities to do the job.

*For a ShowFlopper Answer*

- ✔ Show you're offended by the question — soapbox about unspoken bias.

- ✔ Explain that your coworkers have always set aside their work to assist you with problematic tasks.

- ✔ Without examples to support your claims, assert you have no problems with job performance.

**Because you're our first applicant with a disability, we've never dealt with accommodations before. How much are these accommodations going to cost us?**

*For a ShowStopper Answer*

- ✔ Promise that your requirements are minimal, and give examples of how your skills will merit the company's small investment. According to the Job Accommodation Network (contact on the Internet at janweb.icdi.wvu.edu), roughly 31 percent of all accommodations made cost nothing, while 19 percent cost less than $50.

- ✔ Offer to provide some of your own equipment (you aren't required to, but the offer shows serious interest in contributing to the company).

- ✔ Offer information on accommodations, such as telephone numbers for companies that sell accommodations devices or consultant organizations specializing in accommodations.

*For a ShowFlopper Answer*

✔ Name a costly price for all the equipment you could possibly need, assuming the company can afford the expense. (Remember the company can turn you down if hiring you is an "undue hardship" — defined by the Americans with Disabilities Act as "requiring significant difficulty or expense.")

✔ Act demanding because the ADA is protecting you — the interviewer on the lookout for litigious types won't hire a bad attitude.

✔ Cite the ADA requirements and threaten to sic your attorney on them. If you sue, hope you win enough money to not need a job — ever! (Companies have access to databases of individuals who have sued other employers, and they resist hiring litigious applicants.)

# Chapter 21

# Upstaging Inappropriate Questions

. . . . . . . . . . . . . . . . . . . . . . . . . . . . . . . . . . . . . . . . . . . .

### In This Chapter

▶ Defining discriminatory questions

▶ Profitably answering nonjob questions

. . . . . . . . . . . . . . . . . . . . . . . . . . . . . . . . . . . . . . . . . . . .

**A**re you prepared to answer these questions in a job interview?

*How many sexual partners have you had?*

*Do you insist that your sexual partner use a condom?*

*Do you have experience with bisexuality?*

"Whoa. . . . What's going on here?" you ask. "What kind of questions are these?"

It's hard to believe, but these questions were asked of a female college student interviewing for an internship with an AIDS-related organization. The interviewer justified the privacy-invading queries with the non sequitur that "We can't have people on staff who don't 'practice what they preach.'"

Stunned at what she considered totally unacceptable questions, the student shared the uncomfortable experience with her college counselor. Were these questions illegal? Were they merely inappropriate? How should the student have handled these zingers?

This chapter deals with how to do battle with offensive questions and still get the job offer.

# Defining Illegal Questions

Let's talk terms. An *illegal* question is one that the interviewer has no legal right to ask. Most states and large cities have laws restraining employers from going hog-wild with intrusive questions covering civil rights — age, gender, religion, race, ethnicity, sexual orientation, and so forth. Asking illegal questions can get the interviewer in big trouble.

To find out what's what in your locale, get the facts. You can inquire at your state or city attorney general's office. A library may have a list of questions that shouldn't be asked, according to state or local laws. *Your Rights in the Workplace,* a book from legal specialty publisher Nolo Press and written by attorney Barbara Kate Repa, is an exceptionally good resource.

# Why Interviewers Ask Inappropriate Questions

Although inappropriate questions aren't strictly illegal, they still may lead to lawsuits. Why would anyone ask risky questions?

In small companies where no one has responsibility for the human resource function, the interviewer may not know better and ignorantly violate anti-discrimination laws.

## Club fed's forbidden questions

Discrimination law is ever changing and complex. Contrary to popular understanding, no such thing as a list of illegal questions prohibited by federal law exists, except for these two questions:

1. *Have you ever been arrested?*

2. *How's your health?*

An employer can't ask about your arrest record because an arrest is not an admission of guilt. The Americans with Disabilities Act forbids pre-employment questions asking about a candidate's health, but asking about an individual's ability to perform job-related tasks — *Can you stand for long periods of time?* — is okay.

Other than questions about arrests and health, interviewers can ask any questions they wish as far as the feds are concerned. Federal law merely notes subjects — based on disability and civil rights, such as visible and invisible impairments, race, sex, age, and so forth — that can be the basis for bias complaints and prohibit discriminatory treatment on these grounds.

In large companies where interviewers should know better but don't, interviewers may go on fishing expeditions, hoping that weird, unexpected questions catch candidates without prepared answers, causing them to make unintended revelations.

In companies where interviewers do know better, some go ahead and ask risky questions because they want the information and are willing to gamble that they won't be challenged.

An *inappropriate* question is one the interviewer can legally ask, but probably shouldn't. Depending on whether or not the information is used to discriminate, inappropriate questions set up employers for wealth-draining lawsuits. "Inappropriate" questions range from civil rights and privacy issues to hard-to-classify bizarre inquiries:

> *Is your girlfriend white?*

> *How would you go about making a pizza?*

> *If you were at a departmental meeting and a coworker put his hand on your thigh, what would you do?*

In other words, illegal questions are *always* inappropriate, but inappropriate questions are *not* always illegal.

# Redirect Inappropriate Questions

During the job-rich years of the previous two decades, telling questioners who fired illegal or inappropriate questions at you to back off was fashionable. You used nice language, of course, but passive-aggressive answers like the following amount to telling the interviewer to take a flying leap:

> *How is my marital status a factor in the selection process for this job?*

> *As you know, under Title VII, basing employment decisions on sex is illegal, and I feel that this question is discriminatory in nature.*

If you are a crusader and fighting injustice is your priority, by all means tell the interviewer the illegal or inappropriate question is off-base and shame on you.

But perhaps another, foxier approach appeals to you, especially if you think the interviewer's questions come from ignorance rather than bias. Answer without stirring the pot in a manner that scores points for you. Here is an example of redirecting:

Suppose the interviewer asks a seasoned ace a question about age:

> *I see you went to the University of Colorado. My son's there now. When did you graduate?*

The ace responds:

> *I don't think your son and I know each other. I'm sure he's a fine young man. As for me, fortunately, I've been out of school long enough to have developed good judgment. Would you like to know a little about how my good judgment saved a previous employer $25,000?*

Another way to redirect is to answer the question you *want* to answer, not necessarily the question that's asked. (Politicians do so all the time.) The college internship applicant at the beginning of this chapter could have answered those impertinent questions in this manner:

> *Oh, I am quite familiar with all the "safe sex" precautions. I agree they're very important. Along those lines, would you like to hear more about how I enthusiastically support your organization's mission?*

For purposes of getting a job you want in a job-thinning decade, why waste time trying to separate illegal from inappropriate questions? Why tell interviewers to back off? Answer the question — but do so on your terms. (Chapter 10 explains how to use a question format to beat interviewers to the punch and introduce sensitive issues to the conversation.)

Suppose, for example, you're asked if you'll need time off to celebrate Passover — or any religious holiday. Try this approach:

> *I understand your concern about the time I will need to observe my religious beliefs, but let me assure you that if this time has any bearing on my job performance at all, it will only be positive, because the inspiration of my beliefs will help me stay renewed, fresh, and mentally focused.*

Notice the answer makes no mention of specific religious holidays, it does not refuse to answer, and it does not confront the interviewer with the discriminatory nature of the question.

If a question is repugnant or blatantly discriminatory, don't answer it. I wouldn't. The internship applicant could have said:

> *I do not feel that specific, intimate details of my personal life would be appropriate to discuss here. They do not affect my ability to effectively perform the duties of this position. (Translation: Back off.)*

The AIDS-organization interviewer would have been embarrassed, and when an interviewer is embarrassed, you won't land the job.

If you want the job, avoid becoming confrontational and answer all the questions to your benefit. If the questioner is such a jerk you don't want the job, find a polite way of uttering your back-off exit line.

Even if you decide to answer horrible questions and later suffer candidate's remorse, you still may have the last laugh. The fact that you answered a biased question doesn't disqualify you from filing a legal claim if you believe you've been blitzed by inappropriate questions.

# Red flag questions

If you have doubts about what is or isn't a question that should be off limits, use Internet search engines to find the latest news. For example, go to DirectHit.com (directhit.com), and search on "EEOC guidelines."

Among topics of concern:

**Age:** The Age Discrimination in Employment Act makes it illegal to discriminate in hiring on the basis of age unless age is a bona fide occupational qualification (BFOQ), such as being of the required minimum age to serve alcohol.

**Bankruptcy:** The federal bankruptcy law makes it illegal for employers to discriminate in hiring on the basis of an applicant's bankruptcy. While an employer can run credit checks on applicants, the Fair Credit Reporting Act requires employers to notify job seekers they're doing so.

**Children:** Interviewers who ask applicants about children and child care (especially if the questions are asked only of women and not men) risk charges of discrimination.

**Criminals:** Questions about arrest records (nothing is proven) are illegal, because they may be designed to rule out certain minority groups. Questions about criminal convictions should relate to particulars; a conviction for drunk driving is relevant for a truck-driving job but not for a receptionist job.

**Groups:** Information that might reflect the applicant's race, religion, or national origin can be viewed as discriminatory. Questions about membership should relate to professional groups relevant to the job.

# Chapter 22

# Closing the Show

● ● ● ● ● ● ● ● ● ● ● ● ● ● ● ● ● ● ● ● ● ● ● ● ● ● ● ● ● ● ● ● ● ● ● ● ● ● ●

## In This Chapter

▶ Catching cues to end the interview

▶ After-interview checklist

▶ Following up the interview

▶ Reminding your references

● ● ● ● ● ● ● ● ● ● ● ● ● ● ● ● ● ● ● ● ● ● ● ● ● ● ● ● ● ● ● ● ● ● ● ● ● ● ●

*Y*ou sense it's almost time to go. The interview seems to be winding down. In most instances, a job offer will not be made at this point.

How can you be sure the interview is almost over? Watch for these nonverbal clues: The interviewer may begin shuffling papers, glancing at a wall clock or watch, and, perhaps, standing up. Then you hear words that confirm your hunch.

✔ *Thanks for coming in. We'll be interviewing more candidates through the next week or so. After that, I'll probably get back to you about a second interview.*

✔ *Thanks for talking with me. I think your qualifications make you a definite candidate for this position. Once I'm done with all the initial interviews, I'll get back to you.*

✔ *All your input has been really helpful. Now that I know everything I need to know about you, do you have any questions about the company or the position?* (Careful — only ask job-related questions — you don't have the offer.)

## Make a Strategic Exit

Don't go away from a job interview empty-handed. Remember what you read in this book:

- ✔ Never leave a job interview without reprising your qualifications and the benefits you'll bring to the job.
- ✔ Never leave a job interview without knowing what happens next.
- ✔ Never leave a job interview without propping open the door for your follow-up.

## *Your parting sales pitch*

Haven't you sold yourself enough during this ShowStopper interview? Yes and no. People — including interviewers — often forget what they hear. Start your close with another chorus of your five best skills (see Chapter 4).

Then ask

> *Do you see any gaps between my qualifications and the requirements for the job?*

> *Based on what we've discussed today, do you have any concerns about my ability to do well in this job?*

You're looking for gaps and hidden objections so that you can make them seem insignificant.

When a gap the size of the Grand Canyon exists, accept the fact that the job will go to someone else. Suppose, for instance, that the position requires five years' experience, including two years of supervisory experience. You thought you could talk your way through the gap with your three years of total experience and no years of supervisory experience. Fat chance!

## When a job offer is made at the interview

Once an offer is on the table, bring up your self-interest (vacation, benefits, lunch hours) requests for information. Whip out a note pad and say

> *I'm excited and grateful for your interest. There are just a few issues I'd like to clear up. Can you tell me about — ?*

Unless the circumstances are unusual, accepting or rejecting a job offer on the spot is not in your best interest. You are likely to think of something later that you forgot to negotiate. Improving an offer after you have accepted is difficult.

Even if you have survived multiple interviews and have long known the likely outline of the offer, think about it overnight at least (see Chapter 23).

But if the gaps are not wide and the objections not lethal to your search, attempt to overcome stated shortcomings. You can make this attempt based on what you found out in your earlier research. Here's an effective formula you can use:

1. **Sell your qualifications (benefits — chiefly skills).**

2. **Ask for objections.**

3. **Listen carefully.**

4. **Overcome objections.**

5. **Restate your qualifications (use different words).**

After you restate your benefits, you may find the time is ripe to reaffirm your interest in the job:

> *I hope I've answered your concerns on the _____ issue. Do you have further questions or concerns about my background, qualifications, or anything else at this point? This job and I sound like a perfect match.*

> *I'm very interested in this job, and I'd like to be sure you have all the information you need to consider how I might fit in with the company.*

If it seems appropriate, try to lead subtly toward an offer.

> *The position seems to have my name on it. As I understand, your position requires (give job description with your matching qualifications).*

> *My qualifications fit this position very well, since it requires (give job description with your matching qualifications). Is that right?*

> *There seems to be a good match here. From what you've explained, the job calls for (give job description) — am I right? Then, my qualifications seem tailor-made! Don't you think so?*

> *I'm really glad I had the chance to talk with you. I know that with what I learned at Violet Tech when I established its Internet Web site, I could set up an excellent Web site for you, too.*

## Leaving the door open

How can you tape the door open for a follow-up? You seek the interviewer's permission to call back; with permission, you won't seem intrusive. Use these statements as models to gain the permission:

> *What is the next step in the hiring process, and when do you expect to make a decision? (You're trying to get a sense of the timetable.)*

*I'm quite enthusiastic about this position. When and how do we take the next step?*

*May I feel free to call if I have further questions?*

*I know you're not done reviewing candidates; when can I reach you to check up on the progress of your search?*

*I understand you'll call me back after you've seen every candidate for this position; would you mind if I call you for an update or if I have more questions?*

*I appreciate the time you spent with me; I know you're going to be really busy recruiting, so when can I call you?*

*I look forward to that second interview you mentioned (shake hand firmly but gently, make eye contact) — can I call you later to schedule it after my work hours so I don't have to throw off my current employer's schedule?*

In the final moments, be certain to express thanks to the interviewer for the time spent with you. Say it with a smile, eye-to-nose, and a firm but gentle handshake: *It looks like a terrific opportunity — I look forward to hearing from you.* Don't linger.

As soon as you're alone at a place where you can make notes, write a summary of the meeting. Concentrate especially on material for your follow-up moves, described later in this chapter.

# How Aggressive Should You Be?

How hard should you sell? How eager should you be? That depends — How old are you? How experienced are you? How senior a job are you seeking? No behavior is perfect for every person and every situation.

If you have experience and are offering in-demand skills, allow yourself to be wooed a bit. You don't want to be seen as jumping at every opportunity. It's the old story: The more anxious you seem, the less money you will be offered.

## Recruiters follow up for you

You don't have to follow up with the employer when you were introduced to the company by a recruiter or employment consultant — the recruiter or consultant follows up for you, negotiating the closure or turndown. Usually, you can get a report card from your recruiter or consultant fairly quickly.

# *Your After-Interview Checklist*

Experts in any field become experts because they've made more mistakes than the rest of us. After your interview, take a few minutes to rate your performance. The following checklist can be helpful in curbing bad habits and becoming an expert at job interviewing.

- ❑ Were you on time?
- ❑ Did you use storytelling, examples, results, and measurement of achievements to back up your claims and convince the questioner that you have the skills to do the job?
- ❑ Did you display high energy? flexibility? interest in learning new things?
- ❑ Did the opening of the interview go smoothly?
- ❑ Did you frequently make a strong connection between the job's requirements and your qualifications?
- ❑ Was your personal grooming immaculate? Were you dressed like company employees?
- ❑ Did you forget any important selling points that you can put in a follow-up e-mail, letter, or call-back?
- ❑ Did you smile? Did you make eye contact?
- ❑ Did you convey at least five major qualities the interviewer should remember about you?
- ❑ Did you make clear your understanding of the work involved in the job?
- ❑ Did you show your understanding of the strategies required to reach company goals?
- ❑ Did you use enthusiasm and motivation to indicate that you're willing to do the job?
- ❑ Did you find some common ground to establish that you'll fit well into the company?
- ❑ Did you take the interviewer's clues to wrap it up?
- ❑ Did you find out the next step and leave the door open for your follow-up?
- ❑ After the interview, did you write down names and points discussed?

Think about the following questions to help you clearly identify your strengths and weaknesses on the job interview stage:

- ✔ What did you do or say that the interviewer obviously liked?
- ✔ Did you hijack the interview (grab control or speak too much — more than half the time)?
- ✔ Would you have done something differently if you could replay the interview?

# Follow Up or Fall Behind

Never walk away from an interview telling yourself that Act III is over — that the whole job thing is now out of your hands. That's how unsuccessful job hunters think.

What takes place after the first interview — when the ranking of candidates takes place — decides who has the inside track on winning the job.

Your follow-up may be the tiebreaker with the job going to you over other promising candidates. And even if the employer already planned to offer you the job, your follow-up creates goodwill that can silken your success when you join the company.

Follow up vigorously. It's your caring that counts.

Your basic tools are

- ✔ E-mail
- ✔ Letters
- ✔ Telephone calls
- ✔ References

## Let's hear it for e-mail follow-up!

One of the online discussion lists I monitor recently considered the merit of e-mail versus telephone follow-up to job interviews. The human resource professional was strongly in favor of e-mail: "It saves time, I don't have to call back, I don't have to look up his files, and so forth. Ten years ago we didn't have e-mail technology, and follow-up calls were necessary. No longer."

Not everyone agrees that telephone calls are dead. There are times when the telephone follow-up is much stronger, especially with employers whom you suspect are traditionalists (they like phones, and they like paper), but e-mail does have its charms:

- Use e-mail when you're over age 40 to underscore a contemporary image.

- Use e-mail when you hope to start or continue a dialogue with an interviewer. E-mail is more conversational and easier for a quick reply (but, on the other hand, it's also easier to say no in an e-mail message than on the telephone).

- Use e-mail when quick action matters. The job could be filled while you're waiting for postal mail to be delivered.

- Use e-mail if that's the way you sent your resume and especially if the employer requested electronic communication in a job ad.

- Use e-mail when you are dealing with a high-tech firm; the firm's hiring authority probably doesn't remember what paper is and may think voicemail is a bother.

- Construct e-mail messages differently than you do letters. Keep your e-mail follow-up short and send it in plain text (ASCII), not as an attachment. Limit the message's width to three quarters of the screen. Use appropriate business language. Don't forget your contact information, even though the interviewer can push the reply button and get back to you with ease. One more point: Remember to complete your subject line with sales pizazz: "Thank you for reviewing my qualifications: Sales, 6 yrs, autos."

## *Letters*

Write a thank-you letter for the interview within 24 hours to strengthen the good impression you made in the interview. To suggest the quality of follow-up to make, two sample letters follow.

You need not stop with one letter — if the employer has left you dangling in the wind waiting for a hiring decision, try to think of new facts to add in a second or third follow-up letter (fax, postal mail, or e-mail). After the third letter, try to include a relevant news clipping or even an appropriate cartoon.

The interviewer knows what's going on, but at least you're keeping your name before the decision-maker.

### E-Mail Thank-You for Job Interviews

Dear Brent C. Nababy:

I was impressed with the warmth and efficiency of your offices and your genuine interest in acquainting me with your staff and company goals. We share the priority of "Beating the competition's quality by miles."

We discussed vendors: In addition to those I mentioned, among my favorite suppliers, you may recognize the names of Namath Re-bar, Drywall By-the-Miles, and Lionel Fixtures.

High standards have been so central in my work that I feel compelled to join such a demanding company as yours. Thanks for the interview. I look forward to contacting you next week to check on the progress of your search.

Sincerely, Max Hong


Maxwell Hong
123-D North Circle Drive
Toronto, Canada 44567
22-33-44-55
mhong@aol.com
www.BUILDNET.com

**Thank-You for Job Interviews**

**Maxwell Hong**
123-D North Circle Drive, Toronto, Canada 44567
Telephone: 22-33-44-55
E-mail: mhong@aol.com
WWW.BUILDNET.COM

September 7, 200x

Mr. Brent C. Nababy, Vice President
21st Century Developments
5555 Hassau Broadway
Toronto, Canada 44568

Dear Mr. Nababy:

> Opens with personable style and quick reminder of interview.

Thank you for the opportunity to interview for a subcontractor coordinator position. I was impressed with the warmth and efficiency of your offices, and your genuine interest in acquainting me with your staff and company goals.

> Reviews salient points made during interview.

During our discussion, I told you about my background in sub-contractor coordinating experience. Although our conversation focused on hiring policies, top contacts, and scheduling strategies, I wanted to underscore our mutual priorities. The latest issue of *Building Issues* brings to my attention a priority we share: "Beating the competition's quality by miles."

> Includes interests not fully covered in interview, uses company motto.

I have always strived to reach high-quality results by using the most appropriate materials, and by studying the quality of materials used by other companies. Among my favorite suppliers, you may recognize the following names: Namath Re-bar, Drywall By-the-Mile, and Lionel Fixtures.

> Mentions contacts not included on resume.

Such high standards have been so central in my work that I feel compelled to join such a demanding company as yours. Thanks again for the interview. I look forward to contacting you next week to check on the progress of your search.

> Signs off with intent to follow-up.

Sincerely,

*Max Hong*

## Telephone calls

In the call-back-once-a-week era before the mid-1990s, search experts correctly told job seekers to keep calling interviewers as long as the interviewer didn't threaten them with a kneecap job if they didn't lay off. Today, business has put on running shoes because the ranks of managers are sparse. Managerial survivors are far too busy for a constant, interruptive series of telephone calls.

If you call interviewers too often now, you waste their prime work hours, annoy them, and probably jeopardize your opportunity for the job. Space your follow-up calls — once a month is probably plenty. Fill in the slack with e-mail or letters.

Some search advisers suggest that it's still a good idea to call weekly if you call early in the morning, late in the evening, or on weekends, avoiding prime work hours. I'm not sure that's true. When I come to the office at 7 a.m. on a Saturday, it's because I have a heavy work agenda, not because I want to field telephone calls.

Once upon a time, all that job callers had to worry about was getting past gatekeeper assistants. That problem was solved in various ways. One recommended technique: Adopting a pleasant and honest manner and making an ally of the assistant by revealing the refreshing truth about why you're calling. Another suggestion: Trying to reach the interviewer by calling before 8:30 a.m. and after 5:30 p.m. when the assistant is not likely to be on duty and the interviewer fields phone calls alone.

Those were the good old days. Now, voicemail has joined human gatekeepers in throwing roadblocks in front of job seekers who try to set up interviews or follow-up interviews.

The big voicemail question for job seekers is — *Should I leave a message on voicemail?* Opinions vary, but, as a practical matter, you may have to leave a message if you don't connect after the first few calls. You won't get all your calls returned, but your chances improve when you say something interesting in a 30-second sound bite:

> *This is _____. I'm calling about the (job title or department) opening. After reflecting on some of the issues you mentioned during our meeting, I thought of a facet of one problem you might like to know (create intrigue). My number is _____.*

### Opening the conversation

Here is a sprinkling of conversation starters:

- *Is this a good time to talk?*

- *I think you'll be interested to know _____.*

- *I understand you're still reviewing many applications.*

- *I forgot to go into the key details of* (something mentioned during the interview) *that might be important to you.*

- *While listening to you, I neglected to mention my experience in* (function). *It was too important for me to leave out, since the position calls for substantial background in that area.*

- *I was impressed with your _____.*

- *I appreciate your emphasis on _____.*

### Keeping the conversational ball rolling

Try these approaches to maintain the conversation:

- Remind the interviewer why you're so special, what makes you unique (exceptional work in a specific situation, innovating).

  *Let me review what I'm offering you that's special.*

- Establish a common denominator — a work or business philosophy.

  *It seems like we both approach work in the* (name of) *industry from the same angle.*

- Note a shared interest that benefits the employer.

  *I found a new Web site that may interest you — it's XYZ. It reports on the news items we discussed . . . Would you like the URL?*

# Reminding your references

References can make all the difference. As I advise in Chapter 8, spend adequate time choosing and preparing the people who give you glowing testimonials. What they say about you is more convincing than what you say about yourself.

Call your references and fill them in on your interview:

*I had an interview today with* (person, company). *We talked about the position, and it sounds like a perfect match for me. They wanted* (give a list of key requirements), *and that's just what I can supply.*

*For instance, I have all this experience* (match five key requirements with five of your qualifications) *from when I worked with* (name of company).

*Would you like me to fax you those points I just mentioned? . . . I was so happy about the interview I just wanted to thank you once more for all your help and support. I couldn't have done it without you.*

# Onward and Upward

You've done it all — turned in a ShowStopper performance at your interview and followed up like a pro. Keep following up until you get another job or until you're told you are not a good match for the position — or that while your qualifications were good, another candidate's were better.

Even then, write yet one more thank-you note, expressing your hope that you may work together in the future. Sometimes the first choice declines the job offer, and the employer moves on to the next name — perhaps yours.

# Chapter 23

# When You're Offered the Part

*In This Chapter*

▶ Responding wisely to a job offer
▶ Questions to consider about the job
▶ Evaluating counteroffers
▶ Signing employment agreements

Congratulations, you've been offered the part you auditioned for. A few small things may curb your unbridled enthusiasm: Your salary's so low you have to rent your toothbrush. Your hours are so late that even the cable channels are running test patterns when you get home. Your health benefits consist of you giving up only one of your kidneys. Otherwise, the job is great.

Failing to think through the pros and cons of a job offer is how people become cemented in a routine of disappointing work. This chapter deals with issues to consider in your decision.

# Don't Say Yes Right Away

When you hear those sweet words, "We're offering you the job," bookend your reaction:

1. **Enthusiasm.**

   Act as though you've just won a lottery.

2. **Thoughtfulness.**

   Ask for a day or two to "sleep on it."

3. **Enthusiasm.**

   Act as though you've just won a lottery.

Why should you be so enthusiastic when you're not certain you want the job? Because it's more fun to turn down than to be turned down.

## New grads can ask for three weeks to accept job

Although job changers normally are expected to give a yea or nay to job offers within a few days, college seniors who are trying to figure out where they want to work after graduation should be given plenty of time to explore all their employment options, says the National Association of Colleges and Employers. NACE recommends that employers give graduating students a minimum of three weeks to choose among job offers.

Some employers use a competitive tactic called the "exploding offer," which means the student is given too little time, sometimes only a few days, to accept before the offer is withdrawn. This rush of decision-making backfires on all parties when students make poor, pressured decisions and then renege or resign early. If you're a rookie, quote the NACE policy recommendation when asking for enough time to think clearly and thoroughly. Choosing a first job is a major decision.

You need a little time to get over the excitement of being chosen and calmly consider whether accepting the offer is in your best interests.

The employer probably expects you to take a few days to decide. After all, you're making a major life decision. An immediate response could be seen as impulsiveness or not taking the job seriously.

Even when it's the only game in town and everyone wants the job, your interests are best served by reflecting before giving your answer. Ask for overnight, a few days, or, at most, a week to think over a job offer.

Deliberate on the offer quite carefully before saying "yes." You may still be able to extract one last benefit that didn't come with the original offer. And the additional facts provided by the interview may have opened your eyes to aspects of the job you hadn't considered.

## *Stick to Your Career Script?*

Not so long ago, a key consideration in choosing a job was the opportunity to stay in your career field to follow your personal goals. Zigzagging from career field to career field rather than changing jobs within the same career field was not a smart strategy. The situation has changed. Turning down a job today because it doesn't "fit into your long-term career goals" is still a desirable policy, but not always a practical choice.

Analyzing who you are and what you want to do will always be relevant. Staying within the boundaries of the work you love and are prepared to do is always more satisfying — and better for your career.

## Please stay. We're not kidding.

With labor tight, employers have rediscovered counteroffers when a useful employee quits to take a better job. If you find yourself being wooed back, it's usually best to leave the counteroffer on the table, say thanks, and move on. Here's why:

✔ When substantial financial considerations aren't in the mix, most people leave a job because of a personality rift, blocked advancement, or nonfulfilling work. A generous counteroffer won't fix any of these things.

✔ Once you've announced a departure, count yourself out of the inner circle. You won't be trusted as before.

✔ Renewing your enthusiasm will be challenging — you already know why you want to find the exit. If your current employer wouldn't promote you or give you a decent raise before you put on your walking shoes, don't expect anything different when it's time to move up to your next career level.

✔ If a recruiter connected you with the new offer, and you say "yes" and then "no," your credibility goes up in smoke — a negative that could come back to haunt you.

✔ Ask yourself: Would you join the company that now employs you if you were looking for a good job? (This exercise can help you make the right decision.)

Having said that, economic realities may mean that sometimes to earn a living, you have to do what you can do, rather than what you love to do. Should you find yourself in this situation, try to identify new skills and knowledge you will gain that enhance your original career direction if you return to it.

*What's important to you is that any job you take must allow you to develop and tweak portable skills that you can use in your next job.*

# To Accept or Not to Accept

Once you stop dancing around and whooping it up after finally getting the job offer, you need to think about the particulars of whether or not the job is right for you. Here are the kinds of questions to ask yourself.

## Is the job itself a good one?

Is this job worth one half of your waking hours? Only you can decide. When considering the worthiness of the job itself, ask yourself the following questions:

✔ Does this job allow me to strengthen my marketable skills? Does it offer career mobility?

✔ Will the boss(es) and I get along?

✔ Will this work hold my attention?

✔ Does the job use the best of my talents, skills, and abilities?

✔ Will this work give me a sense of enjoyment?

✔ Is this a job that "makes a difference?" Do I care?

✔ Do I get to make the important decisions about how I do the job?

✔ Will I have to travel? How much? Is that okay with me?

✔ Will I have to work hours when my friends play? Is that okay with me?

✔ Will this job allow me to add to my personal network?

✔ Will I be visible to people who make decisions?

✔ Could this job be a stepping stone to something better?

✔ Do I need a whole new wardrobe for this job? Is that okay with me?

---

# Feedback when you're not offered the part

If you aren't ready for this chapter yet — that is, when you lose the part to another candidate — you may be wondering where you went wrong. Disappointed job seekers often ask interviewers for reasons why they were not selected and for tips on how to do better in the future.

Don't waste your time — almost never will you be given the real reason. Employers have no legal or ethical obligation to explain why you weren't the one.

Instead, they're likely to offer these kinds of innocuous rationales: "We didn't feel you were the best fit for this job" or "We chose another candidate who had more experience" or "Company policy won't allow me to comment."

Why won't interviewers take you behind the scenes and share the truth? Here are some of the reasons they give.

✔ ___Legal exposure: *Companies are extremely wary of lawsuits accusing them of discrimination. The less said, the less to be sued about.*

✔ ___Fast-paced world: *There's no profit in wasting prime hours on a dead end.*

✔ ___Discomfort factor: *Managers dislike giving negative feedback.*

✔ ___Scant information: *HR (human resource) interviewers may not have enough details from hiring managers to give helpful answers, even if they were inclined to do so.*

✔ ___Hassle: *Sales candidates see a turndown as a challenge to their ability to sell and will try to countersell to a level of pesky persistence.*

When you're not offered the part, review the After-Interview Checklist in Chapter 22. If you have the requisite qualifications and your performance doesn't need pumping up, the reason you didn't get an offer may have nothing to do with you. Square your shoulders and get ready for the next interview.

# Is the company a good choice?

Is this a company you admire? When considering the kind of company you may be joining, ask yourself the following questions:

- Does the company culture fit my personality?
- Does the company have room for advancement?
- Are the company policies in writing?
- Can I live with these policies?
- Is the company in a good position to survive and grow in a competitive market?
- What's the company's reputation for consideration of employees? Severance policies?
- Is the company's industry growing or shrinking?

# Is the pay enough?

You can be just as happy with a lot of money as a little. For most of us, getting our hands on any money means working at paid jobs for our material things — home, food, transportation, clothing, entertainment, and education. As I note in Chapter 10, compensation comes in a package of base pay, variable pay (such as bonuses), and indirect pay (employee benefits such as health insurance). Weigh each of these factors when considering the company's compensation package. Ask yourself these questions:

- Am I being offered my fair market value in base pay?
- How valuable are any variable pay opportunities — bonuses, commissions, stock options?
- What good are the benefits? Health insurance (what percentage do I pay; can I choose coverage plans)? Retirement plan? Company car? Vacation time? Sick days? What else?
- What is the basis for raises?

## Poll: Employers expect you to negotiate

When you get a job offer *in a tight labor market*, more than eight out of ten human resource professionals expect you to negotiate it, according to a recent poll by the Society for Human Resource Management (SHRM — the leading voice of the human resource profession) and the *Wall Street Journal's* Interactive Edition, `careers.wsj.com`.

Their findings suggest that you should be skeptical if an employer attempts to convince you that a salary offer is embedded in lucite and cannot be altered upward: A whopping 92 percent of human resource professionals surveyed believe salaries are negotiable!

What's more, about half of HR professionals think you can negotiate specific benefits:

- ✔ Relocation costs reimbursement, 58 percent said "yes."

- ✔ Early reviews with the option for salary increases, 48 percent said "yes."

- ✔ Signing bonuses, 49 percent said "yes."

- ✔ Vacation leave, 50 percent said "yes."

So what are you waiting for? If they expect you to ask for more, far be it from you to disappoint. See Chapter 10 to cop a compensation attitude and become a more confident negotiator.

# Employment Contracts: Theirs and Yours

The "get it in writing" trend is growing — on both sides of the desk. Legally, no iron-clad rules apply, and each contract is different. But here are the basics you need to know.

## Company pre-employment contracts

Employment relationships are increasingly contract-oriented for professional, managerial, technical, and administrative positions. Companies make you sign contracts because they can. If you don't, they'll hire someone else. You have more leverage to negotiate (not just mindlessly sign the boilerplate pre-employment contracts you're given) in tight labor markets; you have less leverage in surplus labor markets when ten people are standing behind you ready to grab the job.

What do these pre-employment agreements cover? Usually the prehiring agreement regulates one or more of these issues: training repayments, nondisclosure of company secrets and customer lists, noncompete clauses preventing you from working elsewhere for a specified time period, and arbitration and other alternate dispute resolutions (ADRs).

The ADR agreements usually come with a muzzle clause that prohibits you from discussing settlement details. Arbitration is a contentious issue with employees often feeling that arbitrators (wishing to be hired again) may side with companies, which are more likely to be repeat customers. St. Louis employment attorney Sheldon Weinhaus comments: "Companies keep track of previous awards. It is much harder for a worker to know the history of any arbitrator."

**Tip:** If you're required to sign a pre-employment agreement that mandates arbitration, ask that language be inserted requiring that the arbitrator be chosen from a list maintained by the American Arbitration Association or another selection organization that operates with a code of ethics.

Generally, pre-employment agreements are legal and enforceable — but not always. If you can't afford to consult a lawyer before signing a pre-employment contract (and most of us can't), bulk up your knowledge. Try these two Web resources: nolo.com, the country's best do-it-yourself legal publisher; and monster.com, where you can seek Sylvia Ho's article, "Everything You Need to Know Before You Sign a Non-Compete Agreement."

## *Your pre-employment contract*

Only management has traditionally been given employment contracts spelling out the conditions of employment — and of severance. But the practice is spidering down and across organizational charts so if you even think you've got a ghost of a chance of getting a contract in your favor, go for it. The minimum you should have in all jobs is a letter of understanding, which outlines the basics of your employment.

Stybel Peabody & Associates, a Boston outplacement consulting firm, offers an instructive article, "Should You Ask For an Employment Contract?" on its Web site, www.stybelpeabody.com.

# *Last Chance to Back Out*

Maybe you've decided to accept the offer. Before popping a champagne cork, *make sure that you have the salary, benefits, and starting date in writing.* This information is particularly important if you're being asked to relocate.

If you received the offer over the telephone, ask if the company can mail you a letter of understanding; If not, you write one (see my book *Cover Letters For Dummies*, 2nd Edition).

Perhaps you've decided the job isn't for you, after all. Don't feel obligated to accept it just because you've been dickering over your potential employment for weeks. If you ultimately back out, send a charming letter stating that fact. Charming letter? That's also covered in my cover letters book.

# Part VI
# The Part of Tens

The 5th Wave          By Rich Tennant

@RICHTENNANT

"They had recruiters working the beach all through Spring break. It's the first time I ever had a job interview cut short by an incoming tide."

## In this part . . .

*I*t's time to bring down the curtain on a challenge that more people than ever face today as the world's economy remakes itself. Job changers often don't find a new connection overnight. Keeping up morale is indispensable in a successful search. Three chapters follow to put a smile on your face.

And finally, you see an Encore written by someone who well understands both job interviews and auditions.

# Chapter 24

# Ten Interviewer Personality Types

*In This Chapter*

▶ Interviewer styles you may encounter

▶ Amusing but useful information

*L*iking people who are like ourselves is human nature. Moreover, job interviewers for companies tend to be representative of the kinds of people at their respective companies.

Using general perspectives (see Chapter 1) as a starting point, look over the following personality types, presented according to my "Latin" designations. Without resorting to a personality transplant, try to strike a pose harmonious with that of your interviewer. For example, if your interviewer is full of courtly charm, let honey drip from your lips; but if your interviewer is brisk to the point of brusqueness, stick to the verbal point with virtually no detours.

Heed this mirroring strategy, and you'll have a better chance of establishing a good rapport.

## Achieveus Youngius (Young Achiever)

A twentysomething, fresh-faced, conservatively dressed, preppie type most commonly seen on college campuses during job fairs; easily tamed; demeanor is cheerful and positive — friendly.

Approach these specimens with down-home charm, and you'll have them eating out of your hand. Encourage conversations about extracurricular activities, common interests, leadership positions, admiration for the company, and lots of enthusiasm. But not for too long.

Specimens of this type have little or no interviewing experience, so help out by asking questions. Doing so puts them at ease. To get the job, focus on demonstrating traits, skills, goals, and experiences that the *achieveus youngius* can relate to.

# Businessius Serious (Serious Businessperson)

Gray-haired, successful, most often seen wearing a slightly rumpled, expensive suit; females are less common than males; demeanor is serious and businesslike.

Approach these specimens with confidence and humility and let them know that you're willing to work your way to the top. Discuss your academic or work achievements, strict work ethic, steadfast dedication to a goal, and leadership skills. Let the *businessius serious* see that you have broad knowledge of the company.

Let this specimen control the interview. To get the job, focus on showing the *businessius serious* exactly what skills you bring to the company and how you can apply those skills toward the position you seek.

**Caution:** Most specimens of this type are friendly. However, a few have a mutant gene that makes them very dangerous. Watch out for the ones who try to bite you with stress-inducing situations and off-the-wall questions.

# Bossus Potentialus (Potential Boss)

Of variegated descriptions; similar to *businessius serious;* usually found at top of department, looking for help; demeanor is serious and practical.

To identify these specimens, ask if the *businessia serious* interviewing you would be your direct boss. If so, ask questions about management philosophy. Then present your skills as compatible with that philosophy. For example, if the *bossus potentialus* mentions teamwork, show yourself as a team player.

The *bossus potentialus* values common sense, work experience, and a positive attitude and despises arrogance and immaturity. Use level-headed practicality when approaching these specimens and let them control the interview.

# Contemplativius Coldius (Cold Contemplator)

Usually found in comfortable, uninteresting clothing in a practical environment; doesn't collect personal items; likes to be alone; methodical, precise, and work-oriented; demeanor is quiet and self-sufficient.

If you have any discrepancies on your resume, beware — *contemplativius coldius* wants a logical explanation. These specimens are thinkers — analytical and critical. Approach them with reserve and self-confidence. Don't talk too much and don't try to be their new best friend. Focus your answers so that you do not stray into irrelevant information — doing so drives *contemplativius coldius* crazy.

Do give plenty of information for them to mull over; they love details, so tell them the who, what, why, when, and how. These specimens love analyzing, but they need something to analyze. Offer your skills, achievements, and experience as a rich analytic possibility, more interesting than any other yet offered, and they'll be happy.

# Fuzzius Warmus (Warm Fuzzies Person)

Nonthreatening, friendly, likes people; several personal items in office; usually involved in several things at once; smiles often and genuinely; demeanor is concerned, comfortable, and thoughtful.

These specimens make sure that you're happy and comfortable before they start the interview. In fact, you may find that they spend so much time caring for you that you never get interviewed.

Start by establishing a connection and then steer the interview toward more serious matters. *Fuzzius warmus* is delighted to follow your lead; after all, they just want you to be happy. Don't expect them to be very skilled at interviewing — they hate making decisions. So be ready to present all of your qualifications for the job.

# Interviewus Incompetus (Incompetent Interviewer)

Of all shapes, colors, and sizes; found in various environments; identified by a poor interviewing technique; demeanor varies.

Unlike its close relative, the *interviewus competus,* the *interviewus incompetus* either has little training or experience in interviewing or has personality problems. If your interview seems unfocused, or you find yourself asked unethical or irrelevant questions, or you're faced with an arrogant brute who never lets you speak, you can be fairly sure that you've entered the lair of *interviewus incompetus.*

To escape this specimen unscathed and leave the best impression possible, gracefully take control of the situation by repeating the questions for focus, asking questions that demonstrate your skills or knowledge in a particular area, staying calm, and initiating discussion of your skills and their application to the position you seek. Don't overestimate this specimen's ability to uncover your potential.

# Intimidatus Serious (Serious Intimidator)

Impeccably dressed, conservative; very neat and organized; prefers expensive, classic furnishings; work-oriented; always on time; demeanor is reserved, dedicated, and critical.

Approach these specimens quietly and seriously. Don't scare them away with chatter, false friendliness, or insincerity. *Intimidatus serious* doesn't go to work to make friends, but to work — only work. So don't waste time with pleasantries; get right to the point as succinctly as possible.

Whatever you do, don't let these specimens see your fear or intimidation. They'll kick you right out and race to the next interview.

# Recruiterus Professionalus (Professional Recruiter)

Suave, professional, well dressed; demeanor is quiet and confident, measuring.

These specimens spend their days interviewing people for specific companies. Their goal is more to screen you out than in, as they narrow their list of applicants. They won't let you ask many questions, so concentrate on answering their questions with as many specifics as possible about your skills, experience, and accomplishments.

To get this specimen on your side, focus on presenting the best possible you. Make sure that your appearance is impeccable and that your enthusiasm and interest in the job shine forth. Answer confidently and communicate clearly.

# Talkus Alotus (Person Talks a Lot)

Fashionable, often individualistic in dress; hoards sentimental items like pictures or mementos; prefers clutter to order; often runs late; demeanor is talkative and upbeat.

The *talkus alotus* enjoys company. These specimens gravitate toward busy offices where they're surrounded by many others. They like to talk and they talk fast, so keep up.

Start by establishing a personal connection with these specimens. They probably won't pay much attention to you if they don't like you, so work on creating a friendly foundation by pasting a wide, sincere smile on your face and exuding enthusiasm. Focus on keeping these specimens interested throughout the interview — beware of boring them.

# Technicus Strictus (Strictly Technical Person)

No definite description; look for pencils, notepads, and gadgets, like a pocket calculator or laptop computer; often found behind a technical title, like accountant, marketing assistant, or chemical engineer; demeanor is friendly but distant.

The *technicus strictus* doesn't mix well with other species, so camouflage yourself in the tools of your trade. Focus on your technical knowledge and achievements. Get this specimen excited by discussing common interests in your field.

These specimens usually have little interviewing experience, so make sure that you discuss your skills in detail. Don't assume that they will be able to uncover all of your strengths — *technica stricta* are undoubtedly skilled in their fields, but not in interviewing, so be ready to ask good questions.

# Too Muchus of a Good Thing?

If you're not flatlined after reading this good but goofyius list of interview types, reinforce your understanding by trying to think of a person you know who fits each category. Or meet with friends and pretend you're trying out for the cast of a sitcom, say the *Drew Carey Show* or *Seinfeld*. Each friend assumes a personality type and role-plays an interview with you. Good luck with *Contemplativus Coldius* and *Technicus Strictus*.

# Chapter 25

# Tens of Interview Lines That Never Made History

. . . . . . . . . . . . . . . . . . . . . . . . . . . . . . . . . . . . . . . . . . . . . . . . . .

### In This Chapter

▶ Wacky quotes from the could-have-been world of famous folks

▶ Have a laugh on me

. . . . . . . . . . . . . . . . . . . . . . . . . . . . . . . . . . . . . . . . . . . . . . . . . .

**Y**ou've dutifully finished a whole book of savvy strategies and astute responses. Your big reward arrives when you get the job offer you want. But your immediate reward follows. . . .

## From the Time Machine: News You Can't Use

Job interviews have been around since God interviewed Noah for ship's captain. Here's a totally made-up collection of what famous figures in history and literature might say to a job interviewer today. Would these comments get the job?

**Zeus** — I know you advertised for someone with three years' experience, and I have way more than that. But I used to be the King of the Gods, for cryin' out loud! There must be something I can bring to the table that helps your department.

**Joan of Arc** — I may look a little wet behind the ears, but I defeated the world's greatest army, liberated my country, changed the course of history, and my last boss called me a saint.

**David** — I'm not into size. When it comes to the competition, my thinking is "The bigger they are, the harder they fall."

**George Washington** — If I can lead a successful rebellion and a fledgling country, I'm sure I can lead your insignificant department.

**Moses** — I can part the red tape to get the job done.

**Thomas Jefferson** — You're looking for growth? Our company doubled in size under my leadership.

**Christopher Columbus** — You bet I can open new markets for your company. Put me on the road, and I'll discover a world of opportunity, the likes of which you've never seen.

**Harriet Tubman** — My specialty is discreet outplacement.

**Lewis & Clark** — Big land development plans? Yes, we have experience in scouting out new real estate.

**Hester Prynne** — Here are my references, including a scarlet letter of recommendation from my last boss.

**Julius Caesar** — My previous job involved a lot of office politics and back-stabbing. I'd like to get away from all that.

**Jesse James** — I can list among my experience and skills: leadership, extensive travel, logistical organization, intimate understanding of firearms, and knowledge of security measures at numerous banks.

**Theodore Roosevelt** — My career record should stand on its own. I speak softly, but I carry a big resume.

**Napoleon Bonaparte** — Okay, I'll start today in the mailroom, but tomorrow . . . the world.

**Marie Antoinette** — My management style has been criticized, but I like to think I'm a people person.

**John F. Kennedy** — In preparation for this interview, I asked myself not what this company can do for me, but what I can do for this company.

**Joseph Guillotine** — I think I can give your company a head start on the competition.

**Al Capone** — So, you're tellin' me dat your business is havin' a few problems. I like you, kid. If you hire me, me an' m'boys will take good care o' you. Of course, if you don', it'll be very unpleasant.

**Wyatt Earp** — I think I can bring some order to this department.

**Douglas MacArthur** — My greatest weakness is that I don't like being micro-managed. *What?* You don't *want* me to return?

**Lenin** — Do I want my boss's job? Are you kidding? I envision a company where *everyone* is the boss.

**Henry VIII** — My record shows that I believe in gender equity. Many of my department heads were women. But if they didn't produce, they were axed.

**Amelia Earhart** — I'd like to start right after I finish my flight around the world.

**Hamlet** — My last position was eliminated in a hostile takeover.

**Robin Hood** — My financial management experience? Some may consider it stealing from the rich and giving to the poor, but I saw it as creative reinvestment of the profits.

**Patrick Henry** — I really, really need this job. Give me employment or give me death!

**Elvis** — My last boss and I . . . say, you gonna eat those fries?

**Lady Godiva** — So, this is *not* what you meant by "business casual"?

**Faust** — I had to make a deal with the devil, but I kept my department under budget.

**Attila the Hun** — How would I describe myself? I'm pretty easygoing, but sometimes I have this urge to do something barbaric and, more or less, just smash things.

**Cleopatra** — The office politics at my last job were a nightmare. I worked with a bunch of snakes.

**Winston Churchill**— My communications skills? I've always been a fair talker.

**Gandhi** — I understand you have a problem with absenteeism. I never take breaks, not even for lunch.

**Lucretia Borgia** — My greatest accomplishment? After I took over the department, our competition just seemed to drop out of sight one by one.

**Macbeth** — Would I go after my boss's job? Do I look like the kind of guy who would knock off his boss for a promotion?

**Pandora** — I think I can bring a lot to your company. I like discovering new things.

**Helen of Troy** — I'm not just another pretty face. Although I've been known to launch a thousand ships, I'd like to be known for the skills I bring to the job.

**Genghis Khan** — My primary talent is downsizing. On my last job I downsized my staff, my organization, and the populations of a number of countries.

**Albert Einstein** — I brought my major research project with me. Do you have time for a demonstration?

Quipmeister: *Jeffrey R. Cox*

# Chapter 26

# Ten Odd Interviews

. . . . . . . . . . . . . . . . . . . . . . . . . . . . . . . . . . . . . . . . . . . .

*In This Chapter*

▶ Ten interviewing stories to brighten your day

. . . . . . . . . . . . . . . . . . . . . . . . . . . . . . . . . . . . . . . . . . . .

No matter how carefully you prepare for your job interview, weird things sometimes happen.

Some are simple slips of the tongue: A young man told an interviewer he "needed part-time work because he was tired of sleeping all day." Rip Van Winkle didn't get an offer.

Others are errors in judgment: Four graduating seniors were interviewed at a lunch hosted by a major brewery; three of the four ordered the host's drink, but the fourth ordered a competitor's brew. The jolly quartette became a trio when offers were passed out.

Still others are pure bad luck: As a new college graduate, I interviewed for a fashion coordinator's job, convincing myself that I looked radiant in a champagne-colored silk suit. Entering the building, a window washer's bucket dropped from the 11th floor, splattering with dirty water my suit, my face, and my confidence. But I made a joke of it and was offered the job.

You see how easily things can go wrong just when you so hope everything will go right. The following ten true stories were sent to me by colleagues to illustrate interviewing train wrecks. **The stories are told from the point of view of the source.** Names of individuals featured in the stories and places where the action occurred have been changed to avoid embarrassment. The anecdotes are instructive or amusing or simply wild.

## More Beans Than You Need to Spill

One of my friends interviewed Jackie, an applicant for a job with a nonprofit organization in North Carolina. Jackie was single and desperate for income and work experience. The interview had gone pretty well and was almost over when the interviewer asked, *So, Jackie, if we offer you the position, could you start work on Monday, the 25th?* Without hesitation, Jackie replied, *No, I must take my baby for a paternity test that day.* Jackie didn't get the job.

**Source: Jimmie Lockman**
**Clyde, North Carolina**

# Signs of Misfortune

My friend Howard had an interview in downtown Seattle. Because he wasn't familiar with the city, we drove in from the suburbs together the night before to figure out where he could park. The next morning Howard arrived ahead of time, parked in the appropriate spot, and went to his interview. He did all the right things to ensure that his interview would go smoothly. The interview started at 10, so he figured he'd be finished by noon.

Six grueling hours later, Howard, exhausted from a full day of interviewing, trudged out of the building toward his car. He couldn't think of anything but getting home and taking a load off his feet. Howard walked to the spot where he had parked his car. Car? What car? Howard was stunned to see a bus in his parking space! Howard jumped onto the bus and demanded to know what had happened to his car. The bus driver pointed to a sign: NO PARKING 3:30 – 6:30 p.m.

Howard had noticed the sign before, but in his preoccupation with succeeding at the interview, he had not focused on its message. A trip to the impound, three hours, and many, many dollars later, Howard finally got home.

**Source: Leslie Dotson**
**Newberg, Oregon**

# Be Funny or Else

After I had spent 20 minutes answering the typical interview questions, my interviewer, a great hulk of a man, suddenly stood up, stared directly down at me, and demanded in a thundering voice, *Give me an example of your sense of humor — NOW!* Being funny is somewhat difficult when you have what feels like a three-thousand-pound rhino bearing down on you. I found out later that it was a stress tactic — he wanted to see how people react in unexpected situations. Of course, I did not want the job after seeing the kind of person I'd report to. Until then, everything seemed to be going so well;

I had forgotten that a few people still think that outmoded stress tactics predict human behavior on the job.

**Source: Pat Seger**
**Minneapolis, Minnesota**

# Beware the Easy Answer

I was in charge of interviewing candidates for a university management position. Our focus was to determine their skills at managing people. We were seeking a team-builder or mentor for a sizable staff.

After reading through more than 100 resumes with the help of a search committee, I managed to narrow the search to three people. The best candidate on paper was Joshua, a man from a prestigious eastern university who held the same position for which we were recruiting. He seemed like a natural.

Because we wanted to hire a team-builder, after outlining the schedule and asking banal questions, I lobbed the first probing question:

> *Imagine this scenario: You have two outstanding but highly opinionated employees. Both have contributed to the department's success many times. You've asked them both to work on the same problem. Both present you with brilliant but totally opposite plans. How do you choose a solution without destroying the team?*

Of course, this dilemma has no right answer. The reasoning process that a candidate uses to explain his actions is what interests us. We look for insight into the candidate's management style.

This candidate's answer was to the point: *Oh, that's easy. I don't deal with situations like that.* The rest of the interview was a chore.

**Source: Gary R. Smith**
**San Francisco, California**

# Forgive Me, I Have Sinned

In my recruiting days, another recruiter and I were talking with dozens of candidates for several jobs. To this day, I am amazed that some people, forgetting to limit their remarks to positive information, can't resist telling an interviewer everything — the good, the bad, and the ugly. As the day wore on, I interviewed one young man who seemed to want to confess to his every sin. Overhearing the young man "going to confession," my colleague motioned me away and whispered, *How many Hail Marys do you think you should give him?*

**Source: Jack Brumbelow**
**Dallas, Texas**

# Name Your Job

This story is a saga of an interview that almost didn't happen — all because of a name.

My daughter, Tracy, was invited to interview for a position in the human resource department of a Chicago company. When she walked into the office, she introduced herself to her interviewer, *Hi, my name is Tracy.* The interviewer responded, *Hi, MY name is Tracy.*

The interviewer told my daughter that she almost didn't get the call for an interview because they shared the same name, and two Tracys in an office could get confusing. Two interviews later, my daughter was offered and accepted the job. Don't ask me how they keep the names straight.

**Source: Gale Owen**
**Syracuse, New York**

# Too Good in the Part

As a career counselor, I once had an interview with a search panel of eight faculty members. With 15 minutes to go, the head of the search committee suddenly stood and said he wanted to see me role-play in a crisis situation, and he set up a scenario. A panelist volunteered to play the client's role, and I the counselor's role. The role-playing must have been realistic because, without warning, the search panelist broke into real tears and became hysterical.

I spent the next ten minutes trying to calm her down, trying to make suggestions for referrals to helping services, while her colleagues sat watching.

I got the job. The search panelist who did the role-play with me as the client never spoke one word to me during my time at the college.

**Source: Pat Seger**
**Minneapolis, Minnesota**

# Never Take No for an Answer

Surfing the Net one day, I ran across this post-interview story — changed somewhat for purposes of confidentiality. You have to give the writer marks for pluck and humor.

It seems that after his interview, Montana D. Glenn was turned down. Never one to take bad news sitting down, Glenn was determined to reject his rejection, sending this message:

> *Dear Ms. Muldoon:*
>
> *Thank you for the interview May 15 and for your letter of June 2. After careful consideration, I regret to inform you that I am unable to accept your letter of refusal to offer me employment with your firm.*
>
> *This year I have been particularly fortunate in receiving an unusually large number of rejection letters. With such a varied and promising field of employers, it is impossible for me to accept all refusals.*
>
> *Despite your firm's outstanding qualifications and previous experience in rejecting applicants, I find that your rejection does not meet my needs at this time. Therefore, I will initiate employment with your firm immediately following graduation. I look forward to seeing you then.*
>
> *Best of luck in rejecting future candidates,*
>
> *Sincerely,*
>
> *Montana D. Glenn*

**Source: William T. Barrett**
**Winston-Salem, North Carolina**

# Why It's Called SLAPstick

I walked into the CEO's (chief executive officer's) office confidently, prepared, and hiding my desperation quite well. I really needed this job and was prepared to give the best interview of my life.

The CEO and I began the interview. Things seemed to be going well when there was a knock at the door. The CEO seemed embarrassed, and as the door flung open, the color in his face drained. He stood up to confront a visibly upset, blond young woman, who was crying and dabbing at a recently busted lip.

Thirty seconds later, an older, sophisticated woman strode into the room, tossed a fat envelope onto the CEO's desk, and turned to leave the room. I was beginning to feel quite uncomfortable and asked the CEO if I might step outside.

*No, that's quite all right, this is your interview. These ladies are leaving!*

I stayed put.

At that remark, the mature woman with the wedding band turned on her heels, rushed over to the desk, and slapped the CEO across the face. Then she turned to me.

*I hope you're not interviewing with this pig!!! If you dye your hair like this one over here, motioning to the blond woman with the bleeding lip, you may just get the position you're looking for! Don't you think he is a filthy, scum-sucking, excuse for a husband?!?!?*

The three of them stared at me, awaiting my response. Talk about the most difficult of interview questions.

My choices were to (1) insult the man who could give me the career opportunity of my life (and I wouldn't be working in the same city as he), (2) insult some bimbo who'd been punched in the mouth, or (3) provoke the wrath of an obviously jilted woman of society. I made an instant decision:

*Yes, I do think he's a pig who has the intelligence to hire an obviously well-qualified woman for a position for which I am the perfect match, rather than face a discrimination suit in the middle of divorce proceedings grounded in adultery. . . .*

I got the job.

**Source: Diana Ascher King**
**Durham, North Carolina**
**(From *Princeton Review Online*)**

# A Storybook Ending to the Interview from Hell

I had been interviewing with the medical products division of a major company in Texas. I was scheduled to drive from San Antonio to Austin for a final interview with the divisional VP (vice president) I'd be working under.

The day before the interview, I was informed by his administrative assistant that he would be unavailable due to a death in the family, but that he had arranged for me to meet with his counterpart in the company's industrial division at a beachfront hotel in Corpus Christi the following day. The deal sounded good to me, so I agreed to go to the interview.

When I arrived at the hotel in Corpus Christi, I was told that the vice president I was to meet had been called to a client site, an oil refinery just outside Corpus, and I was to meet him there. The oil refinery turned out to be one in a long line of oil refineries, each one indistinguishable from the next and served by an unmarked maze of streets. What should have been a ten-minute drive took me nearly an hour.

Upon entering the guard station and stating my business, I was informed that safety considerations required that before I could enter the complex, I must shave my beard, which I had worn for over ten years. I had the guard call to ask if the vice president could possibly meet with me outside of the plant, but the answer was "no." It was a hot job. What could I do? I shaved, and I now had a bright pink ribbon of skin under my Texas-tanned face. I had never expected something like this to happen — but what the hey, it was a great job, I kept telling myself.

After shaving, I watched the "safety video" that all entrants to the facility were required to view. It lasted ten minutes, five of which consisted of blaring horns, played at nearly actual volume, denoting various warning signals. These included the "get inside the nearest building" signal; the "get to the staging area" signal; the "get out of the complex as fast as you can" signal; and, for all I know, my brains having long since been fried by all of the horn blaring, the "kiss your butt goodbye" signal.

Entering the plant also required wearing safety glasses, a hard hat, fireproof clothing, and steel-toed boots, all of which the guard kindly provided. Unfortunately, due to an injury suffered when I was 12, I now wear a size 10 shoe on my right foot and an 8 on my left. The smallest boot available that day was a size 9. My left foot wouldn't stay in the boot, so I was dragging it along, walking like Fester, or whatever his name was, in *Gunsmoke*. What else could go wrong, I wondered? The guard decided the foot dragging was unsafe, so he called my contact, the substitute vice president, to let him know that I couldn't enter the plant, and he would have to come out.

Outside the plant, the only places we could interview were the video viewing room of the guard shack or my car. I could see that this interview was way off track. Since the temperature was 102° outside, we interviewed in the shack. During the interview, we were interrupted three times by people entering the plant, so we ended up sitting through the safety video three times. Matters were going from bad to worse. The interview itself was perfunctory at best, and I was advised after it was over that "somebody" would call me. I shouldn't bother them.

Naturally, I didn't get my hopes up too high, and I spent the next several days trying to decide if I wanted to grow my beard back.

Five days after the interview, the divisional vice president whom I was originally supposed to meet with called to offer me the job!

I asked the VP if he wanted to meet me first, but he said that wasn't necessary. Several of his people had met me, he said. Then the VP explained

> *The way I look at it is this: If you can work half as hard at this job as you've had to work to get it, things will work out fine!*

**Source: Dave Gannon**
**San Antonio, Texas**
**(From *Princeton Review Online*)**

# Encore

• • • • • • • • • • • • • • • • • • • • • • • • • • • • • • • • • • • • • • • • • • • • • • • •

## *An Audition Is Like a Job Interview*

What's an audition like?

The closest thing I can compare it to is a job interview. You dress up to look your best. You arrive and meet your prospective employer. You try to come off as intelligent and interested, but not overly eager or needy. You smile. You answer all their questions. Then you go on your way, hoping you said all the right things, praying that someday soon the telephone will ring and bring you wonderful news.

I'm an actor. Auditioning is a constant part of the profession.

When it happens, your name is called and you are ushered up onto a stage. Under a glaringly bright spotlight, while total strangers watch, you pretend to be somebody else.

I heard about an actor who showed up at an audition in a chicken suit. He wasn't auditioning for the role of a chicken. He just wanted to make sure that the director remembered him.

My worst audition experience happened during my college days at the Boulder Shakespeare Festival. After an exhausting car ride of more than 1,000 miles, I arrived on a bare stage under that ever-glaring spotlight. A voice from the darkness told me to begin. I had prepared a monologue from *Julius Caesar.* When I opened my mouth, I found myself starting somewhere in the middle of the speech, jumping back to the beginning, and then somehow arriving at the end. The voice from the darkness said, "I see you're from Seattle." I confirmed it.

"That is certainly a long way to come. Thank you," the voice replied in dismissal.

The key to a showstopping audition is preparation. Know the role you are auditioning for. Get your hands on a copy of the script and if at all possible, dress the part. For the musical *Jesus Christ Superstar*, one actor entered the auditorium with shoulder-length hair and a full beard, wearing a robe and sandals. He won the lead. (It didn't hurt that he had an incredible singing voice.)

As my next audition approaches, I will learn my audition piece to the best of my ability. I will dress appropriately. When I get on stage, I will give it my best shot and not be intimidated by faceless voices coming out of the dark.

Or, maybe I'll just show up in a chicken suit.

*Douglas Knoop*
*Seattle, Washington*

# Index

### • A •

About.com, 61
academic degrees, 190–193
Advertising Age, 63
after-interview
  checklist for, 233–234
  e-mail follow-up, 234–235
  follow-up, 234–240
  references, 239–240
  telephone calls, 238–239
  thank-you letter, 235, 237
age-related questions
  inappropriate questions, 227
  for older workers, 200–202, 205–207
  for younger workers, 200–205
airport interviews, 47–48
AJR News Link, 63
Alta Vista, 63
American Society of Association
  Executives, 63
America's Corporate Families, 64
aptitude tests, 85
arrest record, questions regarding, 224
Assn. of Internet Professionals, 62
Associations on the Net, 63

### • B •

bankruptcy issues, questions
  regarding, 227
base pay, 120
behavior-based interviews
  answering behavior-based questions,
   42–43
  described, 41–43
body language, 16, 70, 74, 152

business casual clothing, 78–79, 82
Business Periodicals Index, 64
Business Personality Inventory, 90
Business Week, 64
Business Wire, 61

### • C •

camcorder, practicing with, 70
campus recruiters, behavior impressive
  to, 75
candidate specifications, 55
career interests inventories, 85
Career Mosaic, 62
career Web sites, 62
CareerBuilder, 62, 121
CareerPath, 62
Careers.wsj.com, 62
casual attire, 78–79
Chapman, Jack, 120
children, questions regarding, 227
Chronicle of Higher Education, 62
clothing
  business casual, 82
  casual attire, 78–79
  checklists, 80–81
  conservative dressing, 81
  dressing to fit role, 82
  dressing up, 78
  for everyone, 80–81
  first impressions, 79
  guidelines for appropriate, 77–78
  halo effect, 79
  for men, 80–81
  personal style, 79
  trends, 78–79
  for women, 80–81

combination interview, 36
combination tests, 86
commercial videoconferencing
    centers, 145
Companies Online, 61
company cars, 121
company pre-employment contracts,
    246–247
company questions
  applying with company, reason for, 174
  company challenges, 173
  competition, 173
  described, 171–172
  direction of company, 173
  help company, how you will, 174
  market performance of new product,
      predicting, 174
  personal vision, 174
  position, knowledge of, 172–173
company search online, 60
Company WebPages, 60
company's own Web site, 59
compensation
  base pay, 120
  company cars, 121
  compensation package, creativity with,
      129–130
  DirectHit, 122
  dramatic silences in negotiating, 129
  flextime, 121
  Google, 122
  health benefits, 121
  health club membership, 121
  history, 126–128
  indirect pay, 121
  job offer, discussion at time of, 126–130
  JobStar, 122
  market value, 122–123, 130
  negotiating, 119–120, 123
  online salary information, 122
  position, upgrading, 128–129

printed salary information, 122–123
professional group networking, 123
questions, deflecting, 123–125
range, 127–128
rate of pay for your work, finding,
    122–123
recruiters and, 127
retirement packages, 121
stock options, 121
surveys, 122
telephone interviewing, 138
total compensation, 120
tuition reimbursement, 121
vacation leave, 121
variable pay, 121
compensation package, creativity with,
    129–130
competitive position questions, 57
compliments to interviewer, 50
computerized pre-employment tests,
    86–87
conservative dressing, 81
consultant, playing role of, 9
contribution to company, length of time
    for, 183–184
Corporate Window, 61
CorpTech, 60
counteroffers, 243
coworkers, helping, 185
criminal issues, questions regarding, 227
critical incidents, 43–44
culture questions, 57–58

Darling, Scott, 150
decision interview, 35–36
decision-making abilities, 186
demotions, 216–217
DirectHit, 122
direction of company questions, 56
directive interviews, 43–44

*Directory of American Firms Operating in Foreign Countries,* 64
*Directory of Corporate Affiliations,* 64
*Directory of Leading Private Companies,* 64
disabilities, 219–221
discrimination law, 224
discriminatory pre-employment questions, 83–84
discussion groups online, 60
dramatic silences in negotiating, 129
dressing to fit role, 82
dressing up, 78
*Dun & Bradstreet Principal International Business,* 64
*Dun's Top 50,000 Companies,* 64

### • *E* •

education and training questions
  academic degrees, 190–193
  adaptability, 189–190
  changes you would make, 197–198
  courses taken, 198
  degree, lack of, 190–191
  described, 189
  experience, lack of, 193–194
  extracurricular activities, 197
  GPA, 196
  major, choice of, 195
  online study, 191, 193
  school attended, 194
  skills, keeping up to date, 192
EEOC guidelines, 227
e-mail follow-up, 234–235
employee message boards, 61
employer performance questions, 117–118
employment contracts, 246–247
employment gaps, 215–216
*Encyclopedia of Associations,* 64

end of interview
  aggressiveness at, 232
  follow-up interview, setting up, 231–232
  job offer at, 230
  qualifications, restating, 230–231
Excite, 63
experience, lack of, 181–182, 193–194
experience questions
  changes in job, 183
  contribution to company, length of time for, 183–184
  coworkers, helping, 185
  decision-making abilities, 186
  mistakes, learning from, 186–187
  needs of company, matching, 186
  no experience, when you have, 181–182
  problems, resolving, 184
  qualifications, 184
  relevance of experiences, 181–182
  responsibilites, previous, 183
  speeches, preparation for, 185
  supervisor, conflict with, 187
  team-based companies, problems of, 185–186
experienced workers
  benefits of, 201
  myths about, 200
  temporary jobs, 207
  traps for, 202
  younger bosses and, 28
extracurricular activities, 197

### • *F* •

financial Web sites, 59
firings, 212–213
first impressions, 17, 79, 104–106
first-cut interviews, 33–35
flextime, 121
follow-up to interview, 234–240
FreeEDGAR, 61

### • G •

golf course interviews, 47
Google, 60, 63, 122
GPA, 196
group interviews, 39–40

### • H •

halo effect, 79
Headhunter, 62
health benefits, 121
health club membership, 121
health issues, questions regarding, 224
home office, telephone interviewing
    in, 137
Hoover's Online, 61
HotJobs, 62
*How to Make $1,000 a Minute —*
    *Negotiating your Salaries and Raises*
    (Chapman), 120

### • I •

ideal candidate, answering pre-
    employment questions as, 87
illegal questions, 224
inappropriate questions
  age issues, 227
  arrest record questions, 224
  bankruptcy issues, 227
  children, 227
  criminal issues, 227
  discrimination law, 224
  EEOC guidelines, 227
  health questions, 224
  illegal questions, 224
  reasons for, 224–225
  redirecting, 225–227
inconsistencies in answers, 90
indirect pay, 121

industry questions
  applying with company, reason for, 174
  challenges to company, 173
  competition, 173
  described, 171–172
  direction of company, 173
  help for company, how you will
      provide, 174
  market performance of new product,
      predicting, 174
  personal vision, 174
  position, knowledge of, 172–173
Infoseek, 63
integrity tests, 85, 90–91
interview quotes (humorous), 257–260
interview scenarios
  day before, 103–104
  ending interview, 109–111
  first impressions, 104–106
  follow-up to interview, 111–112
  during interview, 106–107
  interviewer reaction, 108–109
interview traps
  behavior not to display, 74
  body language, 74
  for experienced workers, 202
  interference, 73–74
  silent treatment, 74–75
  words not to say, 74
  for younger workers, 202
interviewers
  cold comtemplators, 252–253
  control of interview, 21
  focusing on, 67–68
  friendly, 253
  incompetent, 253–254
  intimidators, 254
  new kinds of, 11–12
  potential boss, 252
  recruiters, 254
  serious business person, 252

similarities with interviewer, showing, 50
talkative, 255
technical person, 255
types of, 251–255
young achiever type, 251
interviewing styles
airport interviews, 47–48
behavior-based interviews, 41–43
combination interview, 36
compliments to interviewer, 50
decision interview, 35–36
directive interviews, 43–44
first-cut interviews, 33–35
golf course interviews, 47
group interviews, 39–40
job fair interviews, 48–49
locations for interviews, 46–49
mealtime interviews, 46–47
mirroring, 46
nondirective interviews, 44–45
note taking, 50
on-campus interviews, 48
one-to-one interviews, 39
party interviews, 47
patterned interviews, 43–44
pauses during interview, 50
promotion interview, 36–37
recruiter courtesy interview, 37
recruiter general screening interview, 37–38
recruiter search interview, 38
screening interview, 33–35
second interviews, 38–39
selection interview, 35–36
serial interviews, 40–41
similarities with interviewer, showing, 50
storytelling, 45
stress interviews, 45–46
structured interviews, 43–44
tips for all, 50

InterviewNow, 146
Inwald Personality Inventory, 90

job fair interviews, 48–49
job hopping, 214–215
job interview tips
for everyone, 50, 71
for experienced workers, 72
for men, 73
for women, 72–73
for younger workers, 72
job interviews
age differences, 25–29
background description matching job, 19
"be yourself," 9–10
behavior-based interviewing, 14–15
big companies, 15–16
body language, 16
communication skills, 17
control of interview, 21
copyrighting ideas, 24
deal moment, 30
educational background, 18
essence of, 7–8
exploitation during, 22–24
first impressions, 17
generational interviewing, 25–29
good fit for job, 7–8
immediate skills, 12
interview ethics, 22–24
interviewers. *See* interviewers
leverage, 30–31
listening skills, 18
loyalty to company, 13–14
natural behavior at, 10
note taking, 18
performance interviews, 22
personality factors, 20–21
positive attitudes, 16

job interviews *(continued)*
  preparation for, 19
  qualifications, ideal, 19
  questions during. *See* questions
  role to take during, 11
  salary. *See* compensation
  scams, examples of, 22–24
  scope of position, 19
  screening interviews, 20
  selection interviews, 20
  self-identity, 9–10
  self-reliance as selling point, 14
  seller/buyer relationship, 29–31
  sensitivity for hiring manager's dislike
    of, 21–22
  small companies, 15–16
  smiling, 16
  storyboarding, 18
  summary of book, 7–31
  technology impacting, 14
  telephone interviews, 14
  tips for, 50, 71–73
  unreasonable demands, 24–25
  younger bosses and older workers, 28
job offers
  acceptance, deciding on, 243–246
  career goals, long-term, 242–243
  company considerations, 245
  company pre-employment contracts,
    246–247
  counteroffers, 243
  discussion at time of offer, 126–130
  employment contracts, 246–247
  good job, determination of, 243–244
  losing job, 244
  negotiating, 246
  obligations to, 248
  pay considerations, 245
  questions to ask before, 113–115
  reaction to, 241–242
  in writing, 247–248
  younger workers and, 242

job relevance, 84
JobOptions, 60, 62
JobStar, 122

## • L •

Law Jobs, 63
listening skills, telephone
    interviewing, 137
locations for interviews, 46–49
Lycos, 63

## • M •

market value, 122–123, 130
MBA Central, 63
mealtime interviews, 46–47
Medzilla, 62
mental tension, 71
Meta List High-Tech Companies, 60
Metcalf, Bill, 150
Minnesota Multiphasic Personality
    Inventory, 90
mistakes, learning from, 186–187
Monster, 62

## • N •

NationJob Network, 62
needs of company, matching, 186
negative characteristics, showing, 88
negotiating, 119–120, 123
nervousness, 67–68
net worth questions, 59
Newspaperlinks, 63
nondirective interviews, 44–45
note taking, 50

## • O •

objections, drawing out, 116–117
odd interviews (true stories), 261–268
older workers. *See* experienced workers

on-campus interviews, 48
one-to-one interviews, 39
online interviewing
  company Web sites with, 146–147
  final hiring decision, 147
  InterviewNow, 146
online research
  company search, 60
  company's own Web site, 59
  described, 59
  discussion groups, 60
  financial Web sites, 59
  trade group sites, 60
online salary information, 122
online study, 191, 193

## • P •

party interviews, 47
patterned interviews, 43–44
pauses during interview, 50
performance tests, 85
personal questions, 113, 115–116
personal style, 79
personality tests, 85, 90
Personnel Decisions, Inc. (Employment
    Inventory), 90
physical tension, minimizing, 70–71
*Plunkett's Research Publications,* 64
position
  analysis of, 55
  upgrading, 128–129
positive characteristics, showing, 87–88
PR Newswire, 61
practicing
  behavior not to display, 74
  body language, 70, 74
  with camcorder, 70
  campus recruiters, behavior impressive
      to, 75
  interference, preparing for, 73–74
  for interview traps, 73–74, 74–75

interviewers, focusing on, 67–68
memorizing list of your skills, 69
mental tension, eliminating, 71
physical tension, minimizing, 70–71
reading aloud list of your skills, 69
relaxation techniques, 70–71
silent treatment, preparing for, 74–75
stage presence, 68–69
words not to say, 74
pre-employment tests
  absolutes on, 86
  answering questions on, 86
  aptitude tests, 85
  Business Personality Inventory, 90
  career interests inventories, 85
  combination tests, 86
  computerized, 86–87
  debate over, 84
  discriminatory questions, 83–84
  ideal candidate, answering as, 87
  inconsistencies in answers, 90
  integrity tests, 85, 90–91
  Inwald Personality Inventory, 90
  job relevance, 84
  Minnesota Multiphasic Personality
      Inventory, 90
  negative characteristics, showing, 88
  performance tests, 85
  personality tests, 85, 90
  Personnel Decisions, Inc. (Employment
      Inventory), 90
  poor performance on, 93
  positive characteristics, showing,
      87–88
  questions to ask before taking, 85–86
  Reliability Scale (Hogan Personnel
      Selection Series), 90
  salespeople and, 89
  sample questions, 91–92
  self-esteem, showing, 89
  skills tests, 85
  stressful situations, adaptability to, 89

pre-employment tests *(continued)*
time constraints, 86
types of, 85
Wonderlic Personnel Test, 90
pre-interview checklist, 112
presumption-phrasing questions, 115
print resources
*America's Corporate Families,* 64
*Business Periodicals Index,* 64
*Directory of American Firms Operating in Foreign Countries,* 64
*Directory of Corporate Affiliations,* 64
*Directory of Leading Private Companies,* 64
*Dun & Bradstreet Principal International Business,* 64
*Dun's Top 50,000 Companies,* 64
*Encyclopedia of Associations,* 64
*Plunkett's Research Publications,* 64
*Standard and Poor's Register of Corporations, Directors and Executives,* 64
*Thomas's Register of American Manufacturers,* 64
*U.S. Industrial Outlook,* 64
*Value Line Investment Survey,* 64
printed salary information, 122–123
prison time, 211–212
problems, resolving, 184
product questions, 56–57
professional group networking, 123
professional organization guides, 63
Project Management Institute, 62
promotion interview, 36–37
psychological readiness, telephone interviewing, 139
Public Relations Society of America, 62
publications
AJR News Link, 63
*Business Week,* 64
*Inc.,* 64
Newspaperlinks.com, 63
*U.S. News and World Report,* 64

## • Q •

qualifications, 184
questions
age-related questions. *See* age-related questions
analytical questions, 13
company questions. *See* company questions
competitive position questions, 57
culture questions, 57–58
direction of company questions, 56
education and training questions. *See* education and training questions
employer performance questions, 117–118
experience questions. *See* experience questions
inappropriate questions. *See* inappropriate questions
industry questions. *See* industry questions
net worth questions, 59
new kinds of, 12–13
objections, drawing out, 116–117
offer, questions to ask before, 113–115
personal questions, 113, 115–116
presumption-phrasing questions, 115
product questions, 56–57
quality of your mind, revealing, 12
questions to ask, 55–59
reputation questions, 57–58
self-revealing questions. *See* self-revealing questions
services questions, 56–57
showing off, 116
size and growth pattern questions, 56
skill questions. *See* skill questions
special issue questions. *See* special issue questions
training questions. *See* education and training questions
work-focused questions, 113–115

## • R •

rate of pay for your work, finding, 122–123
recovery programs, applicants in, 217–218
recruiters
 compenation and, 127
 courtesy interview, 37
 follow up from, 232
 general screening interview, 37–38
 search interview, 38
 telephone interviewing, 135
redirecting inappropriate questions, 225–227
references
 after-interview, 239–240
 accomplishments, recalling, 97
 choosing, 96
 communication with, 98
 confidentiality, 97
 current employer, 97
 Documented Reference Check, 99
 Job Reference, 99
 legal issues, 99
 letter of recommendation, 100
 negligent hiring, 99
 permission to use, 97
 poor references, 98–99, 100
 reference statement, 98, 100
 responses from, coordinating, 97
 resume, having copies of your, 98
 setting up, 95–96
 for younger workers, 96
relaxation techniques
 deep breaths, 70
 pushing wall while grunting, 71
Reliability Scale (Hogan Personnel Selection Series), 90
reputation questions, 57–58
research
 basics, 58–59
 candidate specifications, 55
 career sites, 62
 company history questions, 58
 company Web sites, 60
 Company WebPages, 60
 competitive position questions, 57
 culture questions, 57–58
 direction of company questions, 56
 ease of obtaining, 54
 employee message boards, 61
 *Encyclopedia of Associations,* 64
 Excite, 63
 finding out about companies, 61
 importance of, 65
 *Inc.,* 64
 net worth questions, 59
 niche sites, 62–63
 online research, 59–60
 position analysis, 55
 print resources, 64
 product questions, 56–57
 professional organization guides, 63
 publications, 63–64
 questions to ask, 55–59
 reputation questions, 57–58
 search engines, 63
 services questions, 56–57
 size and growth pattern questions, 56
 tutorial, 65
Researching Companies Online, 65
retirement packages, 121

## • S •

salary. *See* compensation
salespeople, 89
same job, remaining in, 210–211
school attended, 194
screening interview, 33–35
search engines
 Alta Vista, 63
 Excite, 63
 Google, 63
 Infoseek, 63
 Lycos, 63

second interviews, 38–39
selection interview, 35–36
self-esteem, showing, 89
self-identity, 9–10
self-revealing questions
  assets, 165
  changes you would make, 167
  decision-making process, 169
  described, 159–160
  ideal job, 167
  long-term career objectives, 165
  memorable accomplishments, 164–165
  memorize commercial about yourself,
    161–164
  outside interests, 166
  reasons for, 159
  responding to, 160–169
  sample answers, 164–169
  sample questions, 164–169
  sample self commercials, 162–164
  shortened version of self
    commercial, 164
  storytelling, 169
  stressful situations, 168
  success, defining, 167–168
  unique qualities, 168
  weaknesses, 165
  work style, 166
serial interviews, 40–41
services questions, 56–57
sexual orientation, 213–214
showing off questions, 116
silent treatment, 74–75
similarities with interviewer, showing, 50
size and growth pattern questions, 56
skill questions
  about researching, 177
  answering, 176
  group projects, 179
  hired, reasons for being, 179
  oral presentations, 177

problems, tough job, 177
recognizing, 175–176
responsibility, delegating, 178–179
soft skills, need for, 176
storytelling to answer, 176
time organization, 178
unexpected events on job, 178
writing skills, 178
skills
  keeping up to date, 192
  memorizing list of, 69
  questions on. *See* skill questions
  tests on, 85
Society for Human Resource
    Management, 62, 119
special issue questions
  demotions, 216–217
  disabilities, 219–221
  employment gaps, 215–216
  fired, when you've been, 212–213
  job hopping, 214–215
  prison time, 211–212
  recovery, applicants in, 217–218
  same job, remaining in, 210–211
  sexual orientation, 213–214
  for women, 218–219
speeches, preparation for, 185
*Standard and Poor's Register of
    Corporations, Directors and
    Executives,* 64
StarChefs, 62
stock options, 121
storytelling, 45
stress interviews, 45–46
stressful situations, adaptability to, 89
structured interviews, 43–44
SuperPages, 61
supervisor, conflict with, 187

## • T •

team-based companies, problems of, 185–186
telephone calls, 238–239
telephone interviewing
  appointments for, making, 136
  appreciation, expressing, 138
  challenges, 137
  compensation, 138
  described, 134–135
  essential information, gathering, 137
  essentials for, 135–136
  example story, 133–134
  feedback, 138
  flexibility, 137
  home office, using, 137
  important questions, diverting, 138
  in-person meeting, 138
  listening skills, 137
  psychological readiness, 139
  recruiters and, 135
  rushing, 138
  telephone presence, 136
  thank-you letters, 138
  at work, 137
telephone presence, 136
temporary jobs, 207
thank-you letters, 138, 235, 237
Thomas Register Online, 61
*Thomas's Register of American Manufacturers,* 64
time constraints, 86
total compensation, 120
trade group sites, 60
training questions. *See* education and training questions
travel expenses, 139
trends, 78–79
tuition reimbursement, 121

## • U •

U.S. Industrial Outlook, 64
*U.S. News and World Report,* 64

## • V •

vacation leave, 121
*Value Line Investment Survey,* 64
variable pay, 121
Vault, 61
video interviewing
  advantages of, 155
  appearance issues, 150–151
  background, 152
  bandwidth needed for, 142–143
  benefits of, 143
  body language, 152
  clothing, 151
  commercial videoconferencing centers, 145
  cosmetics and, 150
  delay-time, 153
  described, 141–142
  disadvantages of, 144
  equipment, 144, 154
  eye contact, 151
  facial expression, 150–151
  financial reasons for, 143
  jewelry, 151
  lighting, 152
  nervousness, 153
  pausing for effect, 153
  popularity of, 142
  posture, 152
  readiness, 153–154
  resume, displaying, 154
  self-viewing, 153
  speech, 153
  system requirements, 144
  timeliness, 152
  types of jobs using, 144
  videophones and, 145

## • W •

Web sites
  Advertising Age, 63
  Assn. of Internet Professionals, 62
  Career Mosaic, 62
  CareerBuilder, 62
  CareerPath, 62
  Careers.wsj.com, 62
  Chronicle of Higher Education, 62
  company's own Web site, 59
  financial Web sites, 59
  Headhunter, 62
  HotJobs, 62
  JobOptions, 62
  Law Jobs, 63
  MBA Central, 63
  Medzilla, 62
  Monster, 62
  NationJob Network, 62
  Project Management Institute, 62
  Public Relations Society of America, 62
  Society of Human Resource
    Management, 62
  StarChefs, 62
  WetFeet, 60
women
  clothing, 80–81
  job interview tips, 72–73
  special issue questions, 218–219
Wonderlic Personnel Test, 90
work-focused questions, 113–115

## • Y •

Yahoo!, 61, 63
younger workers
  benefits of, 200–201
  job offers, 242
  myths about, 200
  references, 96
  tips for, 72
  traps for, 202

# FOR DUMMIES®

## The easy way to get more done and have more fun

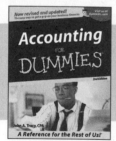

# FOR DUMMIES®

## A world of resources to help you grow

## HOME, GARDEN & HOBBIES

**Feng Shui**
0-7645-5295-3

**Gardening**
0-7645-5130-2

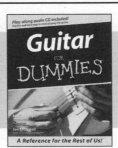

**Guitar**
0-7645-5106-X

**Also available:**

Auto Repair For Dummies
(0-7645-5089-6)

Chess For Dummies
(0-7645-5003-9)

Home Maintenance For
Dummies
(0-7645-5215-5)

Organizing For Dummies
(0-7645-5300-3)

Piano For Dummies
(0-7645-5105-1)

Poker For Dummies
(0-7645-5232-5)

Quilting For Dummies
(0-7645-5118-3)

Rock Guitar For Dummies
(0-7645-5356-9)

Roses For Dummies
(0-7645-5202-3)

Sewing For Dummies
(0-7645-5137-X)

## FOOD & WINE

**Cooking**
0-7645-5250-3

**Cookies**
0-7645-5390-9

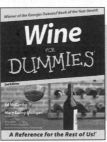

**Wine**
0-7645-5114-0

**Also available:**

Bartending For Dummies
(0-7645-5051-9)

Chinese Cooking For
Dummies
(0-7645-5247-3)

Christmas Cooking For
Dummies
(0-7645-5407-7)

Diabetes Cookbook For
Dummies
(0-7645-5230-9)

Grilling For Dummies
(0-7645-5076-4)

Low-Fat Cooking For
Dummies
(0-7645-5035-7)

Slow Cookers For Dummies
(0-7645-5240-6)

## TRAVEL

**Italy**
0-7645-5453-0

**Hawaii**
0-7645-5438-7

**Las Vegas**
0-7645-5448-4

**Also available:**

America's National Parks For
Dummies
(0-7645-6204-5)

Caribbean For Dummies
(0-7645-5445-X)

Cruise Vacations For
Dummies 2003
(0-7645-5459-X)

Europe For Dummies
(0-7645-5456-5)

Ireland For Dummies
(0-7645-6199-5)

France For Dummies
(0-7645-6292-4)

London For Dummies
(0-7645-5416-6)

Mexico's Beach Resorts For
Dummies
(0-7645-6262-2)

Paris For Dummies
(0-7645-5494-8)

RV Vacations For Dummies
(0-7645-5443-3)

Walt Disney World & Orlando
For Dummies
(0-7645-5444-1)

**Available wherever books are sold. Go to www.dummies.com or call 1-877-762-2974 to order direct.**

# FOR DUMMIES®

## Plain-English solutions for everyday challenges

### COMPUTER BASICS

0-7645-0838-5

0-7645-1663-9

0-7645-1548-9

**Also available:**

PCs All-in-One Desk Reference For Dummies (0-7645-0791-5)

Pocket PC For Dummies (0-7645-1640-X)

Treo and Visor For Dummies (0-7645-1673-6)

Troubleshooting Your PC For Dummies (0-7645-1669-8)

Upgrading & Fixing PCs For Dummies (0-7645-1665-5)

Windows XP For Dummies (0-7645-0893-8)

Windows XP For Dummies Quick Reference (0-7645-0897-0)

### BUSINESS SOFTWARE

0-7645-0822-9

0-7645-0839-3

0-7645-0819-9

**Also available:**

Excel Data Analysis For Dummies (0-7645-1661-2)

Excel 2002 All-in-One Desk Reference For Dummies (0-7645-1794-5)

Excel 2002 For Dummies Quick Reference (0-7645-0829-6)

GoldMine "X" For Dummies (0-7645-0845-8)

Microsoft CRM For Dummies (0-7645-1698-1)

Microsoft Project 2002 For Dummies (0-7645-1628-0)

Office XP For Dummies (0-7645-0830-X)

Outlook 2002 For Dummies (0-7645-0828-8)

## Get smart! Visit www.dummies.com

- **Find listings of even more *For Dummies* titles**

- **Browse online articles**

- **Sign up for Dummies eTips™**

- **Check out *For Dummies* fitness videos and other products**

- **Order from our online bookstore**

**Available wherever books are sold. Go to www.dummies.com or call 1-877-762-2974 to order direct.**

# FOR DUMMIES®

## Helping you expand your horizons and realize your potential

---

## INTERNET

**0-7645-0894-6**

**0-7645-1659-0**

**0-7645-1642-6**

### Also available:

America Online 7.0 For Dummies
(0-7645-1624-8)

Genealogy Online For Dummies
(0-7645-0807-5)

The Internet All-in-One Desk Reference For Dummies
(0-7645-1659-0)

Internet Explorer 6 For Dummies
(0-7645-1344-3)

The Internet For Dummies Quick Reference
(0-7645-1645-0)

Internet Privacy For Dummies
(0-7645-0846-6)

Researching Online For Dummies
(0-7645-0546-7)

Starting an Online Business For Dummies
(0-7645-1655-8)

---

## DIGITAL MEDIA

**0-7645-1664-7**

**0-7645-1675-2**

**0-7645-0806-7**

### Also available:

CD and DVD Recording For Dummies
(0-7645-1627-2)

Digital Photography All-in-One Desk Reference For Dummies
(0-7645-1800-3)

Digital Photography For Dummies Quick Reference
(0-7645-0750-8)

Home Recording for Musicians For Dummies
(0-7645-1634-5)

MP3 For Dummies
(0-7645-0858-X)

Paint Shop Pro "X" For Dummies
(0-7645-2440-2)

Photo Retouching & Restoration For Dummies
(0-7645-1662-0)

Scanners For Dummies
(0-7645-0783-4)

---

## GRAPHICS

**0-7645-0817-2**

**0-7645-1651-5**

**0-7645-0895-4**

### Also available:

Adobe Acrobat 5 PDF For Dummies
(0-7645-1652-3)

Fireworks 4 For Dummies
(0-7645-0804-0)

Illustrator 10 For Dummies
(0-7645-3636-2)

QuarkXPress 5 For Dummies
(0-7645-0643-9)

Visio 2000 For Dummies
(0-7645-0635-8)

---

**Available wherever books are sold. Go to www.dummies.com or call 1-877-762-2974 to order direct.**